above the dreamless dead

world war I in poetry and comics

edited by chris duffy

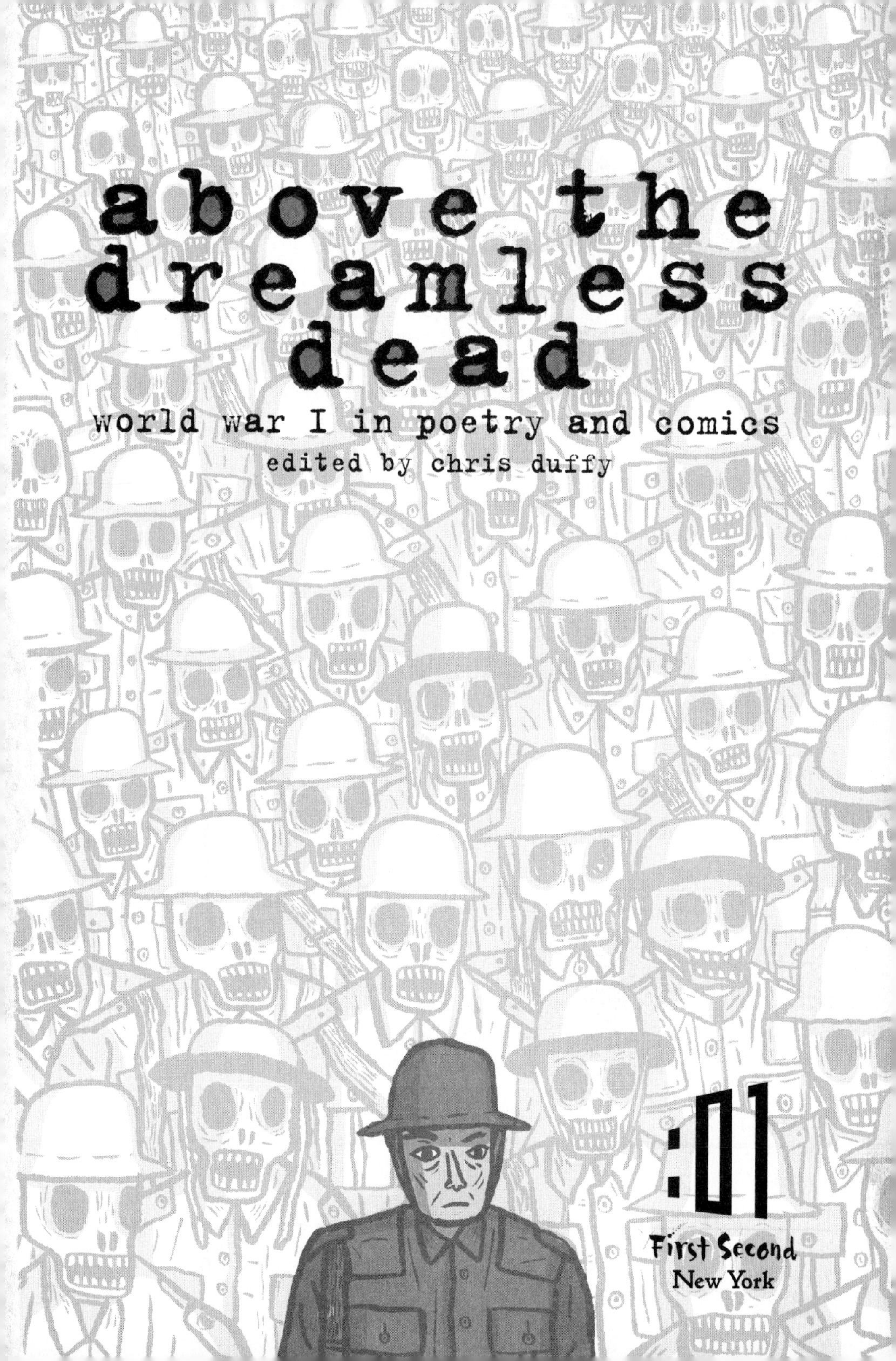

:01
First Second
New York

:01
First Second
New York

Published by First Second
First Second is an imprint of Roaring Brook Press,
a division of Holtzbrinck Publishing Holdings Limited Partnership
175 Fifth Avenue, New York, New York 10010

Edited by Chris Duffy
Book design by Colleen AF Venable
Special thanks to Perry Metzger

Cataloging-in-Pubication Data is on file at the Library of Congress.

ISBN: 978-1-62672-065-7

First Second books may be purchased for business or promotional use. For information on bulk purchases please contact Macmillan Corporate and Premium Sales Department at (800) 221-7945 x5442 or by email at specialmarkets@macmillan.com.

FIRST EDITION

First edition 2014

Printed in the United States of America

10 9 8 7 6 5 4 3 2 1

BY ART WE LIVE

CONTENTS

I—THE CALL TO WAR

II—IN THE TRENCHES

III—AFTERMATH

INTRODUCTION

This is an anthology of comics adaptations of World War I poetry. I've talked to many intelligent people while putting this book together and have learned that most folks (especially in the United States) know very little about World War I—and less about that war's poets. That certainly applied to me at the project's start. I now know just enough about the poets and their work to feel very pleased to be part of a project that draws attention to this important and moving body of writing. I think it's safe to say the comics artists and writers who contributed to this book feel the same.

The English soldier-poets of World War I are known collectively as the Trench Poets. Wilfred Owen is the most famous of these, arguably followed by Siegfried Sassoon and Isaac Rosenberg. The Trench Poets are often thought of as a group, but that's more or less a fiction created in the years after the war, as people tried to make sense of the huge conflict. Some of the Trench Poets were friends, but on the whole they came from many classes, had different educational backgrounds, wrote in a variety of styles, and held different religious and political beliefs. (Please see the notes, biographical glosses, and further reading resources in the back of this book for more background.)

What the Trench Poets did have in common was their subject and their setting: the war's Western Front. This consisted of almost unmoving lines of trenches that stretched nearly 500 miles across Belgium and northern France from autumn 1914 to spring 1918. Trench warfare has become nearly synonymous with World War I, and it's what comes to mind when almost anyone thinks of that war. It's worth reviewing, though:

Machine guns and artillery made rapid advances of troops on land impossible for most of the war. In the conflict's first year, the German Empire's forces and the Allied troops found themselves dug in, facing each other from trenches that were from 100 to 600 yards apart. Trenches were usually 10 feet deep, with sand bags in front and behind raising the walls even higher. The front line of trenches connected to two lines of trenches behind them—one for support troops, the other for reserves. The men in the trenches could experience constant shelling and sniper attacks, depending on their location, and shell shock (now known as post-traumatic stress disorder) was common. Flooding, disease, and pestilence (in the form of rats, lice, mites, frogs, and slugs) were constant problems. Corpses were often left unburied for weeks, as any activity could invite attacks from the enemy line.

Life in the trenches was legendarily miserable. The narrative of that misery has been challenged in recent decades by some writers and historians who want us to know that the Western Front wasn't a setting of nonstop terror and disease. It's telling, though, what "comforting" facts these writers cite: that there were actual dressing stations nearby to treat the sick and wounded; that the average soldier only spent 55 percent of his time in the trenches; that only 1 in 10 soldiers died on the front.

In the notes at the end of this book, Eddie Campbell says about his comics adaptation of Patrick McGill's lyrical last chapter of *The Great Push*: "It's a bit preposterous us thinking we can illustrate this stuff that we know nothing of." That feeling is probably echoed, one way or another, by each of the comics artists and writers who have adapted a World War I poem for this book. However, it's important to remember that the Trench Poets were creating literature; they were artists creating worlds filled with characters and stories. Cartoonists do much the same thing, even if the tools are different. In this way, I think the adapters in this book—some of the best comics creators working in Europe and North America—are well-suited for the task of bringing these poems to new readers.

A few examples: Cartoonist Kevin Huizenga's comics adaptation of Charles Sorley's "All the Hills and Vales Along" is a pitch-perfect graphic equivalent of the poem's text, with all the distance and irony of the poem (as well as its rhythm) beautifully transformed into panels. Peter Kuper's expressive, paranoid layouts add urgency to Isaac Rosenberg's already desperate poem "The Immortals," while perfectly setting up the gruesome punch line. Hannah Berry's detailed and layered portrayal of Wilfrid Gibson's protagonist in "The Question" makes that work even more human and sympathetic as a comic. George Pratt's approach to three Wilfred Owen poems is to let the text stand out, even push forward, while providing haunting accompaniment in beautiful paintings that are somehow vivid and muted at the same time. As a whole, the comics contributors engaged these works with a passion and a sincerity that's palpable in the original poems—maybe none more than Carol Tyler in her touching take on "Two Fusiliers" by Robert Graves.

That feeling of inadequacy in the face of warriors' tales, though, is hard to dismiss. Soldiers in war experience things civilians can only try to understand. And all of the comics creators in this book are civilians, though some have more experience with soldiers and war than others. In drawing comics from the poetry of Sassoon, Owen, Rosenberg, and their contemporaries, the contributors are doing what we all do when faced with the words of soldiers: bearing witness to those who bear witness. It is the least we can do.

—Chris Duffy

I

The Call to War

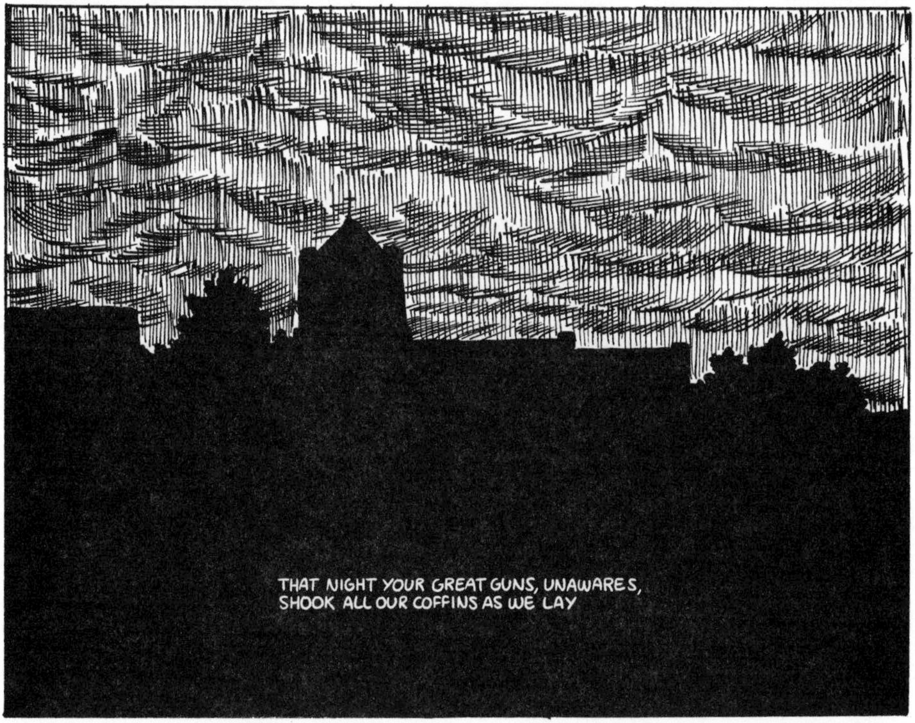
THAT NIGHT YOUR GREAT GUNS, UNAWARES,
SHOOK ALL OUR COFFINS AS WE LAY

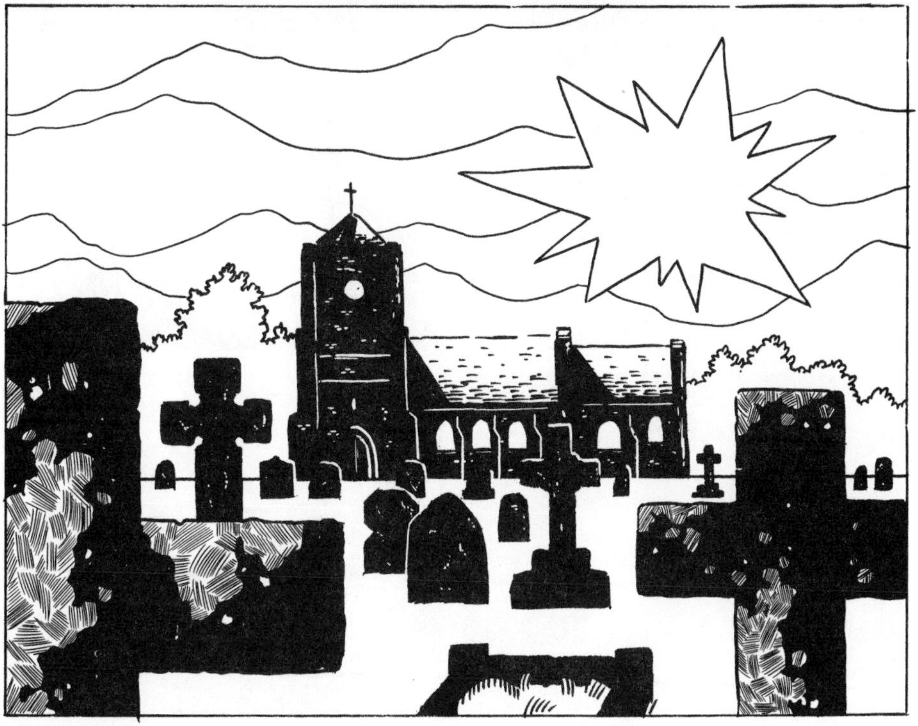

AND BROKE THE CHANCEL WINDOW SQUARES

WE THOUGHT IT WAS THE JUDGMENT DAY

AND SAT UPRIGHT

WHILE DREARISOME AROSE THE HOWL OF WAKENED HOUNDS

THE MOUSE LET FALL THE ALTAR-CRUMB

THE WORMS DREW BACK INTO THEIR MOUNDS

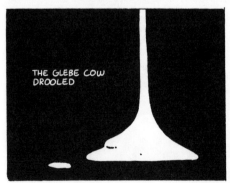

THE GLEBE COW DROOLED

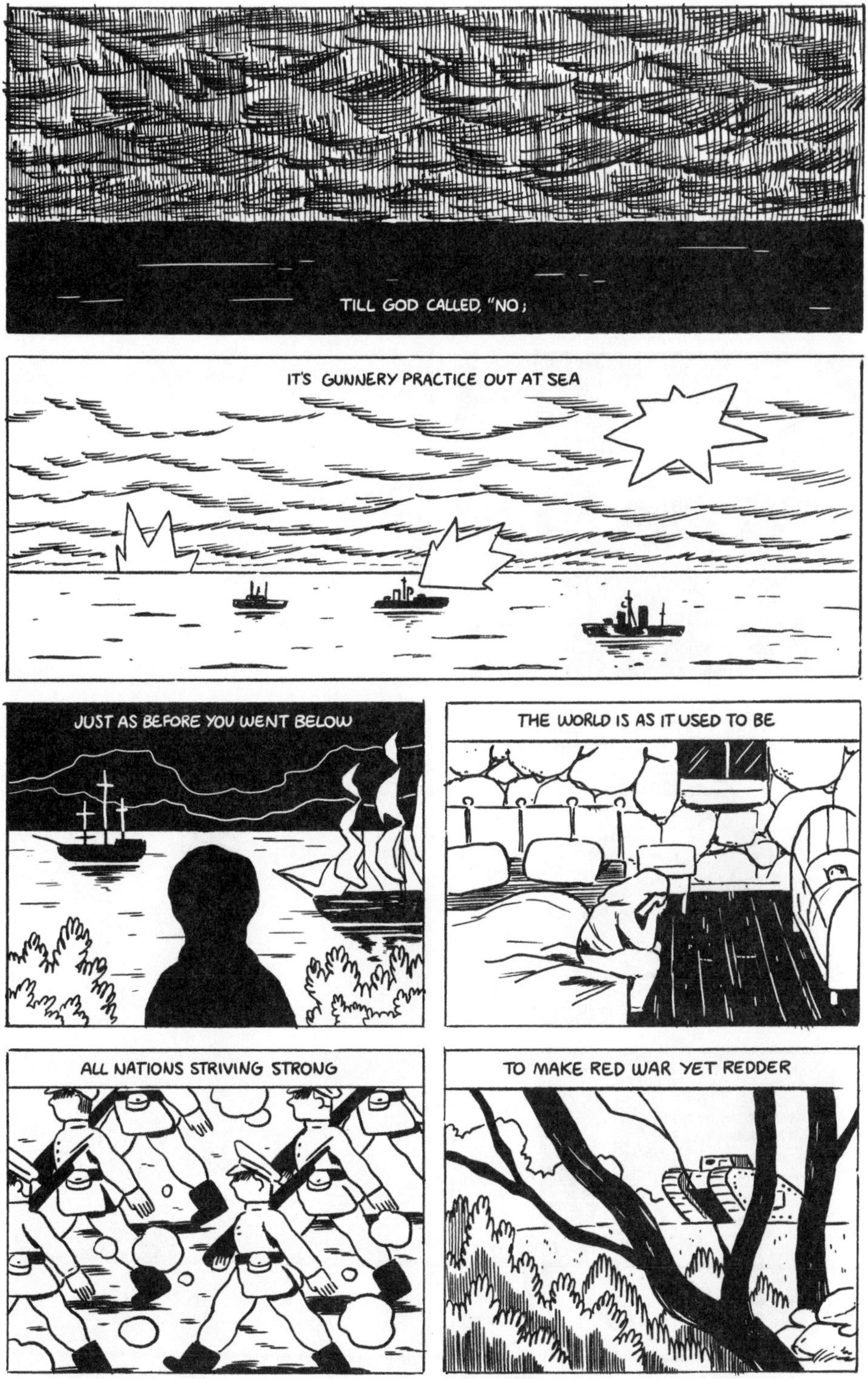
TILL GOD CALLED, "NO;
IT'S GUNNERY PRACTICE OUT AT SEA
JUST AS BEFORE YOU WENT BELOW
THE WORLD IS AS IT USED TO BE
ALL NATIONS STRIVING STRONG
TO MAKE RED WAR YET REDDER

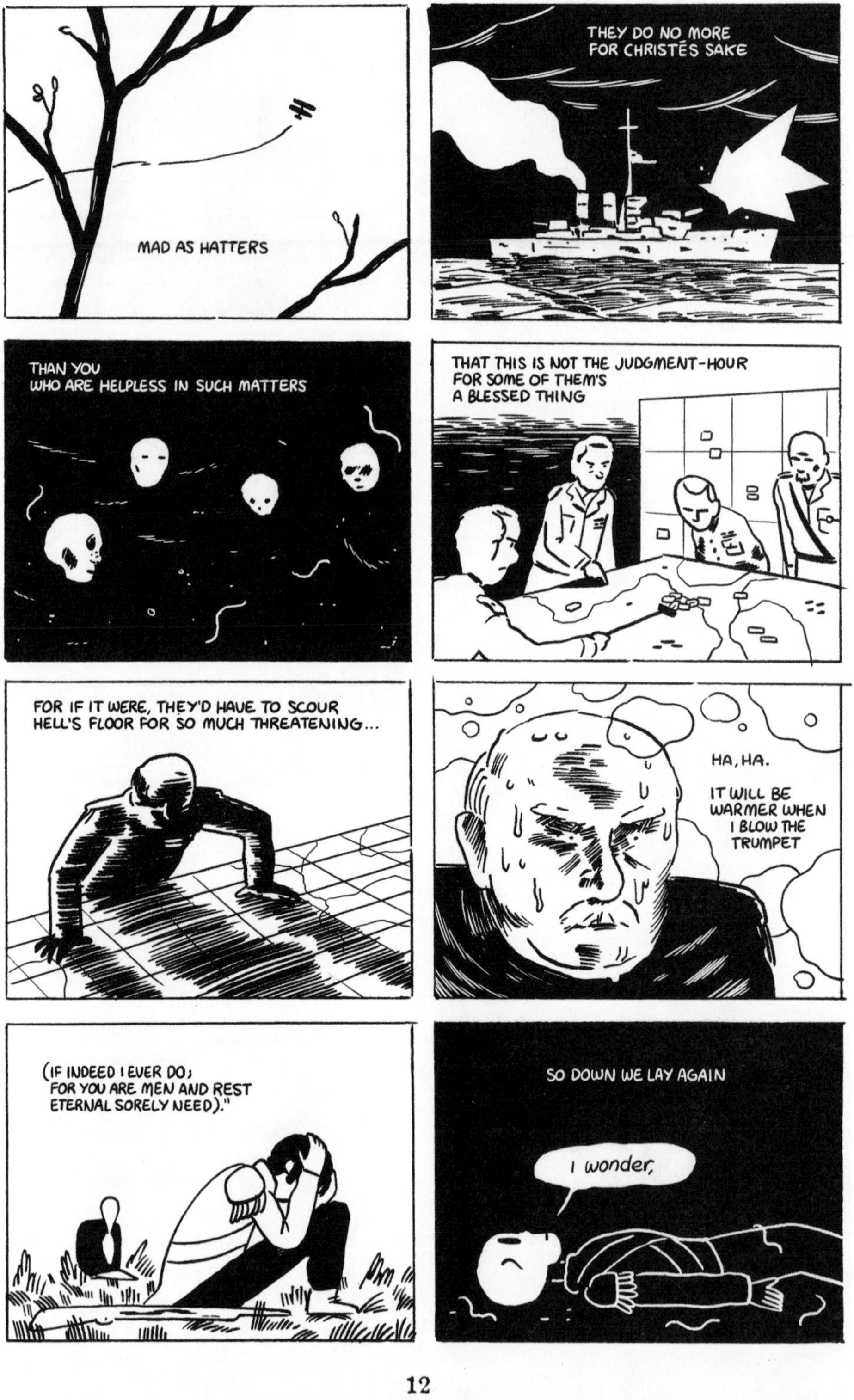
MAD AS HATTERS
THEY DO NO MORE
FOR CHRISTÉS SAKE
THAN YOU
WHO ARE HELPLESS IN SUCH MATTERS
THAT THIS IS NOT THE JUDGMENT-HOUR
FOR SOME OF THEM'S
A BLESSED THING
FOR IF IT WERE, THEY'D HAVE TO SCOUR
HELL'S FLOOR FOR SO MUCH THREATENING...
HA, HA.
IT WILL BE
WARMER WHEN
I BLOW THE
TRUMPET
(IF INDEED I EVER DO;
FOR YOU ARE MEN AND REST
ETERNAL SORELY NEED)."
SO DOWN WE LAY AGAIN
I wonder,

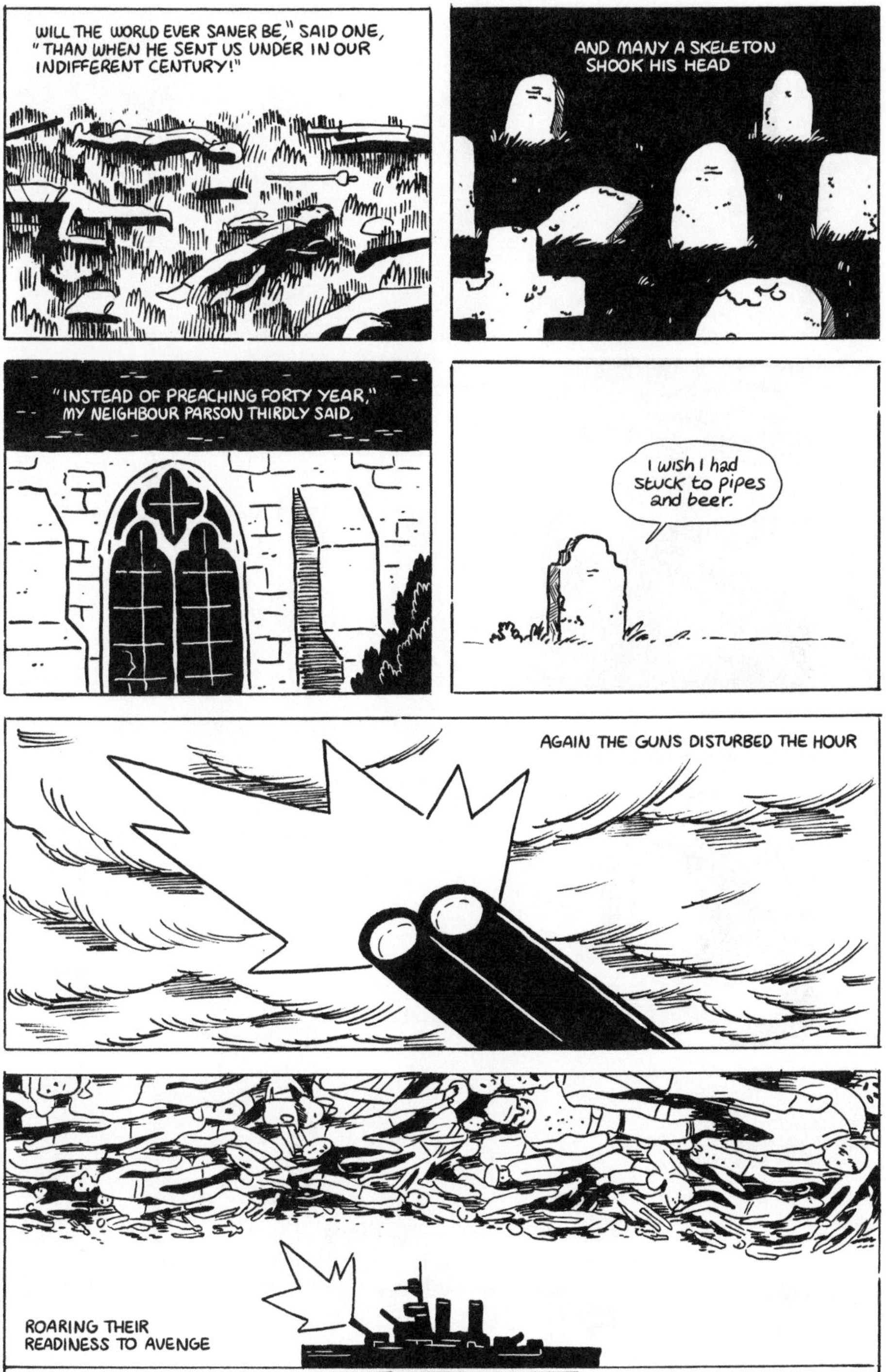
WILL THE WORLD EVER SANER BE," SAID ONE, "THAN WHEN HE SENT US UNDER IN OUR INDIFFERENT CENTURY!"
AND MANY A SKELETON SHOOK HIS HEAD
"INSTEAD OF PREACHING FORTY YEAR," MY NEIGHBOUR PARSON THIRDLY SAID,
I wish I had stuck to pipes and beer.
AGAIN THE GUNS DISTURBED THE HOUR
ROARING THEIR READINESS TO AVENGE

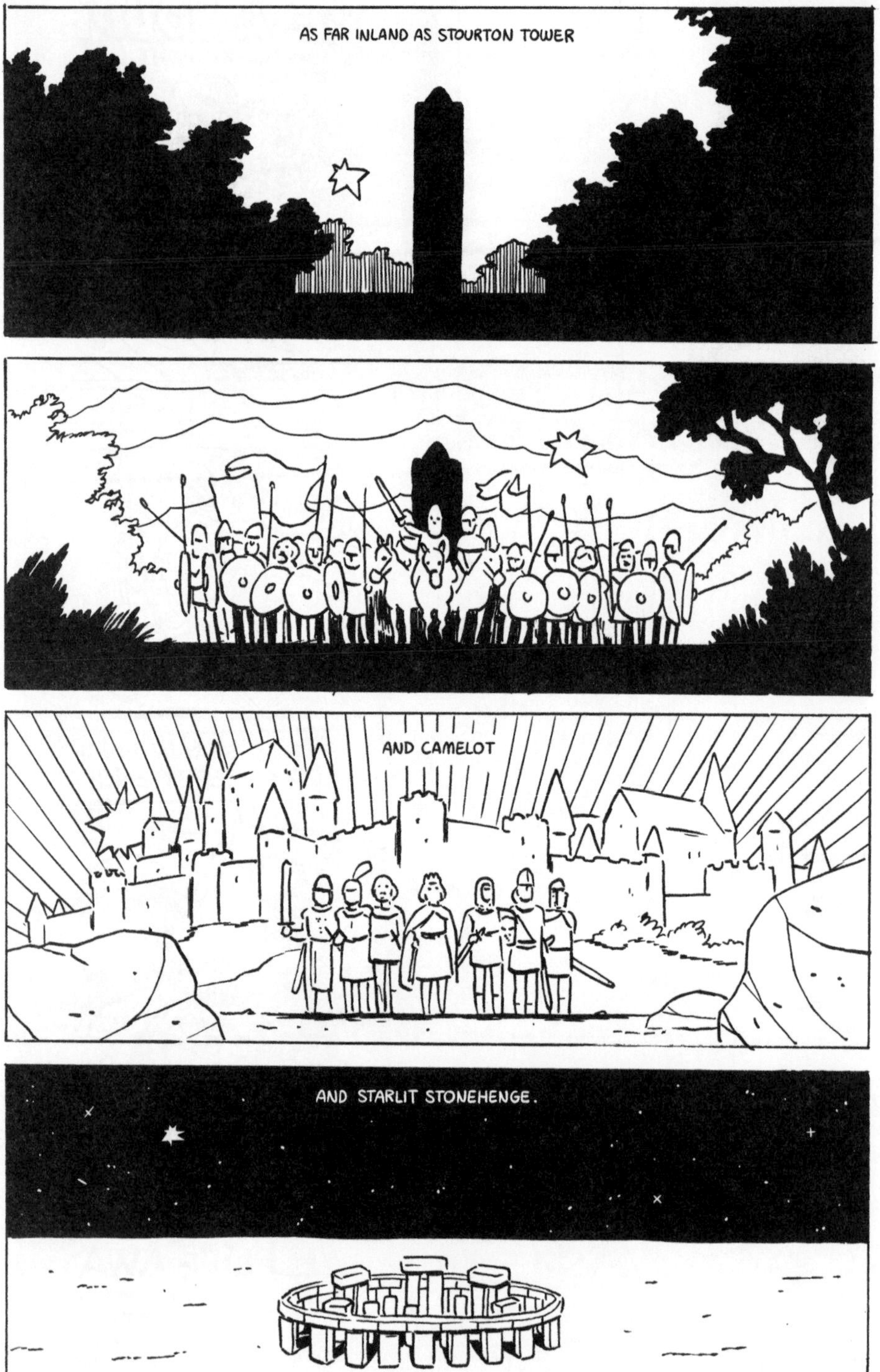
AS FAR INLAND AS STOURTON TOWER
AND CAMELOT
AND STARLIT STONEHENGE.

I DON'T WANT TO BE A SOLDIER

SOLDIERS' SONG ADAPTED BY HUNT EMERSON

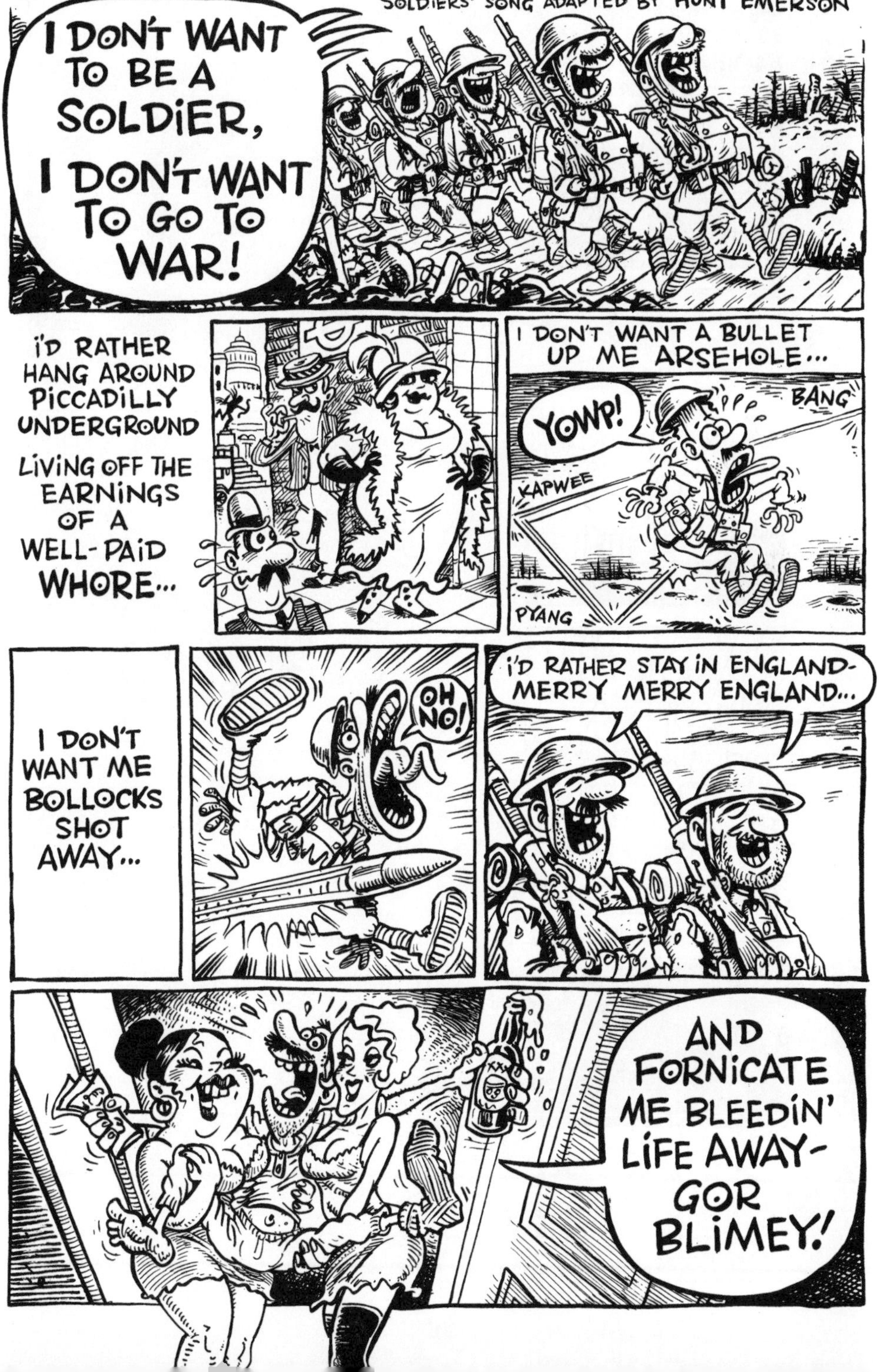

I DON'T WANT TO BE A SOLDIER, I DON'T WANT TO GO TO WAR!
I'D RATHER HANG AROUND PICCADILLY UNDERGROUND
LIVING OFF THE EARNINGS OF A WELL-PAID WHORE...
I DON'T WANT A BULLET UP ME ARSEHOLE...
YOWP!
BANG
KAPWEE
PYANG
I DON'T WANT ME BOLLOCKS SHOT AWAY...
OH NO!
I'D RATHER STAY IN ENGLAND- MERRY MERRY ENGLAND...
AND FORNICATE ME BLEEDIN' LIFE AWAY- GOR BLIMEY!

Peace by RUPERT BROOKE • Adapted by Simon Gane

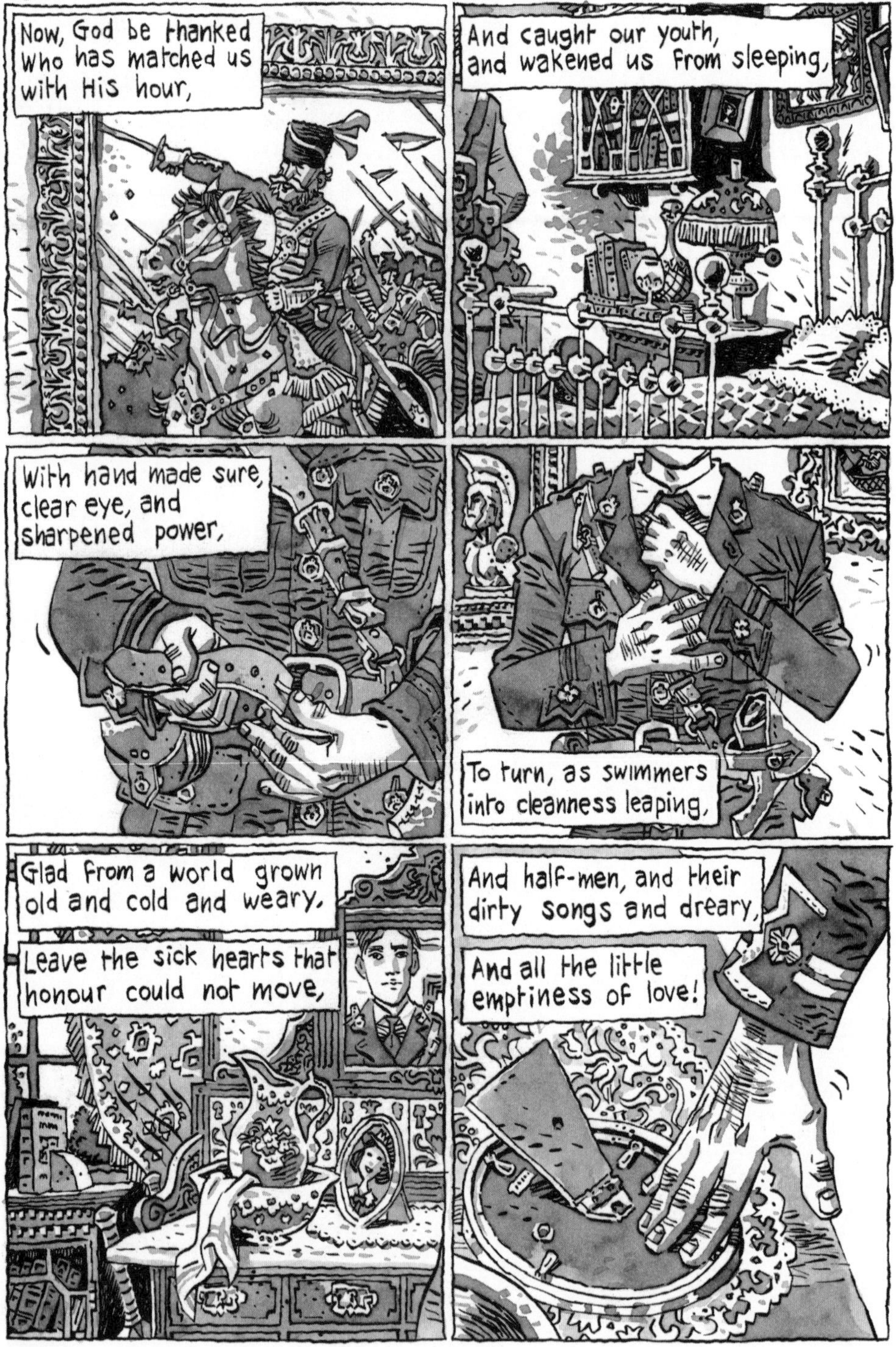
Now, God be thanked who has matched us with His hour,
And caught our youth, and wakened us from sleeping,
With hand made sure, clear eye, and sharpened power,
To turn, as swimmers into cleanness leaping,
Glad from a world grown old and cold and weary,
Leave the sick hearts that honour could not move,
And half-men, and their dirty songs and dreary,
And all the little emptiness of love!

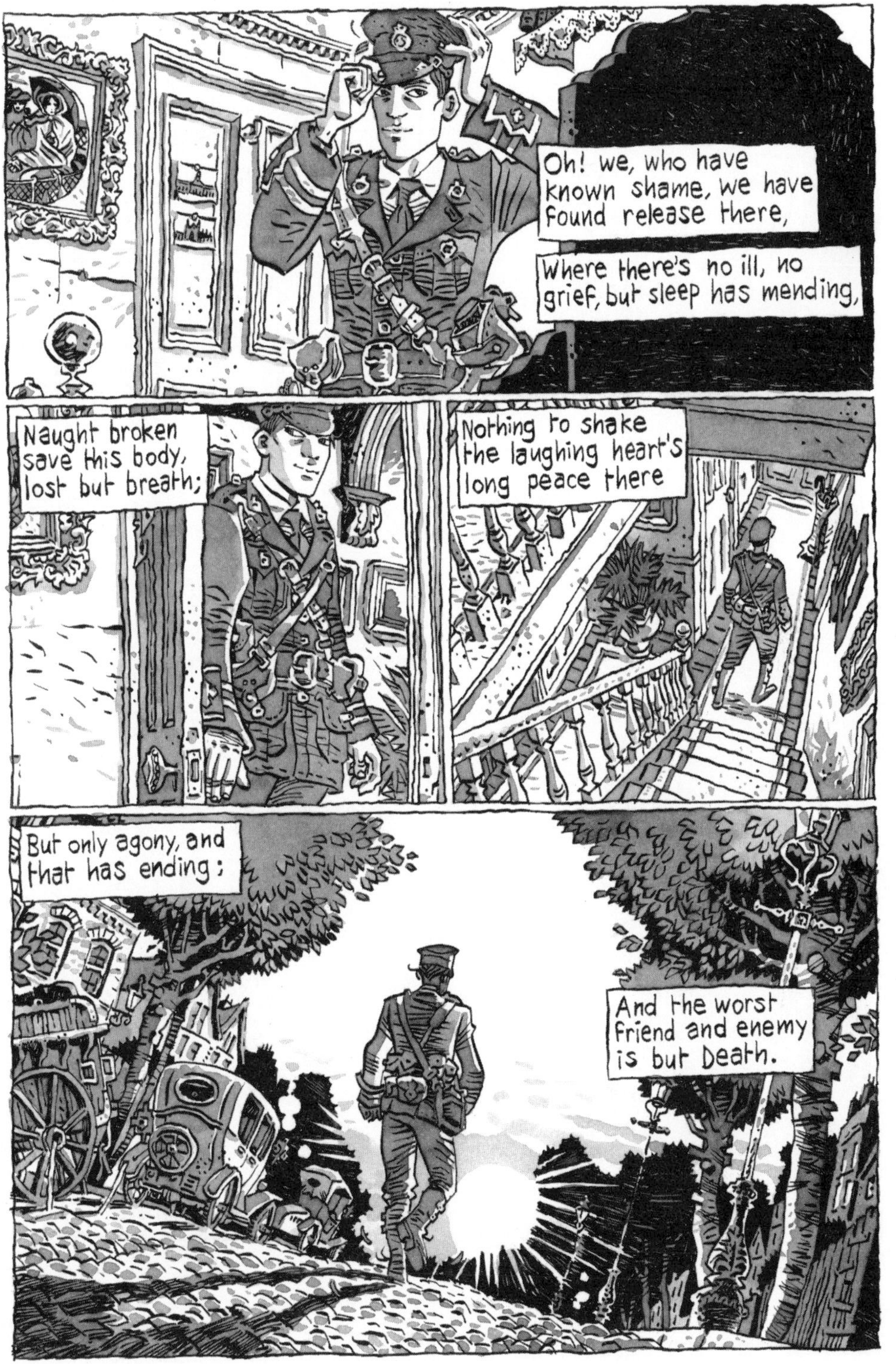
Oh! we, who have known shame, we have found release there,
Where there's no ill, no grief, but sleep has mending,
Naught broken save this body, lost but breath;
Nothing to shake the laughing heart's long peace there
But only agony, and that has ending;
And the worst friend and enemy is but Death.

WAR

FRANCIS EDWARD
LEDWIDGE

ADAPTED BY S. HARKHAM

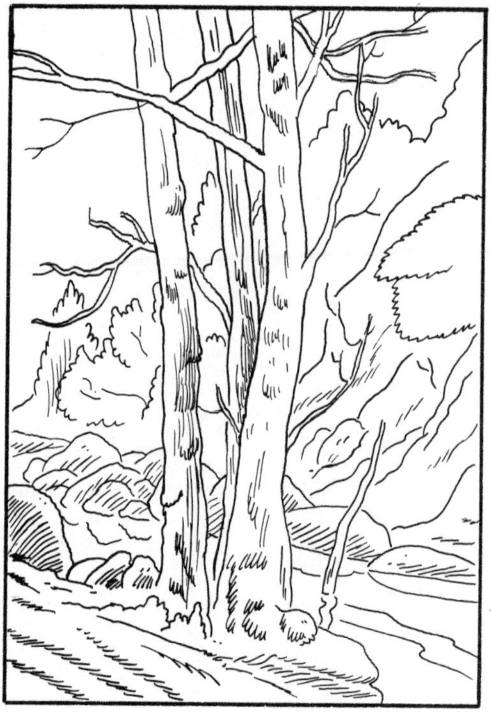

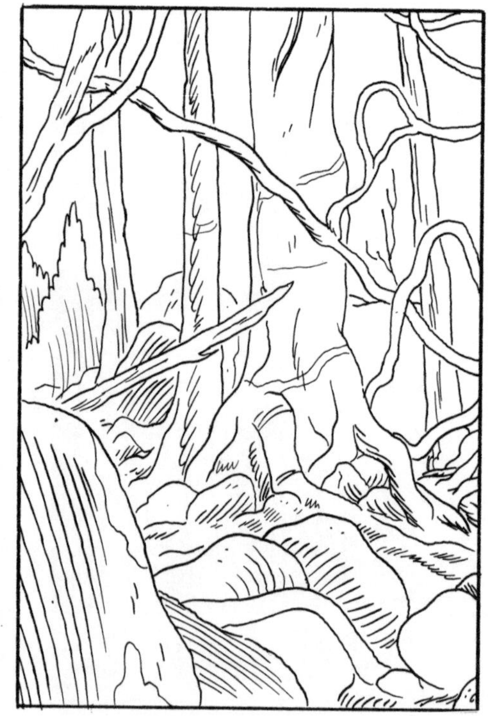

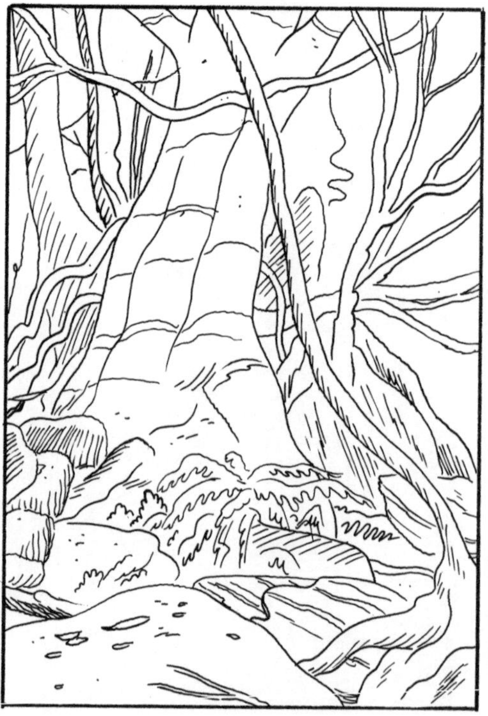

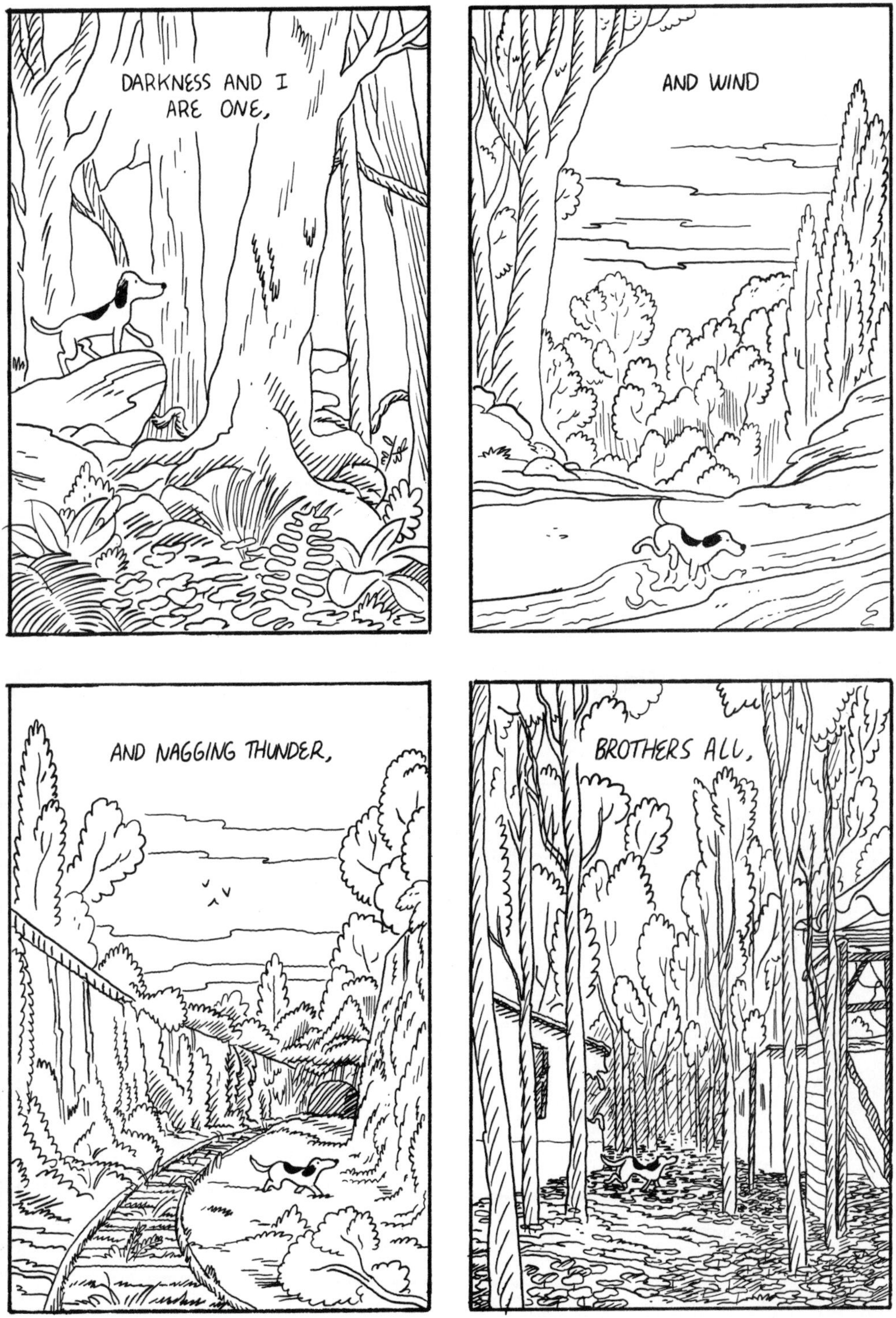
DARKNESS AND I
ARE ONE,
AND WIND
AND NAGGING THUNDER,
BROTHERS ALL,

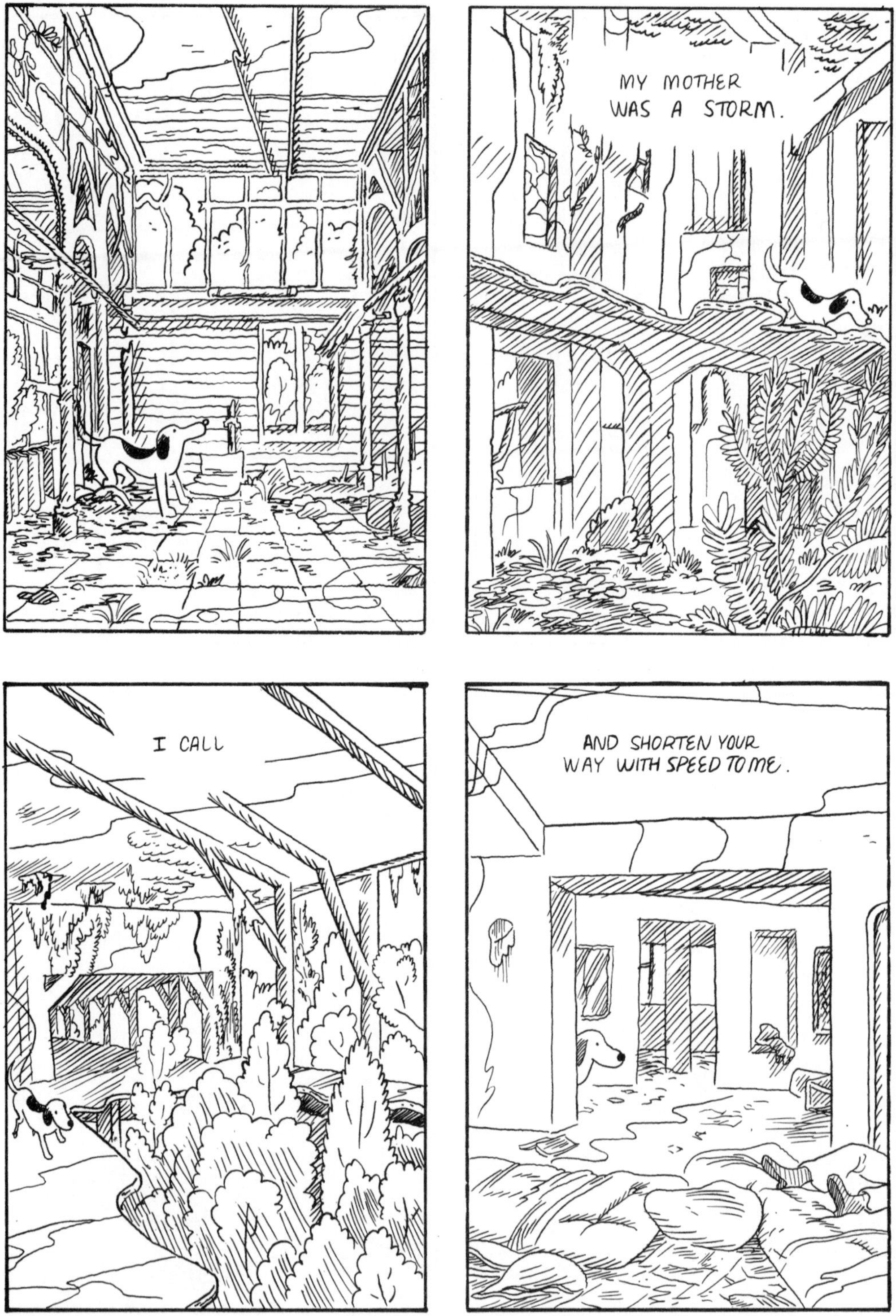
MY MOTHER WAS A STORM.
I CALL
AND SHORTEN YOUR WAY WITH SPEED TO ME.

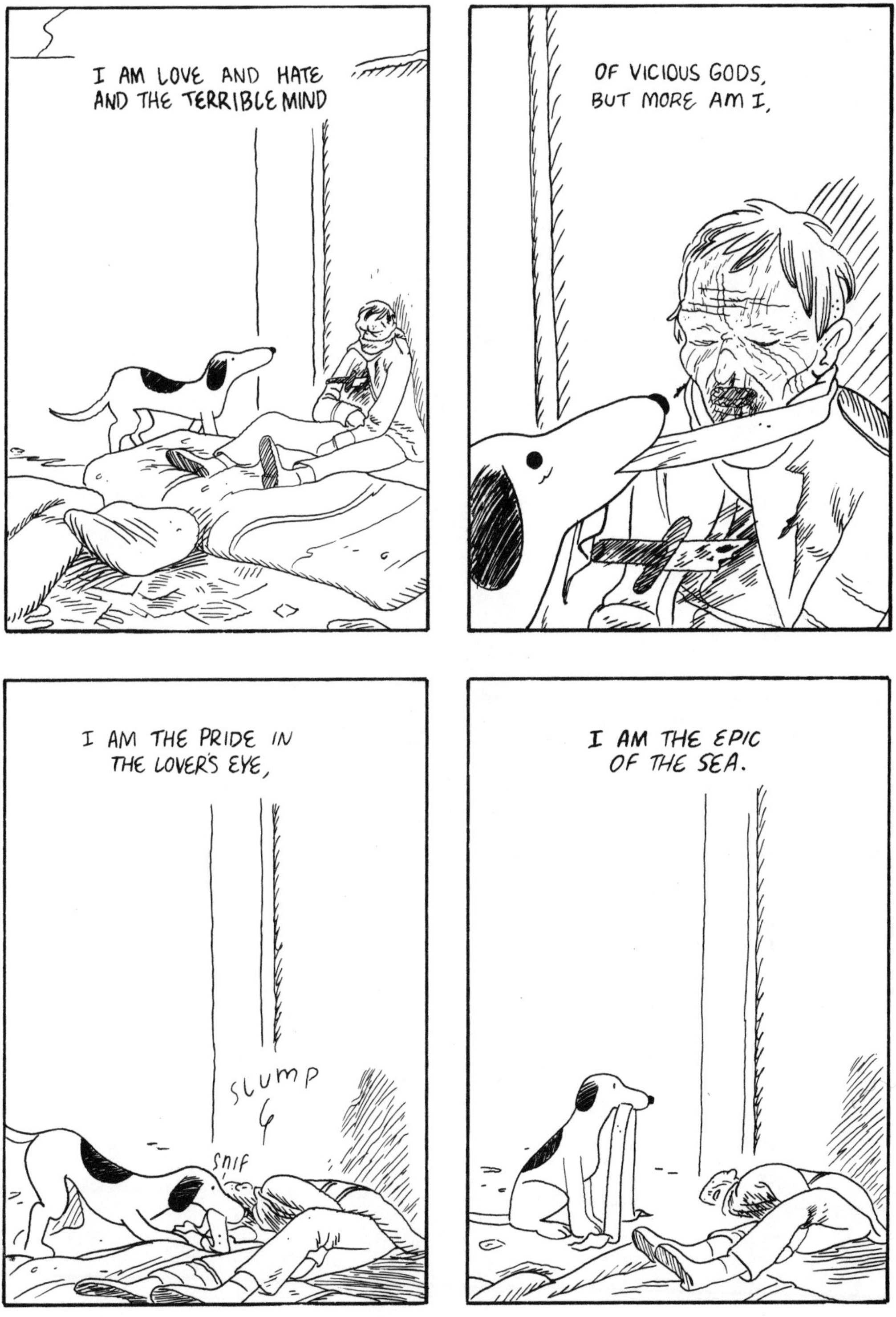
I AM LOVE AND HATE AND THE TERRIBLE MIND
OF VICIOUS GODS, BUT MORE AM I,
I AM THE PRIDE IN THE LOVER'S EYE,
SLUMP
SNIF
I AM THE EPIC OF THE SEA.

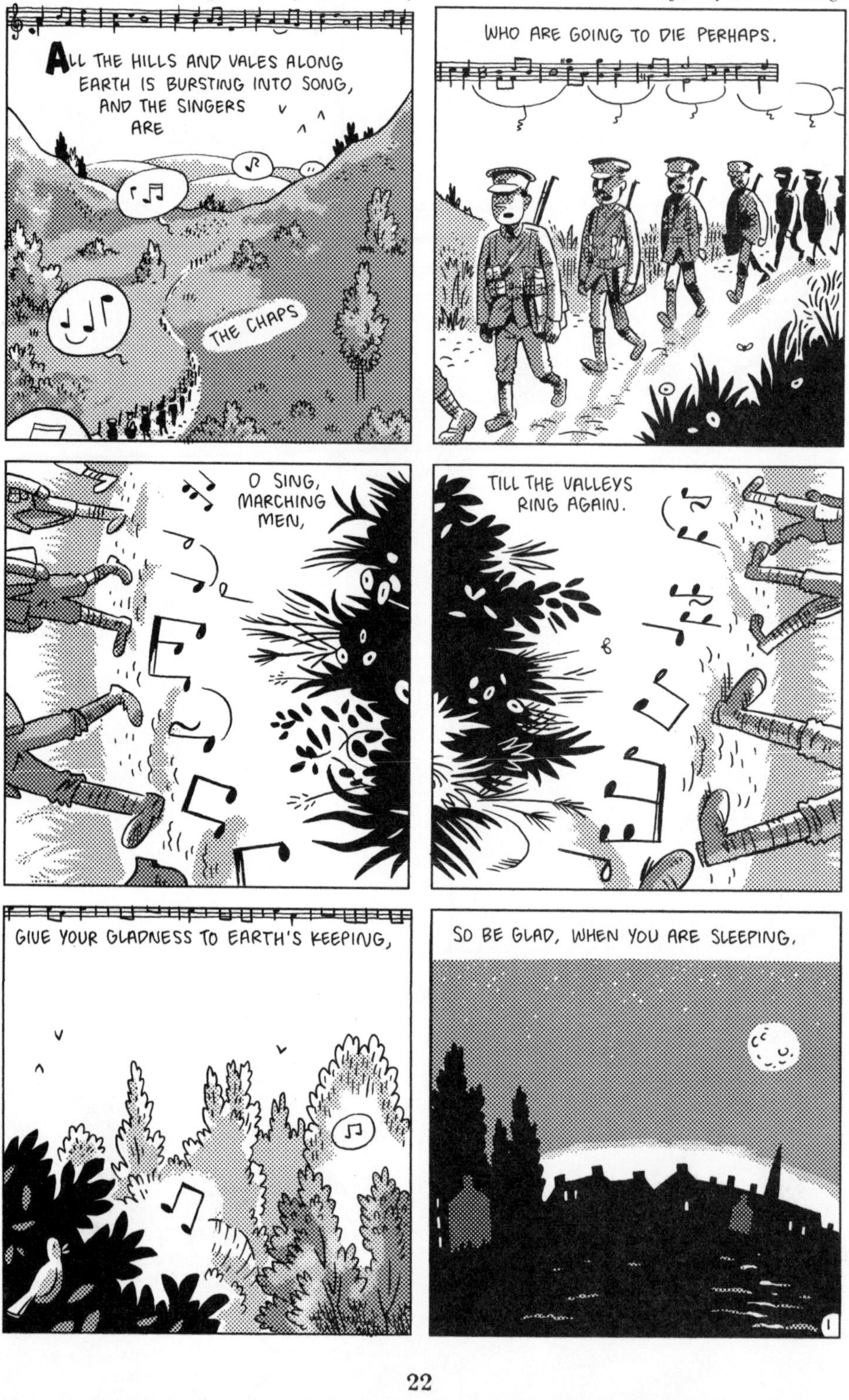
ALL THE HILLS AND VALES ALONG
EARTH IS BURSTING INTO SONG,
AND THE SINGERS ARE
THE CHAPS
WHO ARE GOING TO DIE PERHAPS.
O SING, MARCHING MEN,
TILL THE VALLEYS RING AGAIN.
GIVE YOUR GLADNESS TO EARTH'S KEEPING,
SO BE GLAD, WHEN YOU ARE SLEEPING.
1

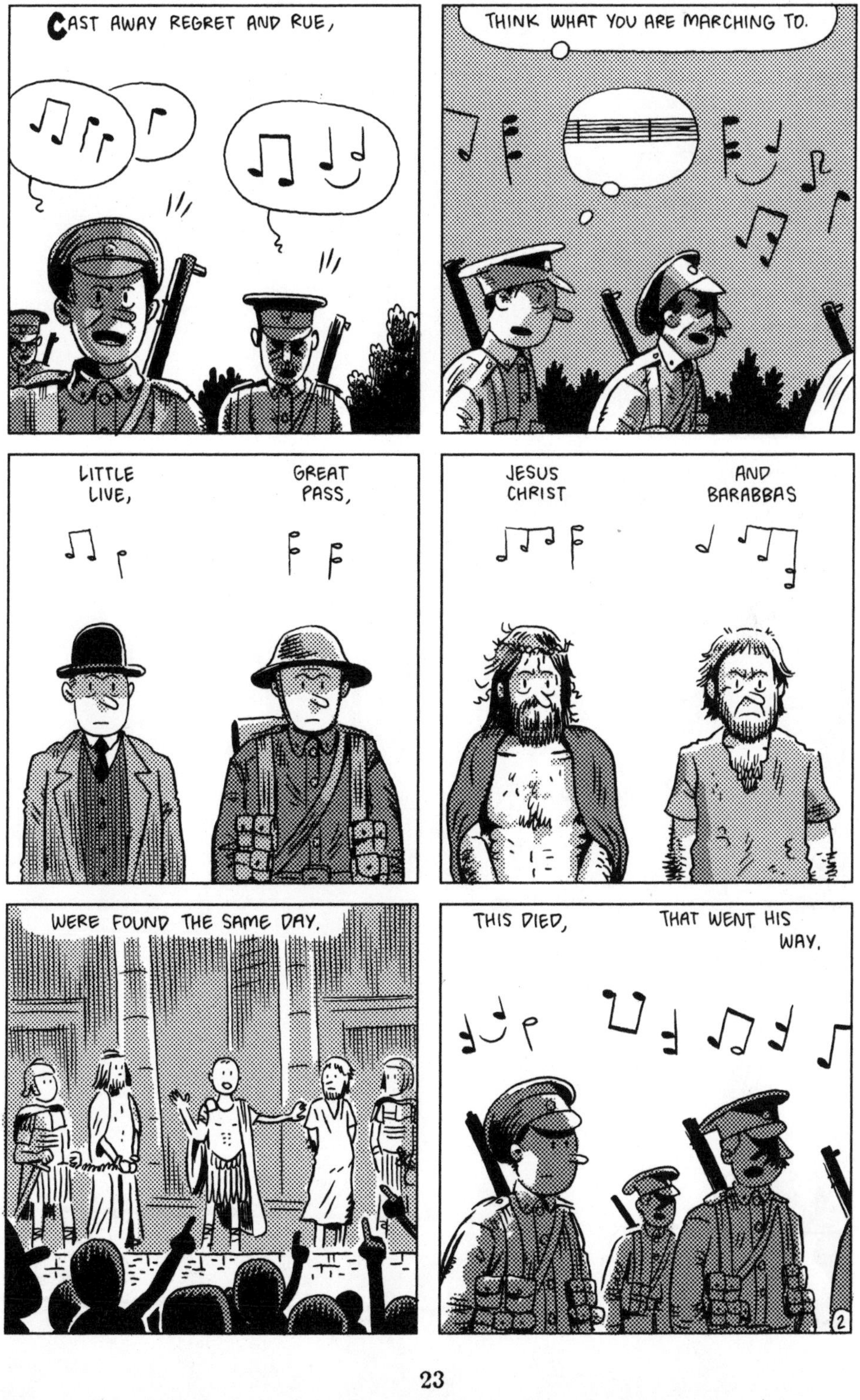
CAST AWAY REGRET AND RUE,
THINK WHAT YOU ARE MARCHING TO.
LITTLE LIVE,
GREAT PASS,
JESUS CHRIST
AND BARABBAS
WERE FOUND THE SAME DAY.
THIS DIED,
THAT WENT HIS WAY.
2

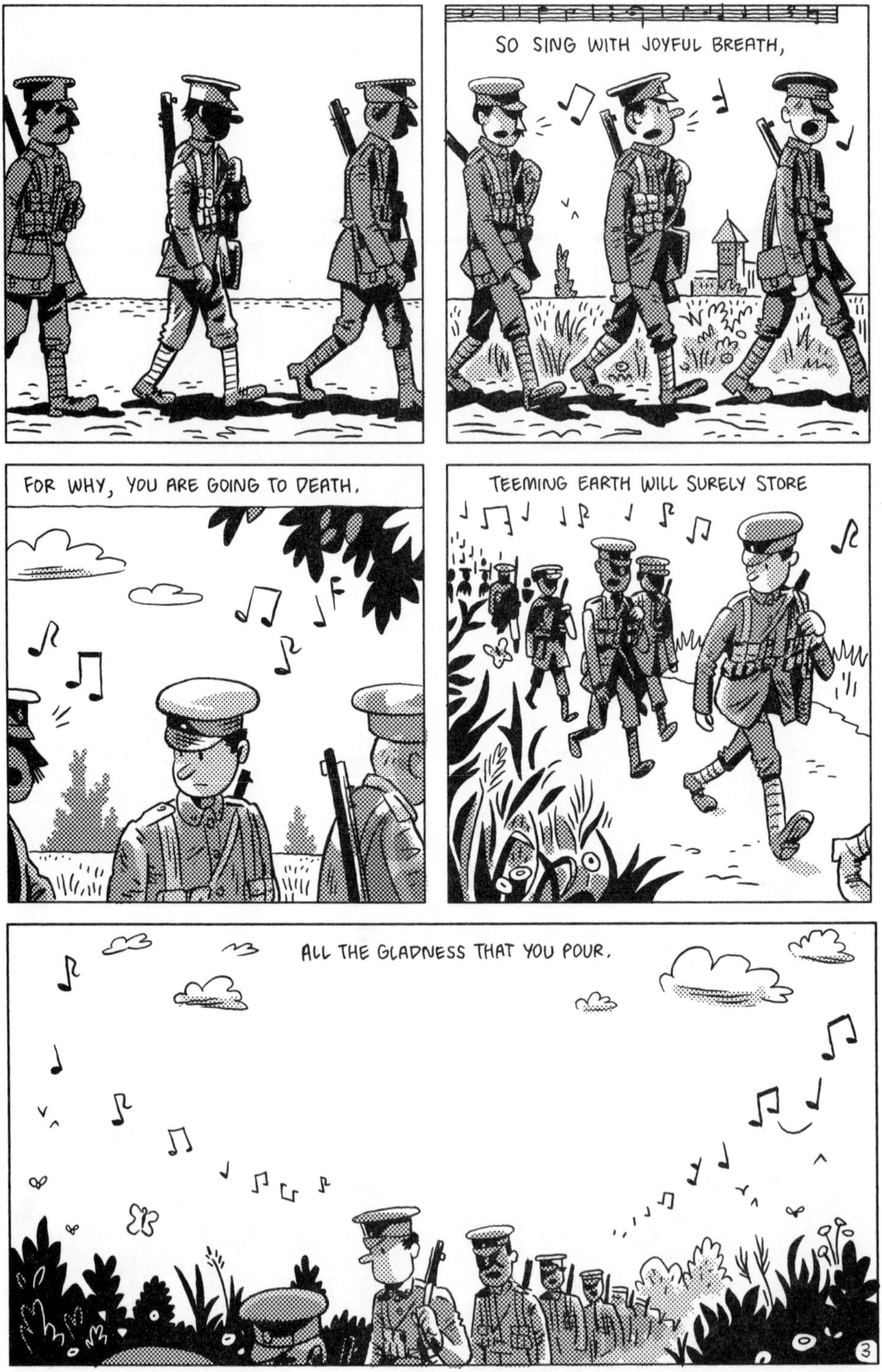
SO SING WITH JOYFUL BREATH,
FOR WHY, YOU ARE GOING TO DEATH.
TEEMING EARTH WILL SURELY STORE
ALL THE GLADNESS THAT YOU POUR.
3

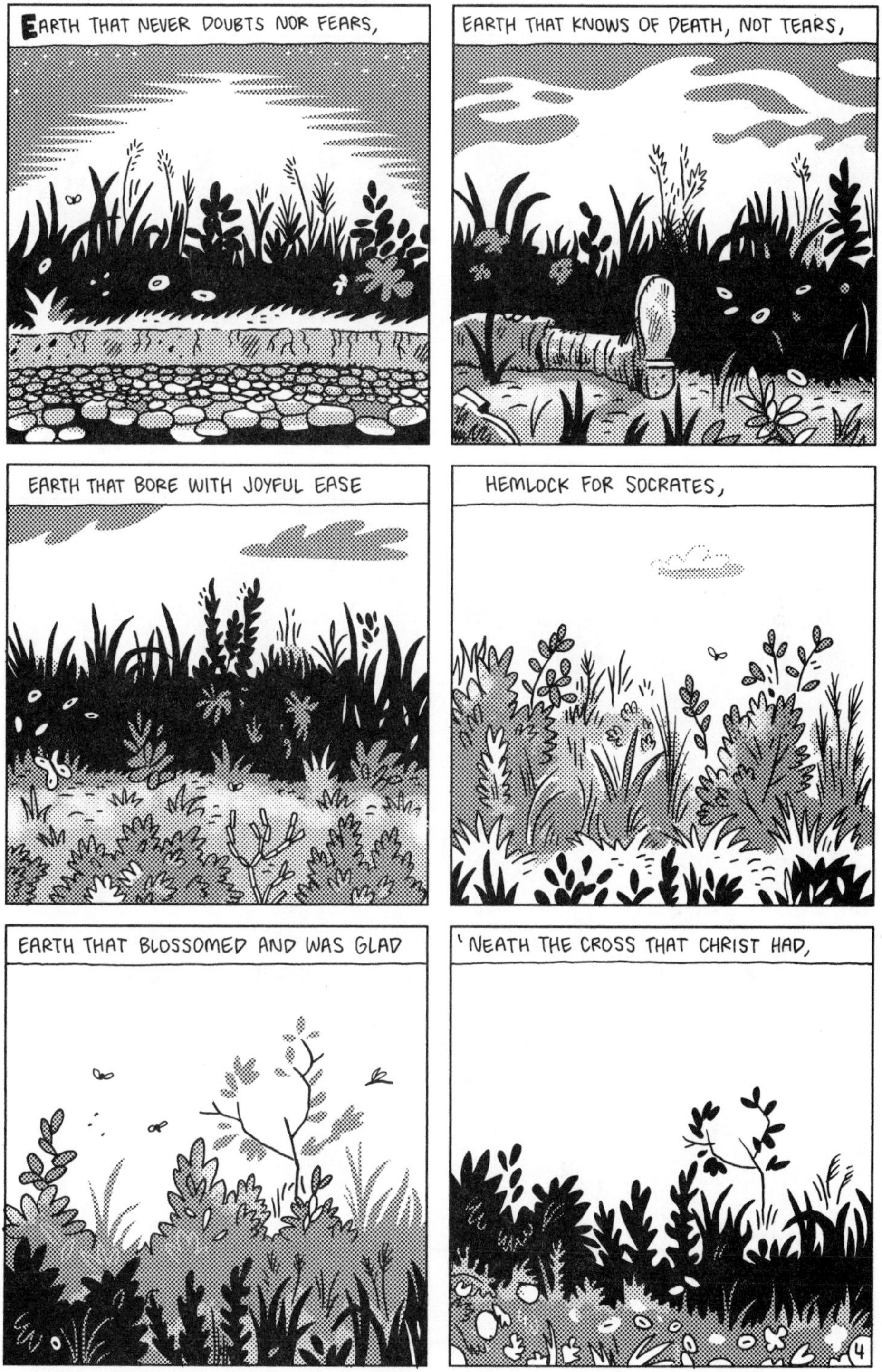
EARTH THAT NEVER DOUBTS NOR FEARS,
EARTH THAT KNOWS OF DEATH, NOT TEARS,
EARTH THAT BORE WITH JOYFUL EASE
HEMLOCK FOR SOCRATES,
EARTH THAT BLOSSOMED AND WAS GLAD
'NEATH THE CROSS THAT CHRIST HAD,
4

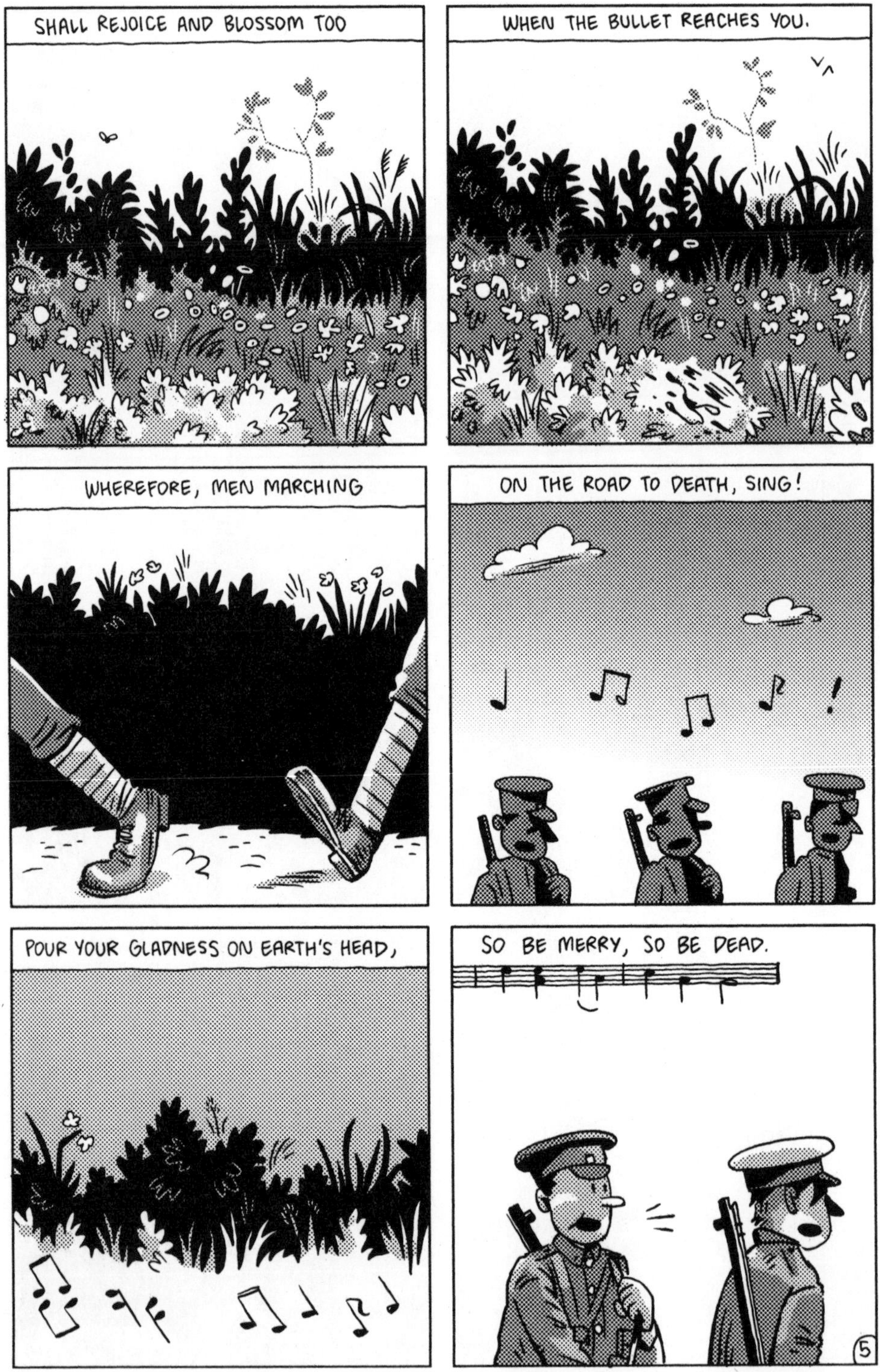
SHALL REJOICE AND BLOSSOM TOO
WHEN THE BULLET REACHES YOU.
WHEREFORE, MEN MARCHING
ON THE ROAD TO DEATH, SING!
POUR YOUR GLADNESS ON EARTH'S HEAD,
SO BE MERRY, SO BE DEAD.
5

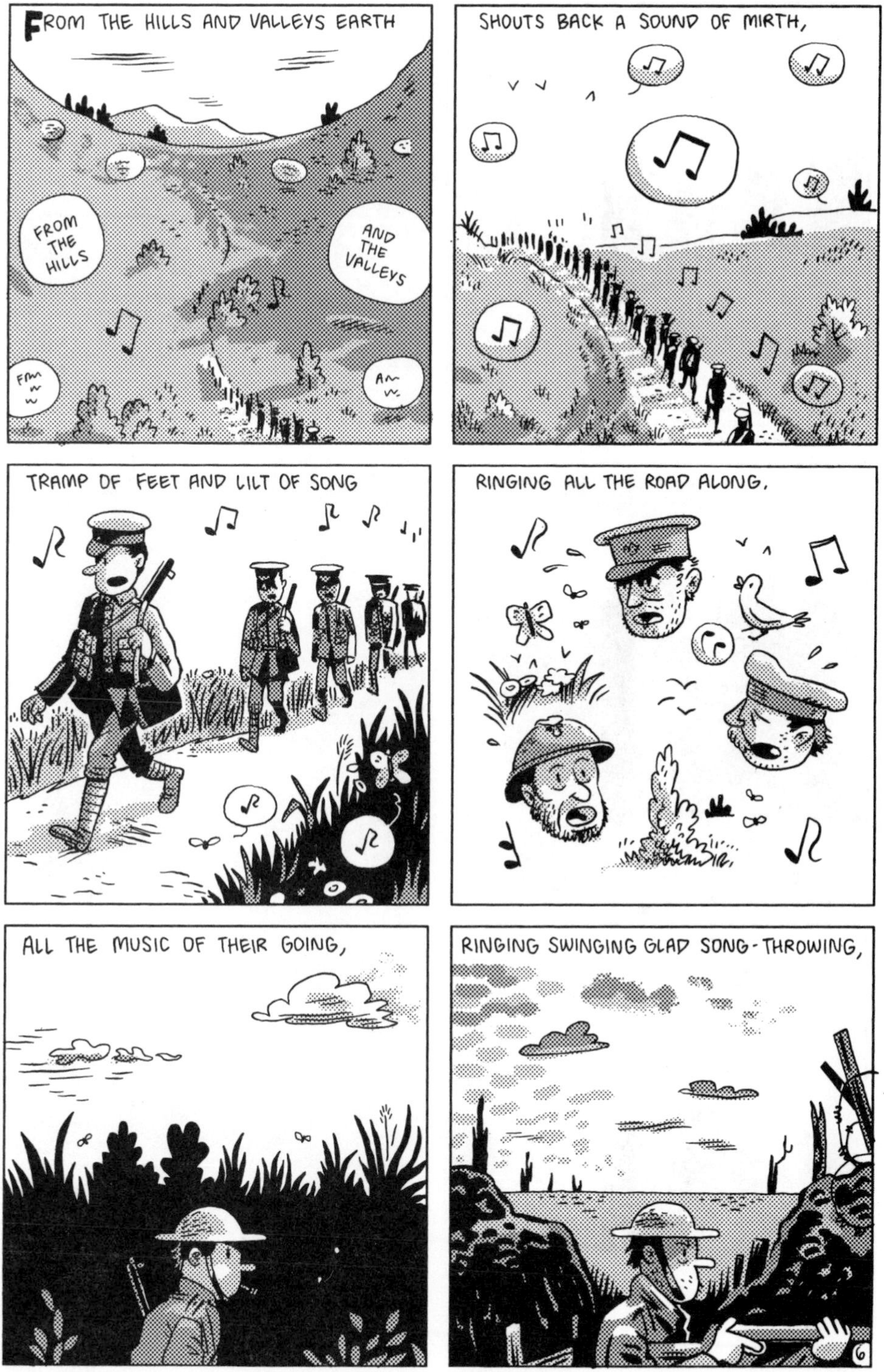
FROM THE HILLS AND VALLEYS EARTH
FROM THE HILLS
AND THE VALLEYS
SHOUTS BACK A SOUND OF MIRTH,
TRAMP OF FEET AND LILT OF SONG
RINGING ALL THE ROAD ALONG.
ALL THE MUSIC OF THEIR GOING,
RINGING SWINGING GLAD SONG-THROWING,

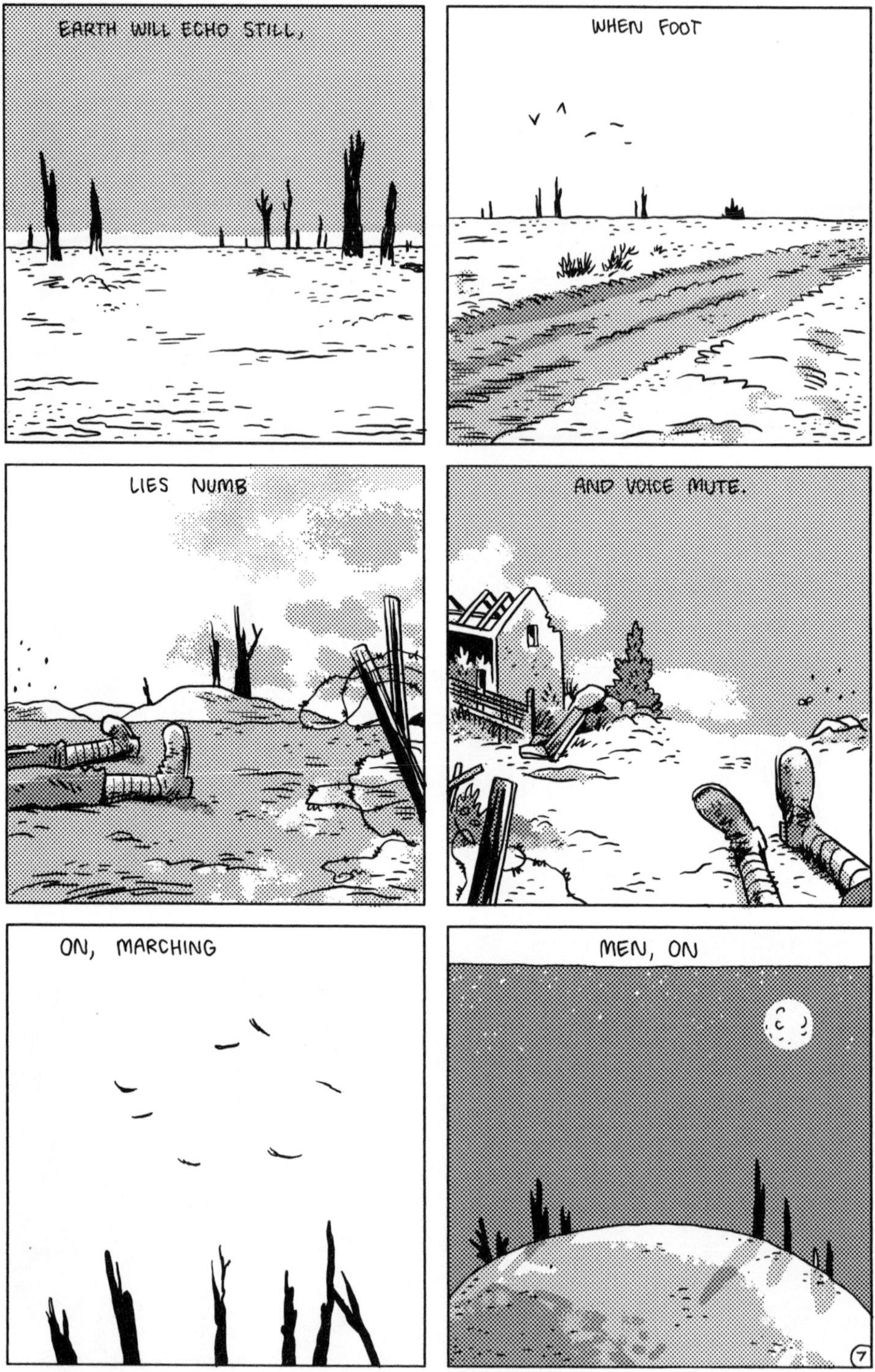
EARTH WILL ECHO STILL,
WHEN FOOT
LIES NUMB
AND VOICE MUTE.
ON, MARCHING
MEN, ON
7

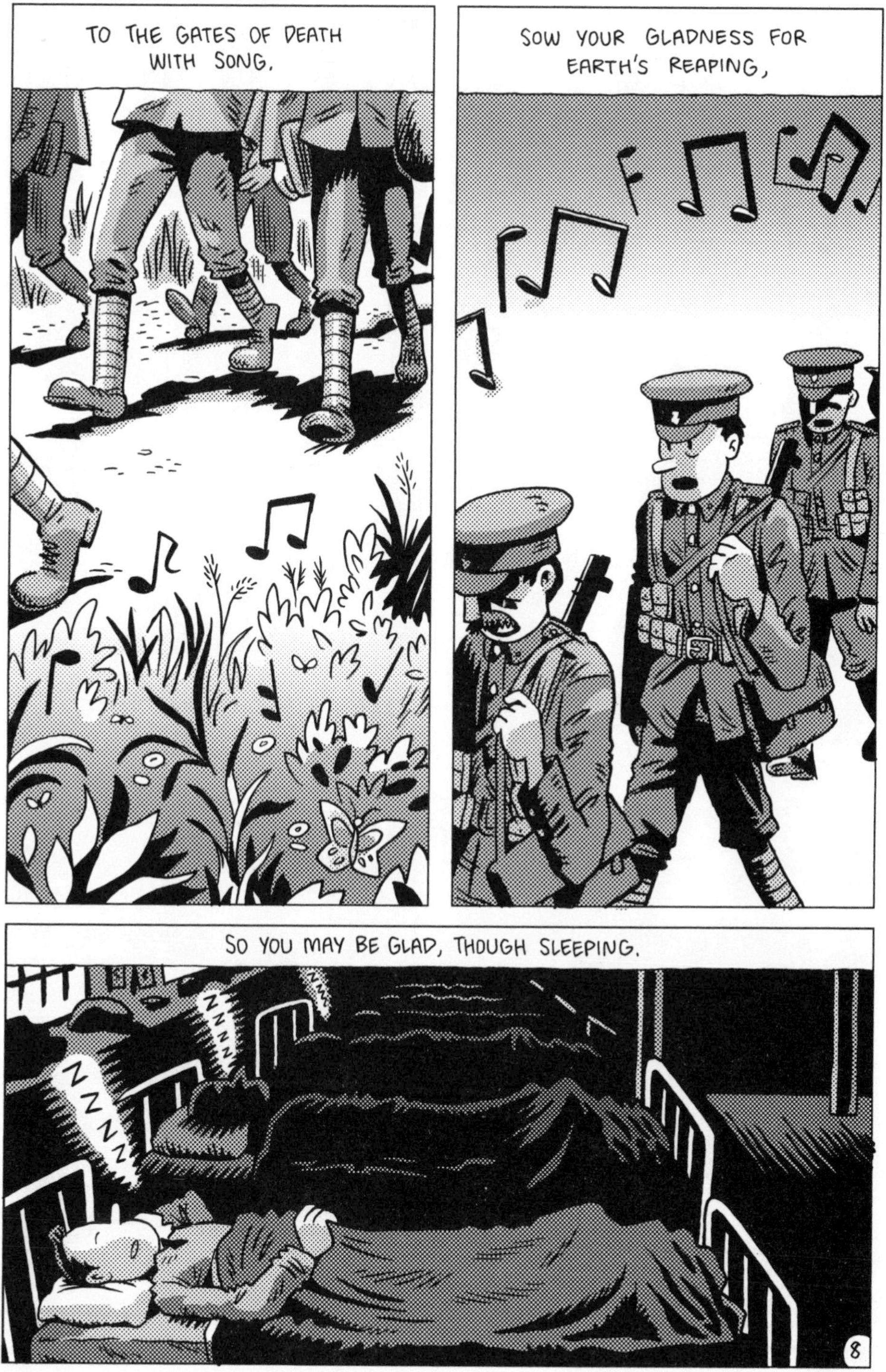
TO THE GATES OF DEATH WITH SONG.
SOW YOUR GLADNESS FOR EARTH'S REAPING,
SO YOU MAY BE GLAD, THOUGH SLEEPING.
ZZZZ
ZZZZ
8

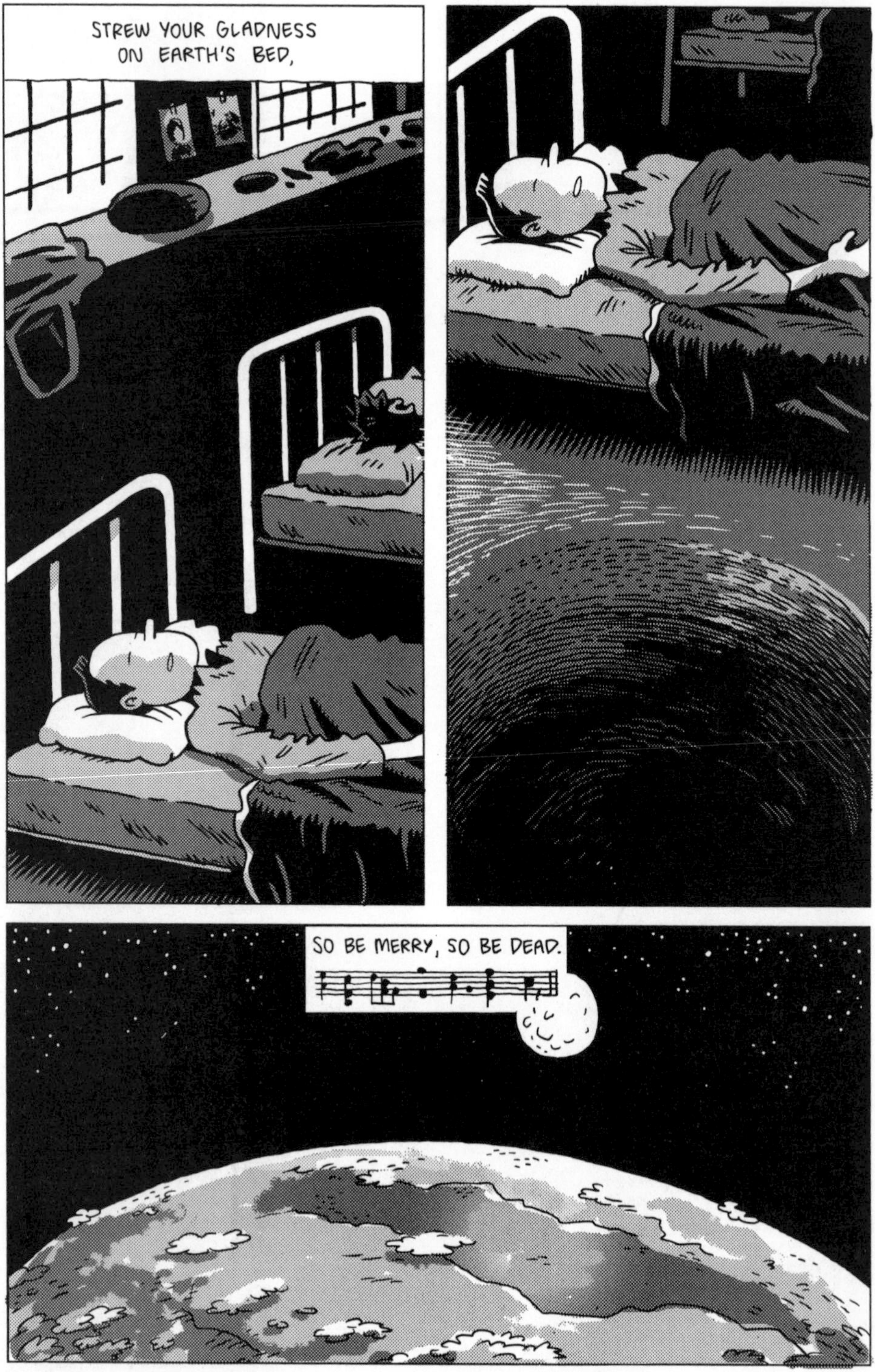
STREW YOUR GLADNESS ON EARTH'S BED,
SO BE MERRY, SO BE DEAD.

II

In the Trenches

The Great Push

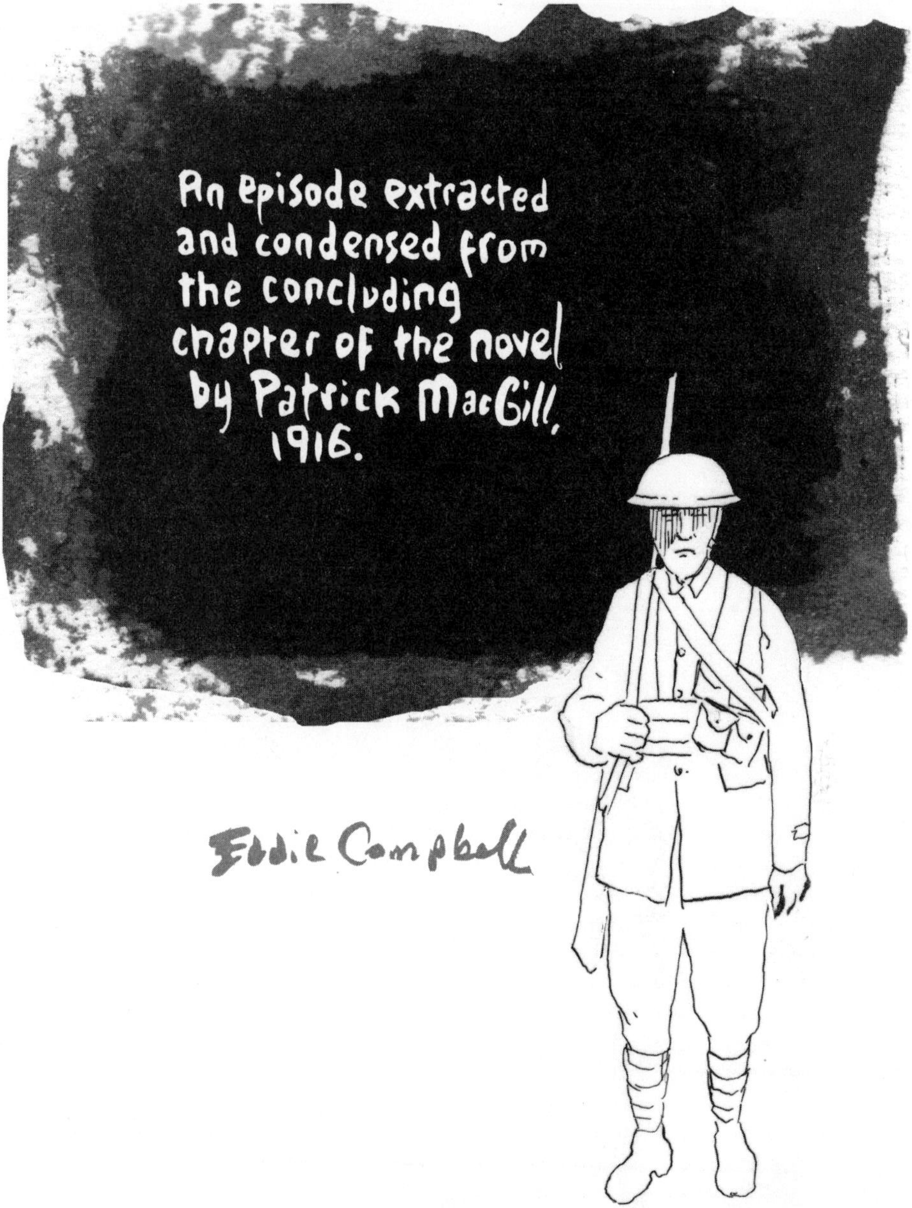
An episode extracted and condensed from the concluding chapter of the novel by Patrick MacGill, 1916.

Eddie Campbell

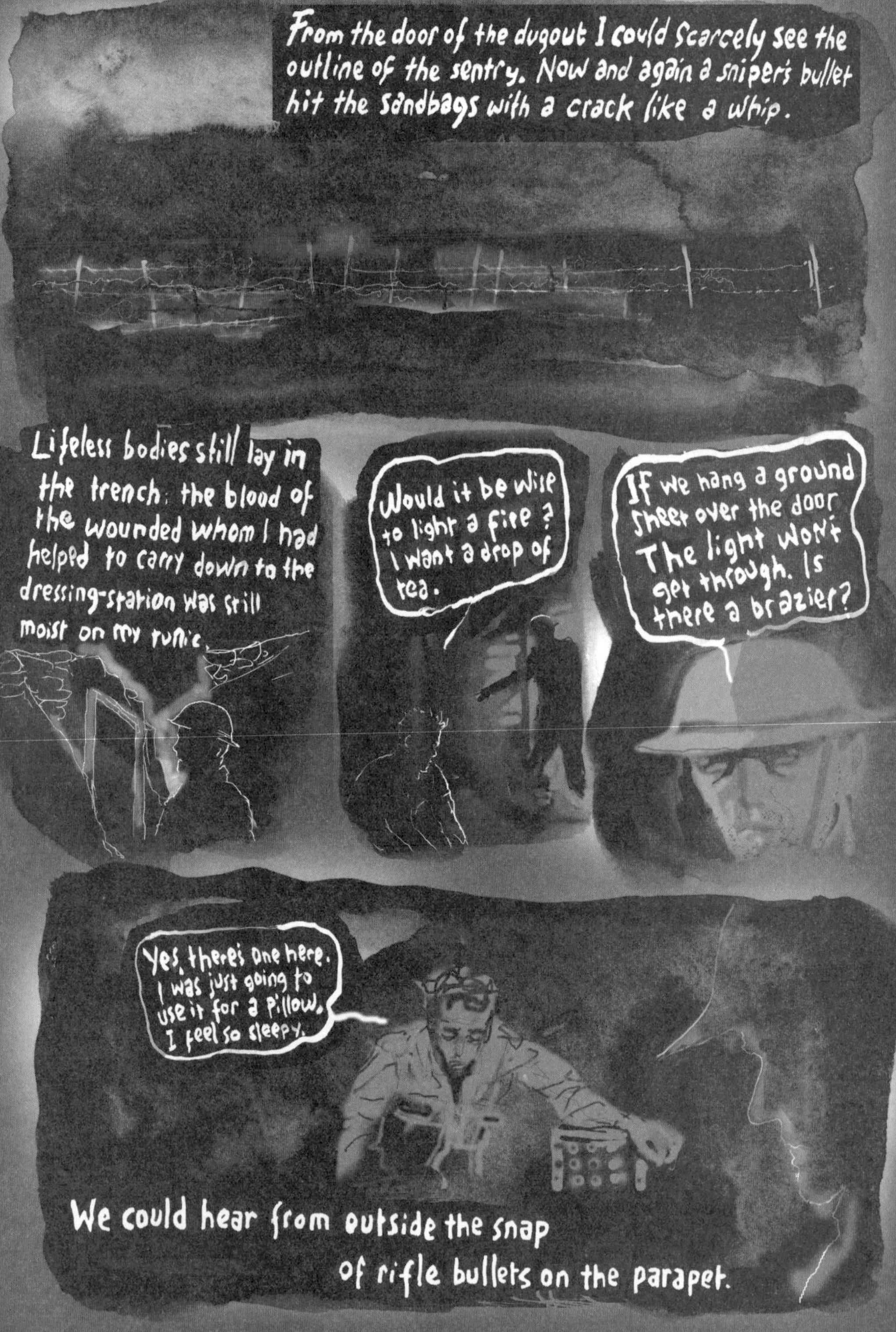
From the door of the dugout I could scarcely see the outline of the sentry. Now and again a sniper's bullet hit the sandbags with a crack like a whip.
Lifeless bodies still lay in the trench: the blood of the wounded whom I had helped to carry down to the dressing-station was still moist on my tunic.
Would it be wise to light a fire? I want a drop of tea.
If we hang a ground sheet over the door the light won't get through. Is there a brazier?
Yes, there's one here. I was just going to use it for a pillow. I feel so sleepy.
We could hear from outside the snap of rifle bullets on the parapet.

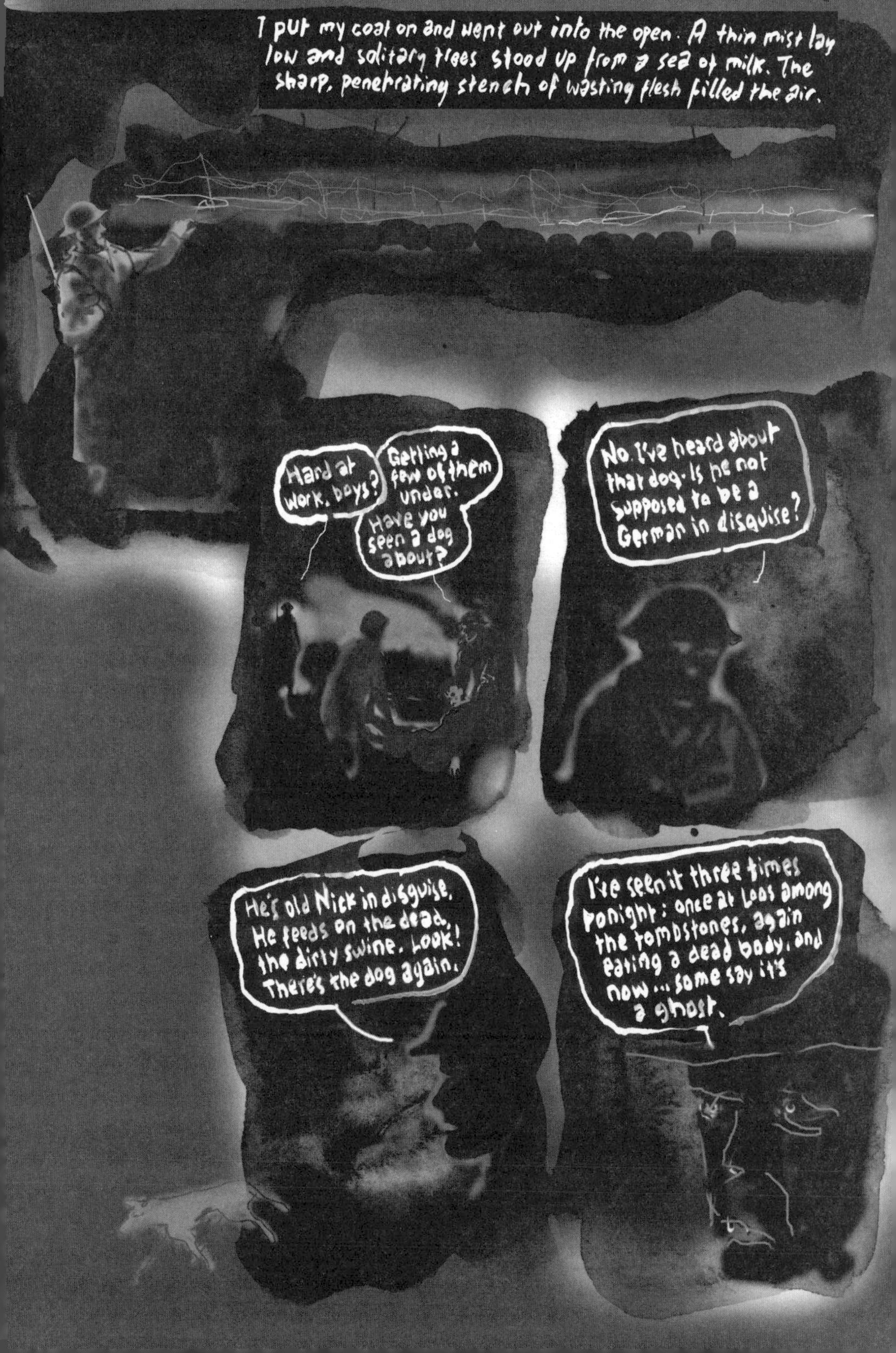
I put my coat on and went out into the open. A thin mist lay low and solitary trees stood up from a sea of milk. The sharp, penetrating stench of wasting flesh filled the air.
Hard at work, boys?
Getting a few of them under.
Have you seen a dog about?
No. I've heard about that dog. Is he not supposed to be a German in disguise?
He's old Nick in disguise. He feeds on the dead, the dirty swine. Look! There's the dog again.
I've seen it three times tonight: once at Loos among the tombstones, again eating a dead body, and now... some say it's a ghost.

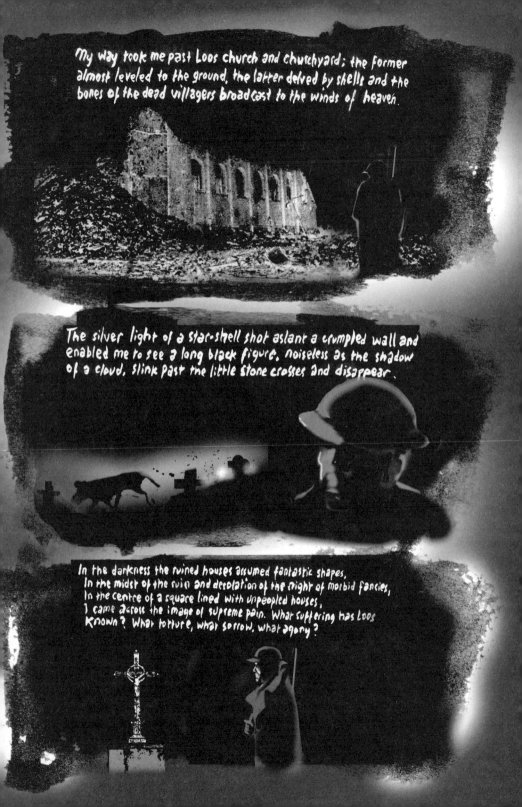

My way took me past Loos church and churchyard; the former almost leveled to the ground, the latter delved by shells and the bones of the dead villagers broadcast to the winds of heaven.

The silver light of a star-shell shot aslant a crumpled wall and enabled me to see a long black figure, noiseless as the shadow of a cloud, slink past the little stone crosses and disappear.

In the darkness the ruined houses assumed fantastic shapes.
In the midst of the ruin and desolation of the night of morbid fancies,
In the centre of a square lined with unpeopled houses,
I came across the image of supreme pain. What suffering has Loos known? What torture, what sorrow, what agony?

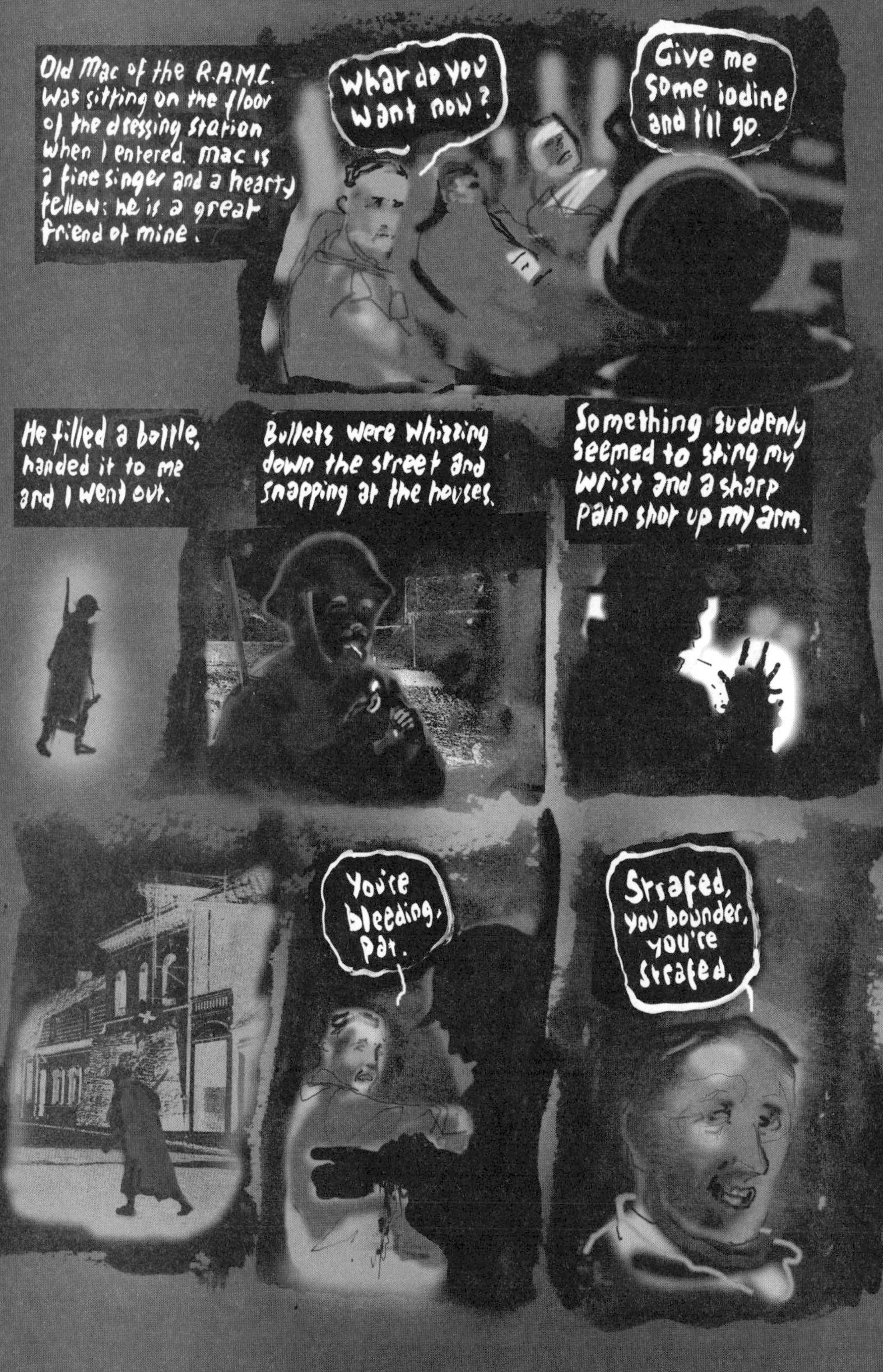
Old Mac of the R.A.M.C. was sitting on the floor of the dressing station when I entered. Mac is a fine singer and a hearty fellow: he is a great friend of mine.
What do you want now?
Give me some iodine and I'll go.
He filled a bottle, handed it to me and I went out.
Bullets were whizzing down the street and snapping at the houses.
Something suddenly seemed to sting my wrist and a sharp pain shot up my arm.
You're bleeding, Pat.
Strafed, you bounder, you're strafed.

Lucky dog. You're for Blighty, man. I wish to God I was. Is it raining now?

It is just starting to come down. How am I to get out of this?

There'll be an ambulance up here in a wee. Suppose it gets blown to blazes?

I'm finished with the war for a few weeks at least.

I'm pleased. I hope I get to England. Another casualty from Loos. The dead are lying all around here; civilians and soldiers.

A dead child lying in a trench near Hulluch. I suppose somebody has buried it. I wonder how it got there.

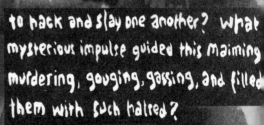

Who is going to benefit by the carnage, save the rats, which feed now as they have never fed before? Why have millions of men come here from all corners of Europe...

to hack and slay one another? What mysterious impulse guided this maiming murdering, gouging, gassing, and filled them with such hatred?

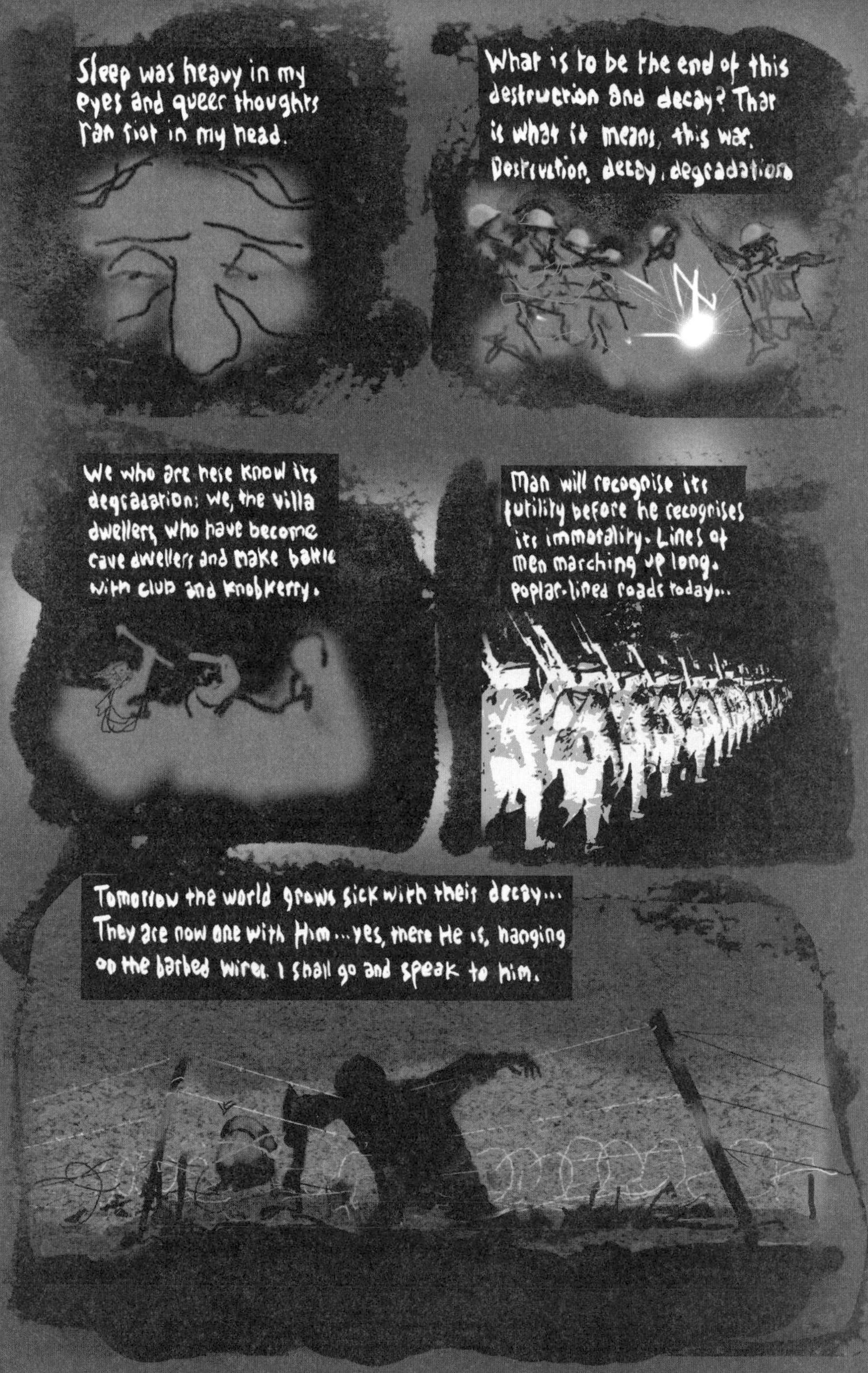
Sleep was heavy in my eyes and queer thoughts ran riot in my head.
What is to be the end of this destruction and decay? That is what it means, this war. Destruction, decay, degradation.
We who are here know its degradation: we, the villa dwellers, who have become cave dwellers and make battle with club and knobkerry.
Man will recognise its futility before he recognises its immorality. Lines of men marching up long, poplar-lined roads today...
Tomorrow the world grows sick with their decay... They are now one with Him... yes, there He is, hanging on the barbed wire. I shall go and speak to him.

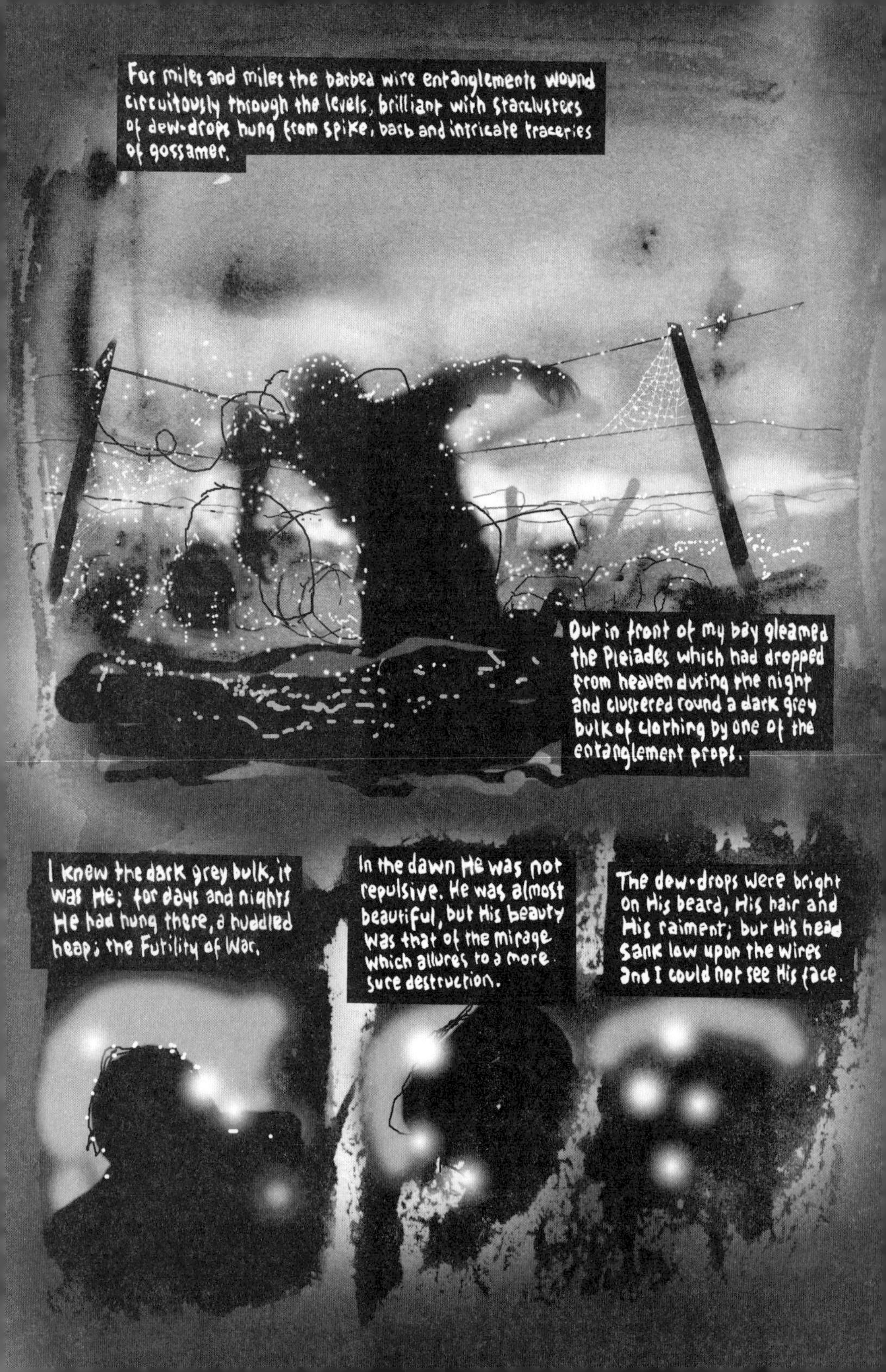
For miles and miles the barbed wire entanglements wound circuitously through the levels, brilliant with starclusters of dew-drops hung from spike, barb and intricate traceries of gossamer.
Out in front of my bay gleamed the Pleiades which had dropped from heaven during the night and clustered round a dark grey bulk of clothing by one of the entanglement props.
I knew the dark grey bulk, it was He; for days and nights He had hung there, a huddled heap; the Futility of War.
In the dawn He was not repulsive. He was almost beautiful, but His beauty was that of the mirage which allures to a more sure destruction.
The dew-drops were bright on His beard, His hair and His raiment; but His head sank low upon the wires and I could not see His face.

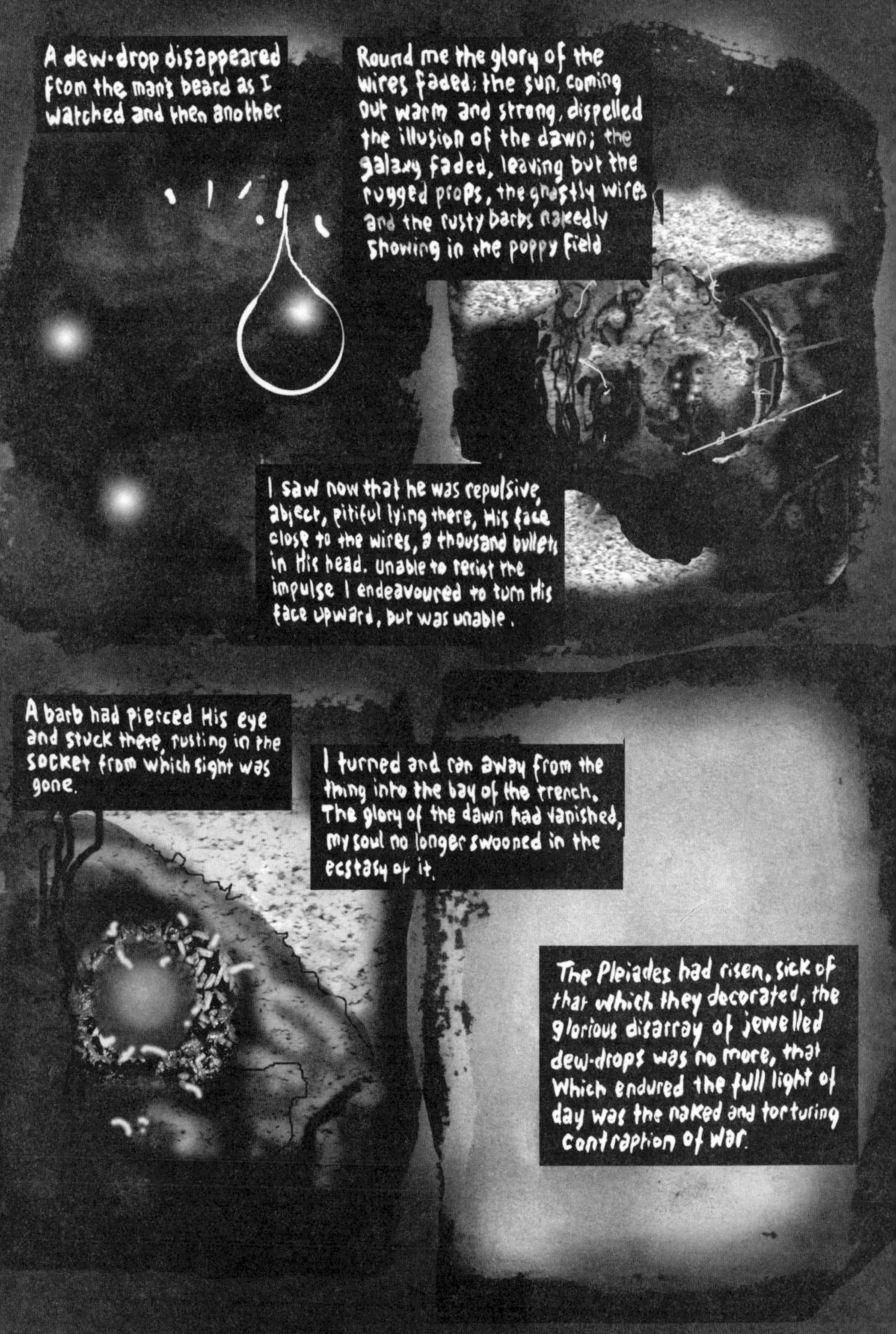
A dew-drop disappeared from the man's beard as I watched and then another.
Round me the glory of the wires faded; the sun, coming out warm and strong, dispelled the illusion of the dawn; the galaxy faded, leaving but the rugged props, the ghastly wires and the rusty barbs nakedly showing in the poppy field.
I saw now that he was repulsive, abject, pitiful lying there, His face close to the wires, a thousand bullets in His head. Unable to resist the impulse I endeavoured to turn His face upward, but was unable.
A barb had pierced His eye and stuck there, rusting in the socket from which sight was gone.
I turned and ran away from the thing into the bay of the trench. The glory of the dawn had vanished, my soul no longer swooned in the ecstasy of it.
The Pleiades had risen, sick of that which they decorated, the glorious disarray of jewelled dew-drops was no more, that Which endured the full light of day was the naked and torturing contraption of War.

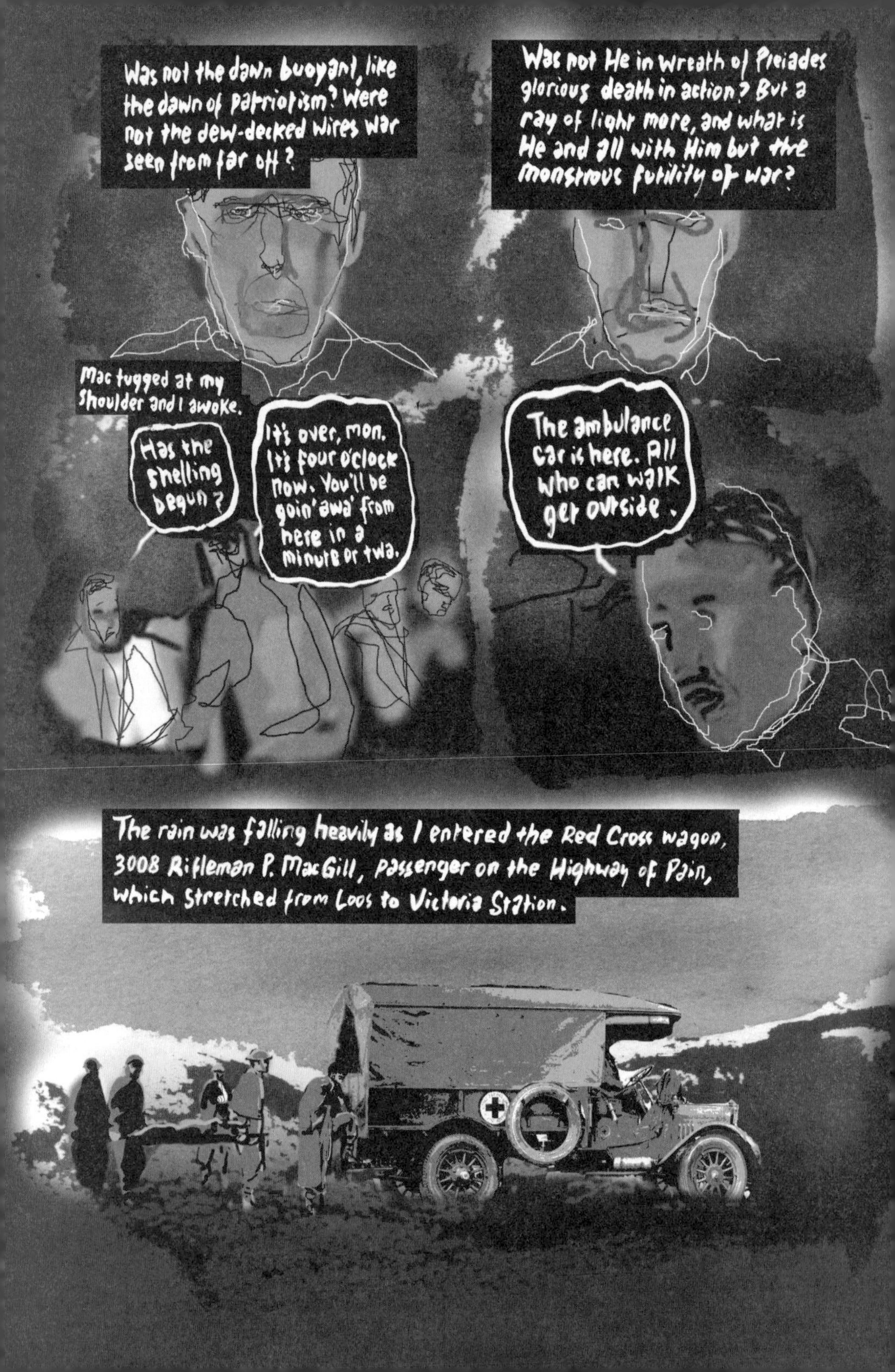
Was not the dawn buoyant, like the dawn of patriotism? Were not the dew-decked wires war seen from far off?
Was not He in wreath of Pleiades glorious death in action? But a ray of light more, and what is He and all with Him but the monstrous futility of war?
Mac tugged at my shoulder and I awoke.
Has the shelling begun?
It's over, mon. It's four o'clock now. You'll be goin' awa' from here in a minute or twa.
The ambulance car is here. All who can walk get outside.
The rain was falling heavily as I entered the Red Cross wagon, 3008 Rifleman P. MacGill, passenger on the Highway of Pain, which stretched from Loos to Victoria Station.

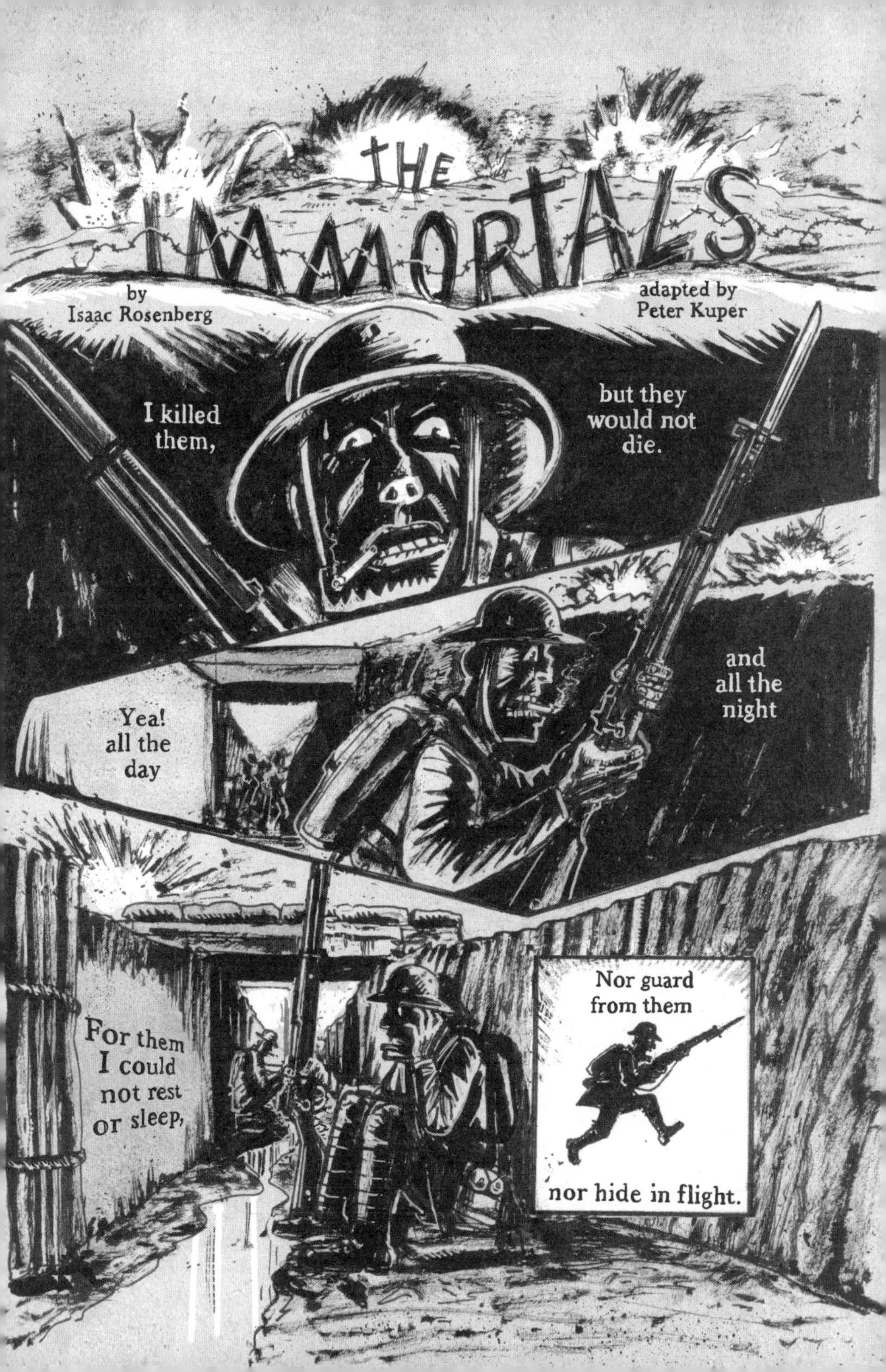
THE IMMORTALS
by Isaac Rosenberg
adapted by Peter Kuper
I killed them,
but they would not die.
Yea! all the day
and all the night
For them I could not rest or sleep,
Nor guard from them
nor hide in flight.

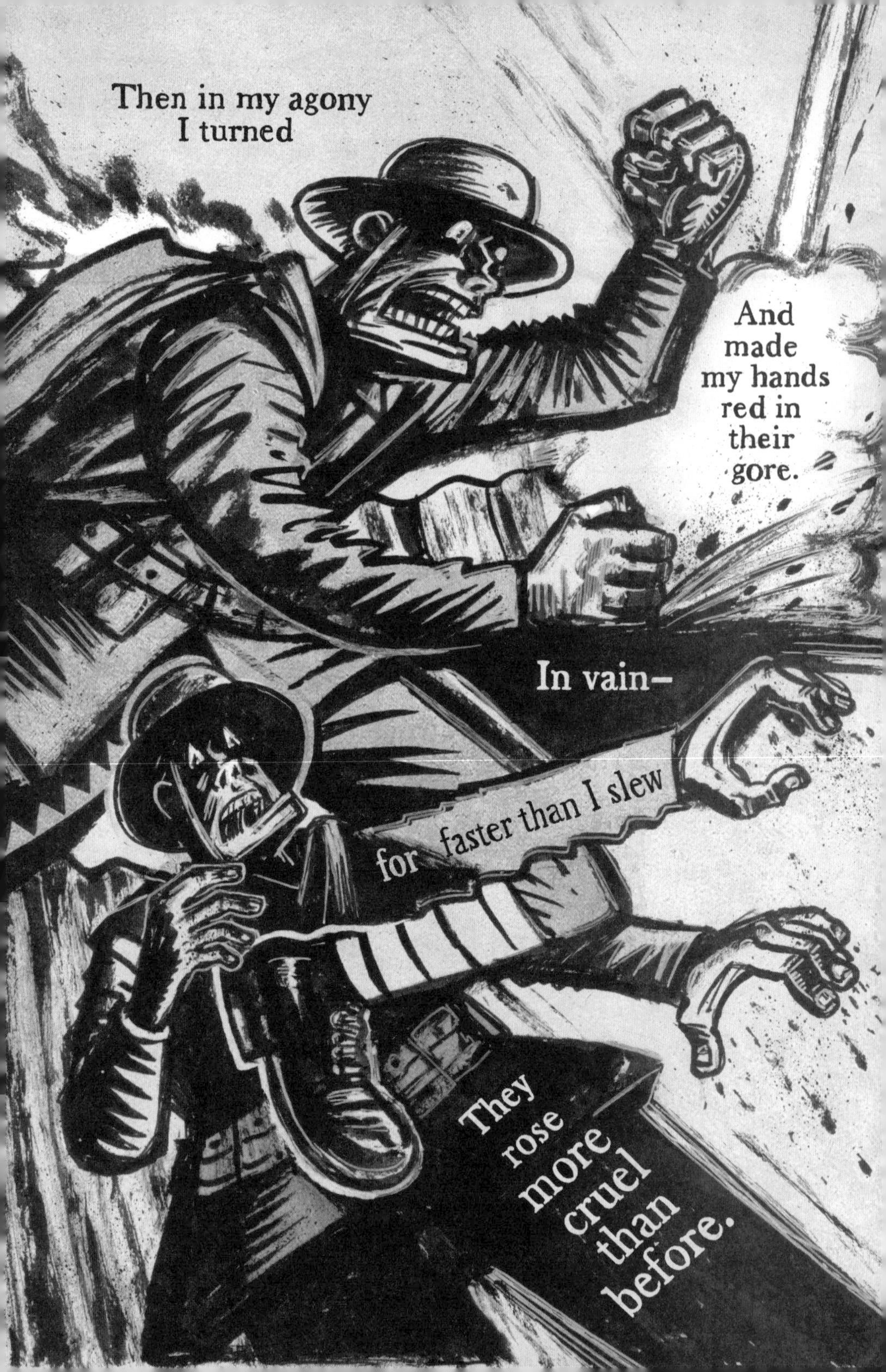
Then in my agony
I turned
And made my hands red in their gore.
In vain–
for faster than I slew
They rose more cruel than before.

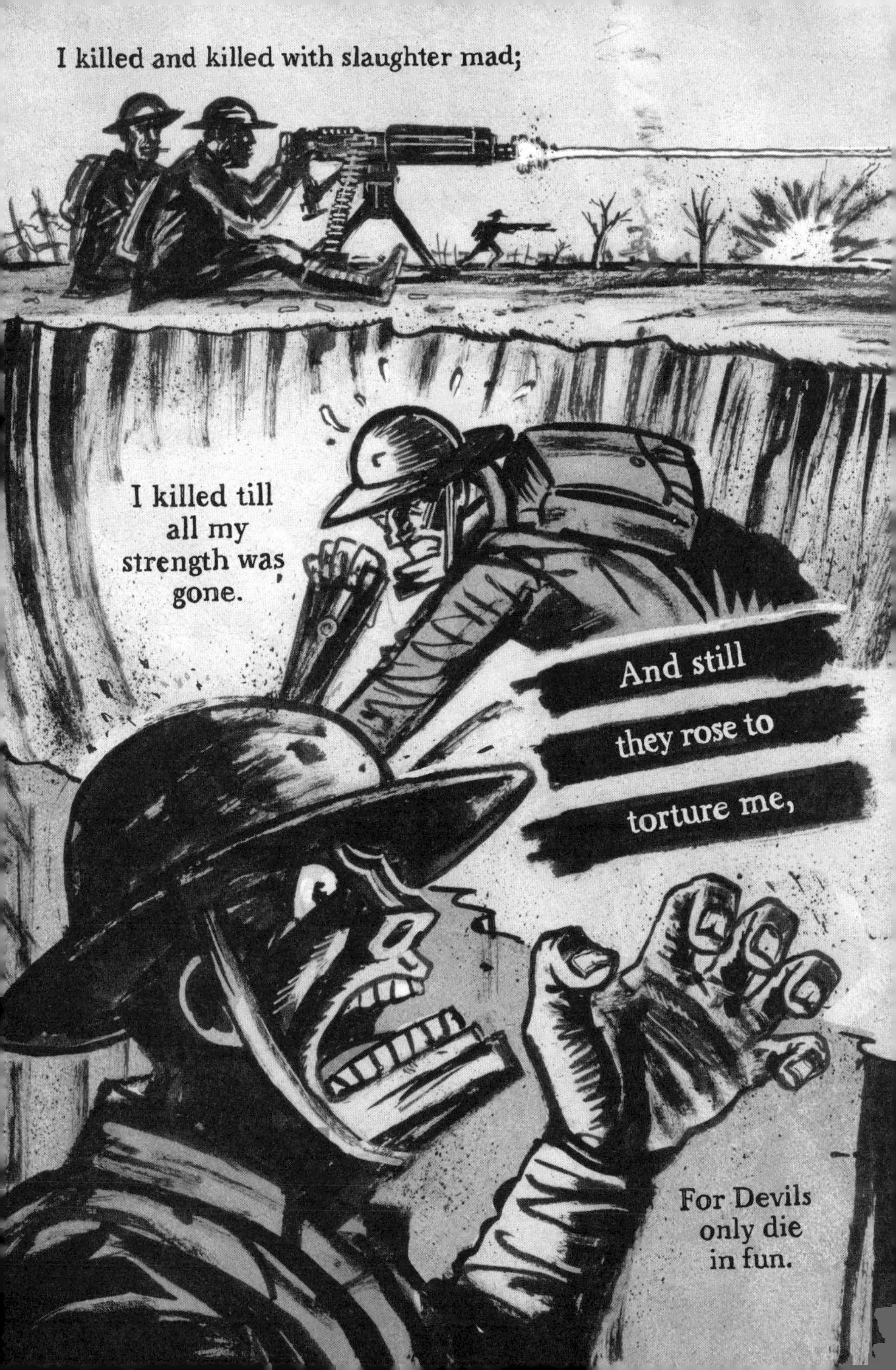
I killed and killed with slaughter mad;
I killed till all my strength was gone.
And still they rose to torture me,
For Devils only die in fun.

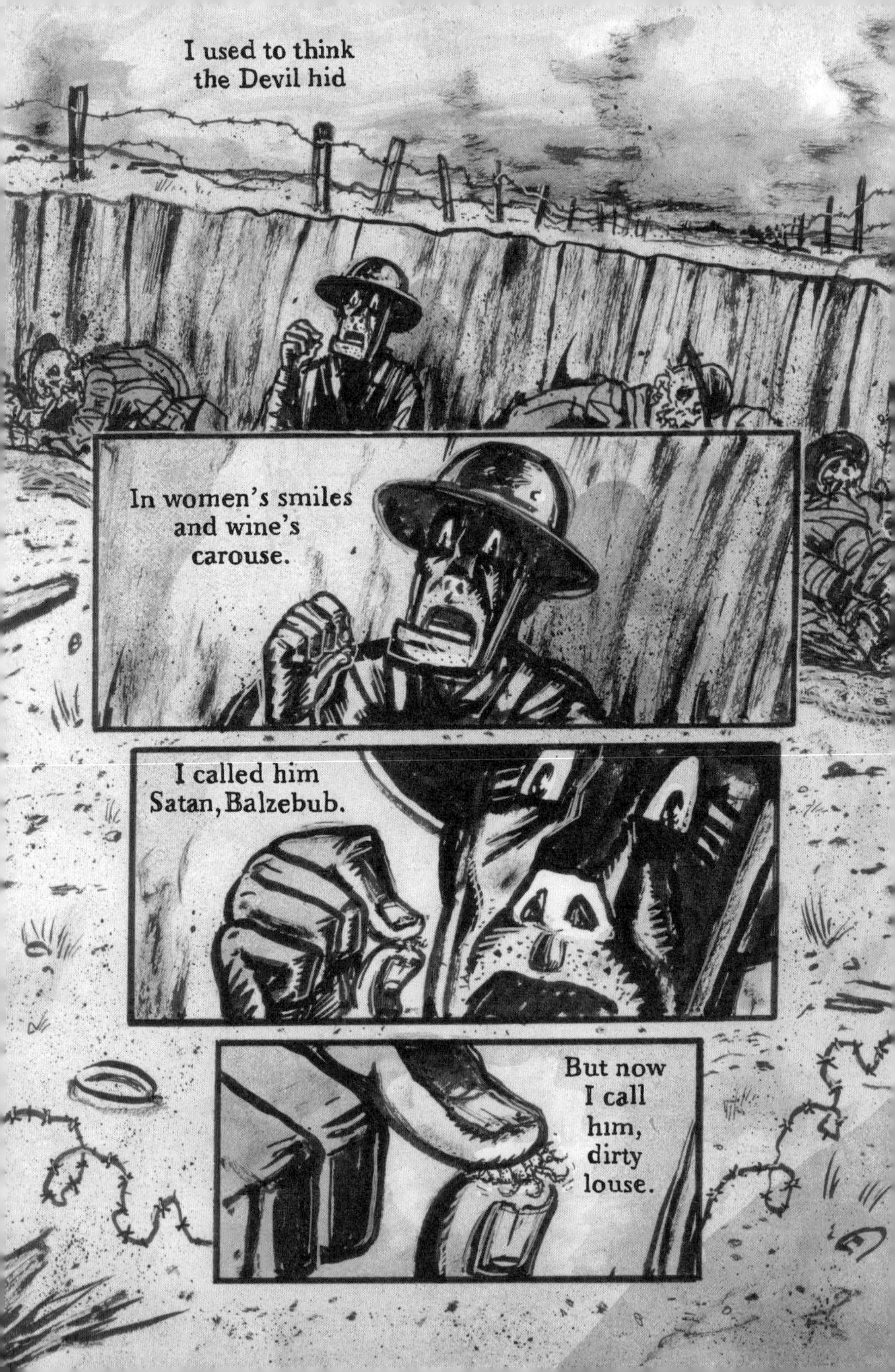
I used to think the Devil hid
In women's smiles and wine's carouse.
I called him Satan, Balzebub.
But now I call him, dirty louse.

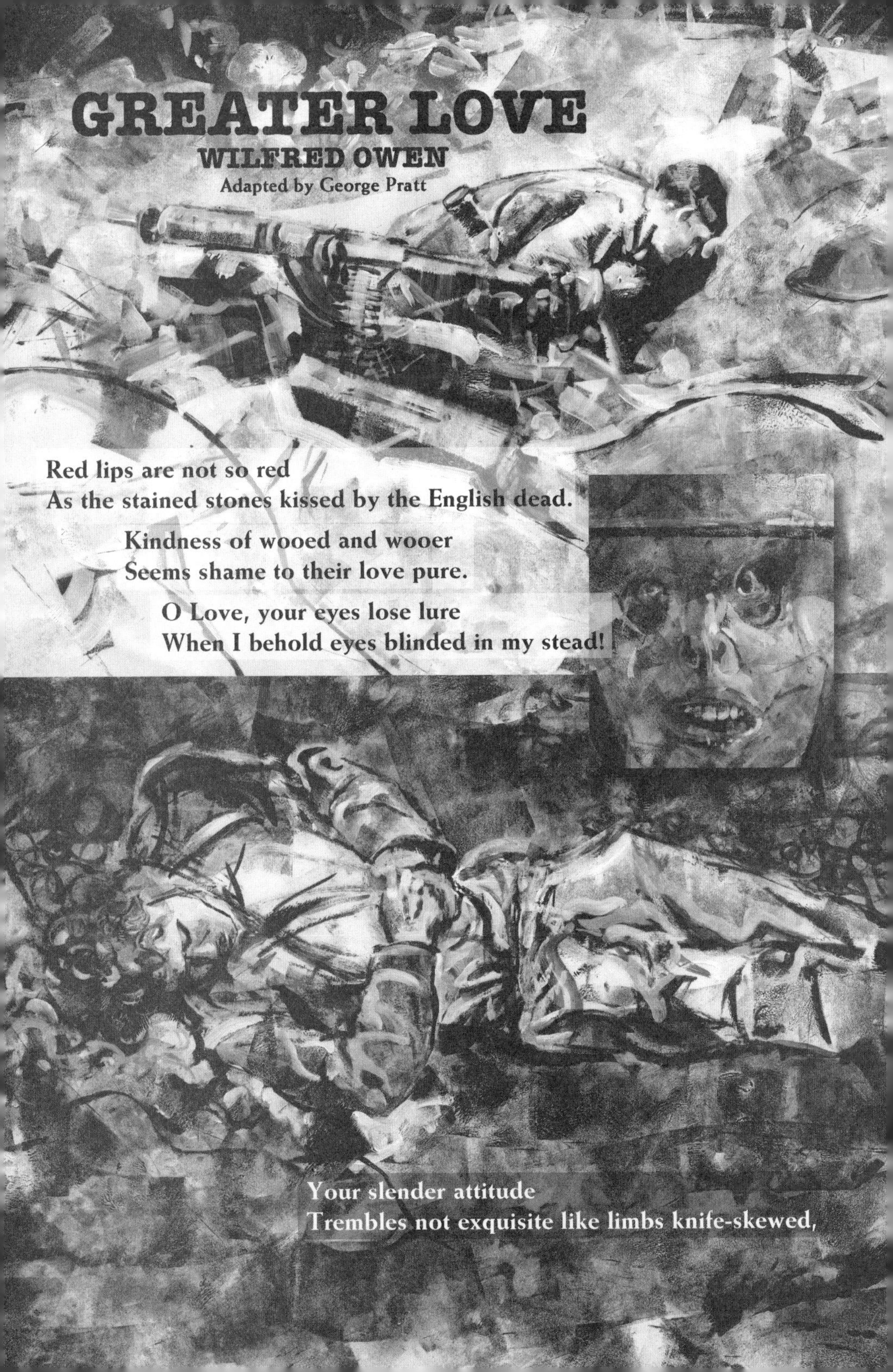
GREATER LOVE
WILFRED OWEN
Adapted by George Pratt
Red lips are not so red
As the stained stones kissed by the English dead.
Kindness of wooed and wooer
Seems shame to their love pure.
O Love, your eyes lose lure
When I behold eyes blinded in my stead!
Your slender attitude
Trembles not exquisite like limbs knife-skewed,

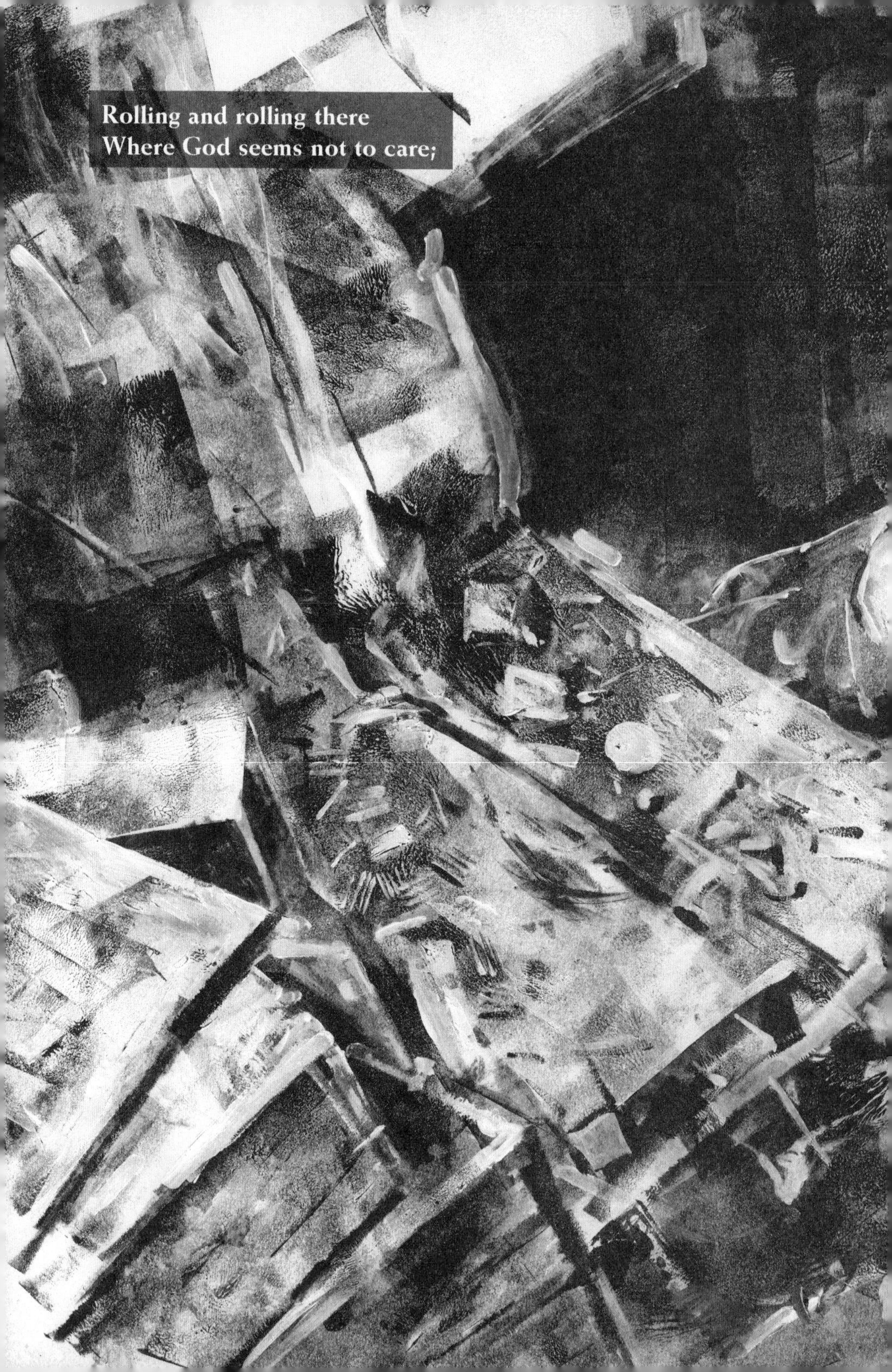
Rolling and rolling there
Where God seems not to care;

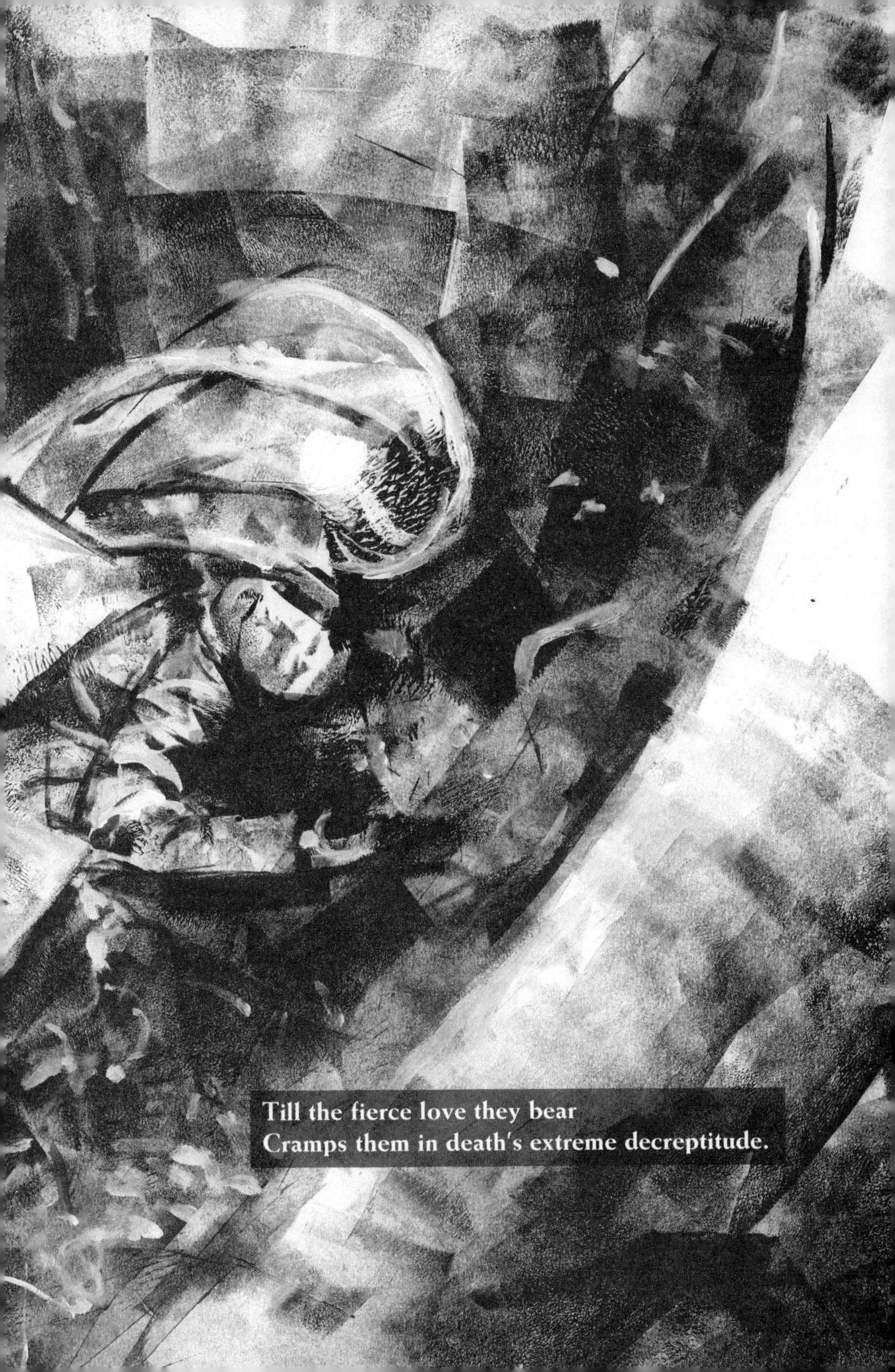

Till the fierce love they bear
Cramps them in death's extreme decreptitude.

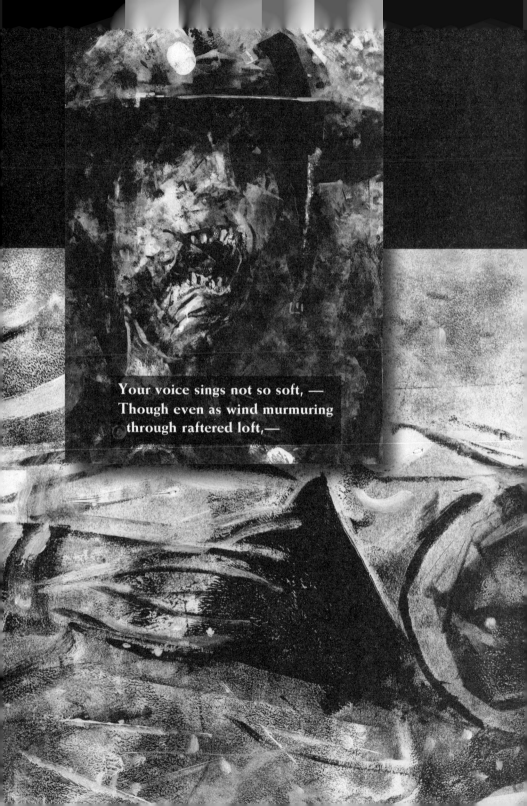

Your voice sings not so soft, —
Though even as wind murmuring
through raftered loft, —

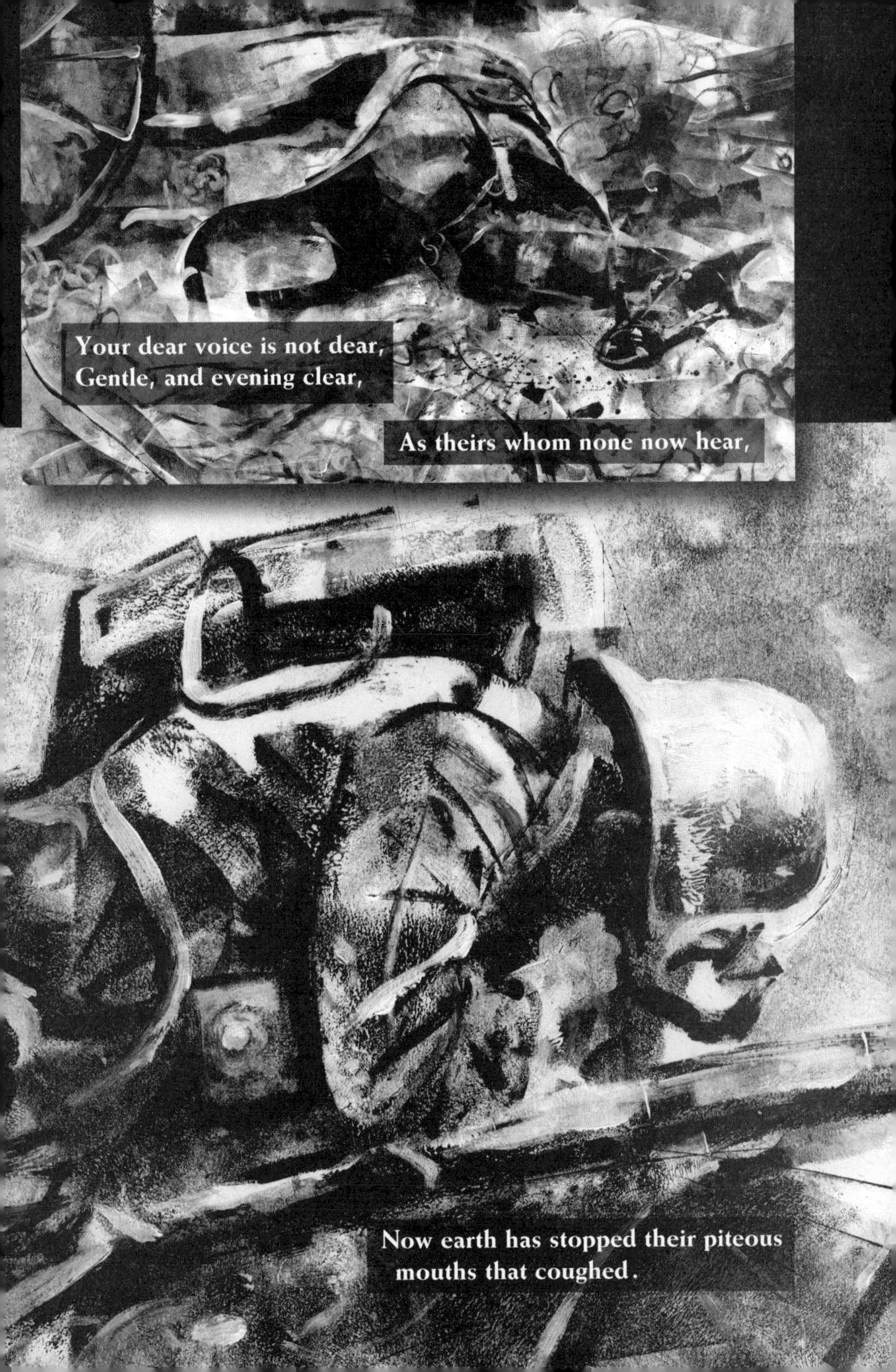
Your dear voice is not dear,
Gentle, and evening clear,
As theirs whom none now hear,
Now earth has stopped their piteous mouths that coughed.

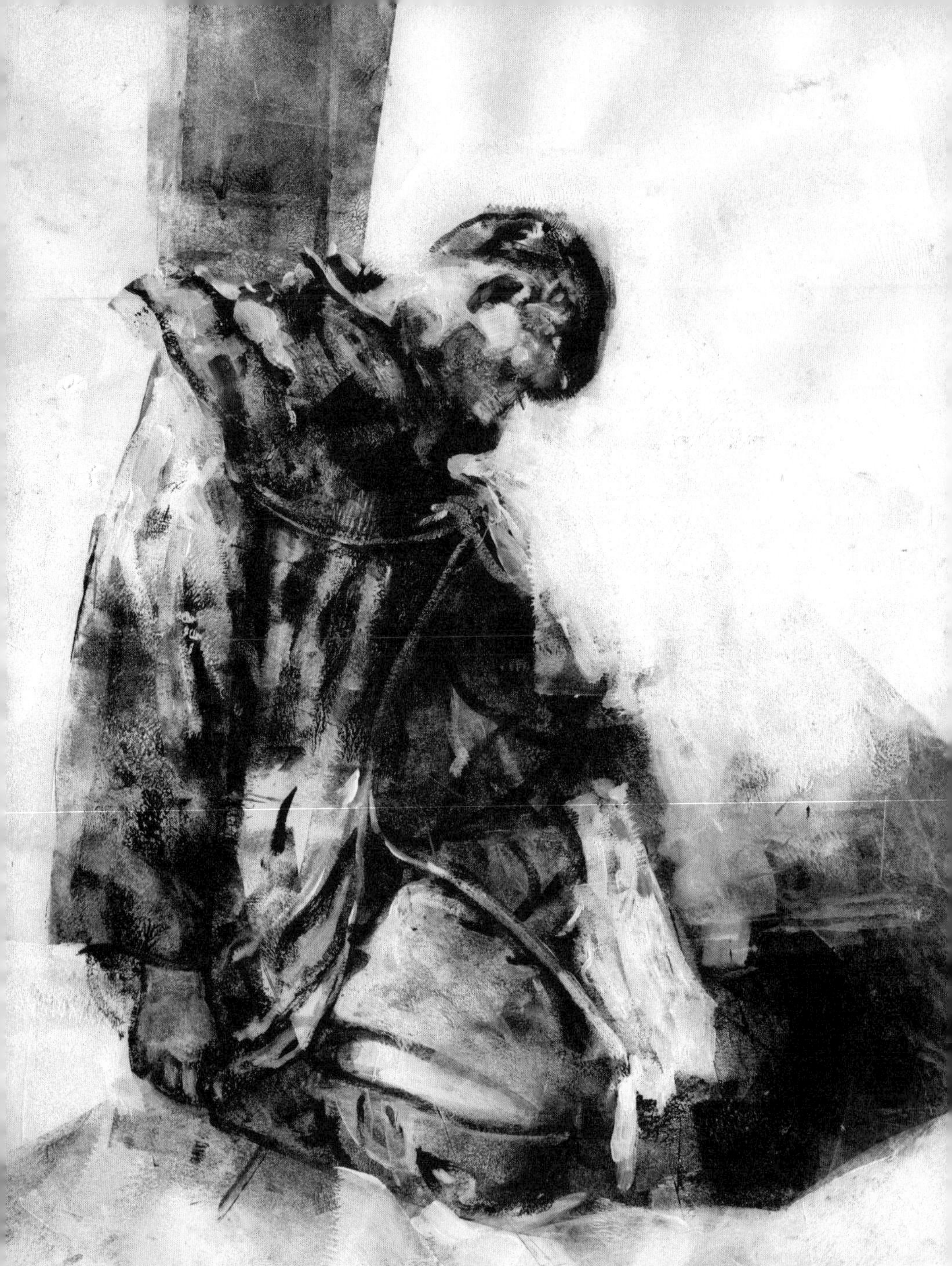

Heart, you were never hot
Nor large, nor full like hearts made great with shot;

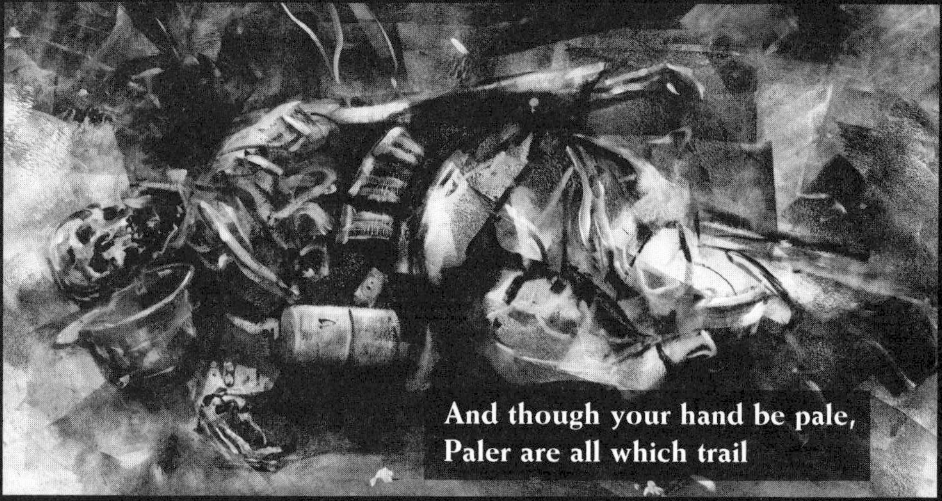
And though your hand be pale,
Paler are all which trail

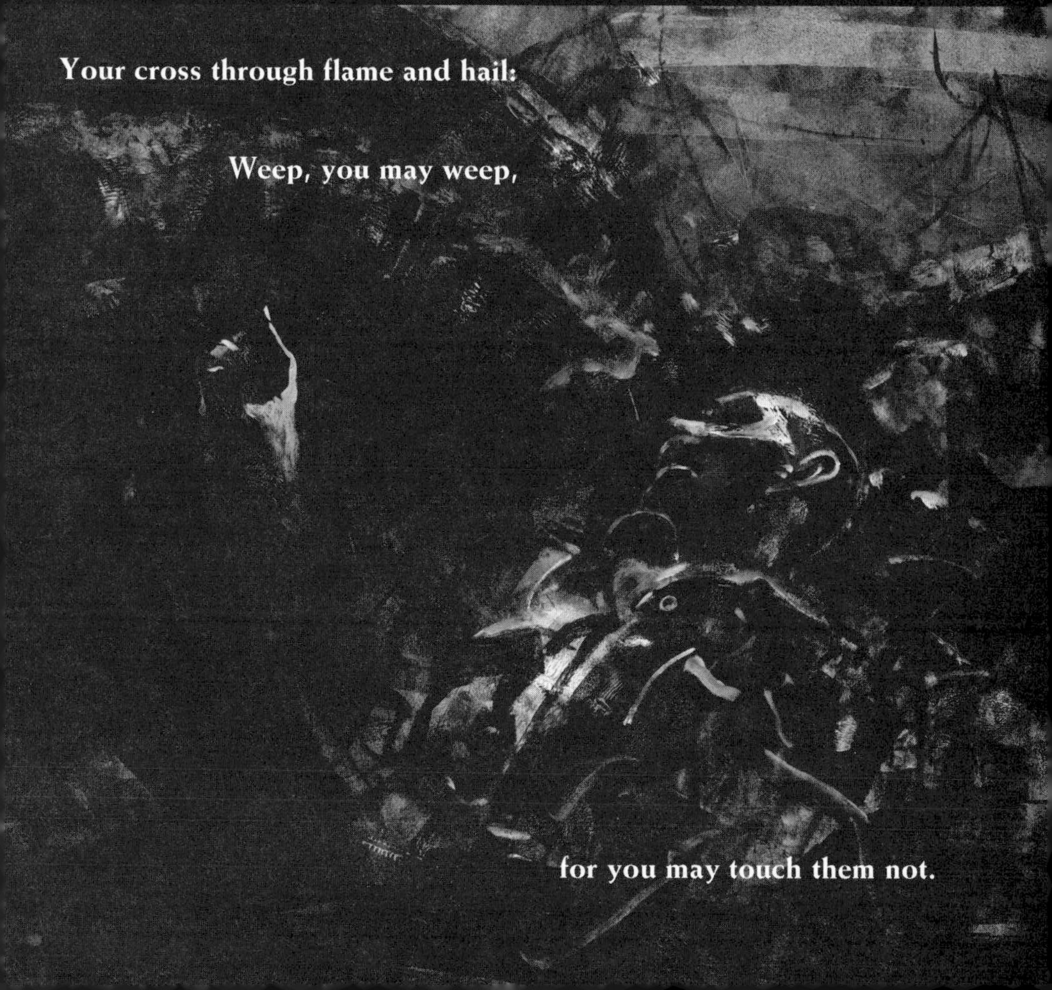
Your cross through flame and hail:
Weep, you may weep,
for you may touch them not.

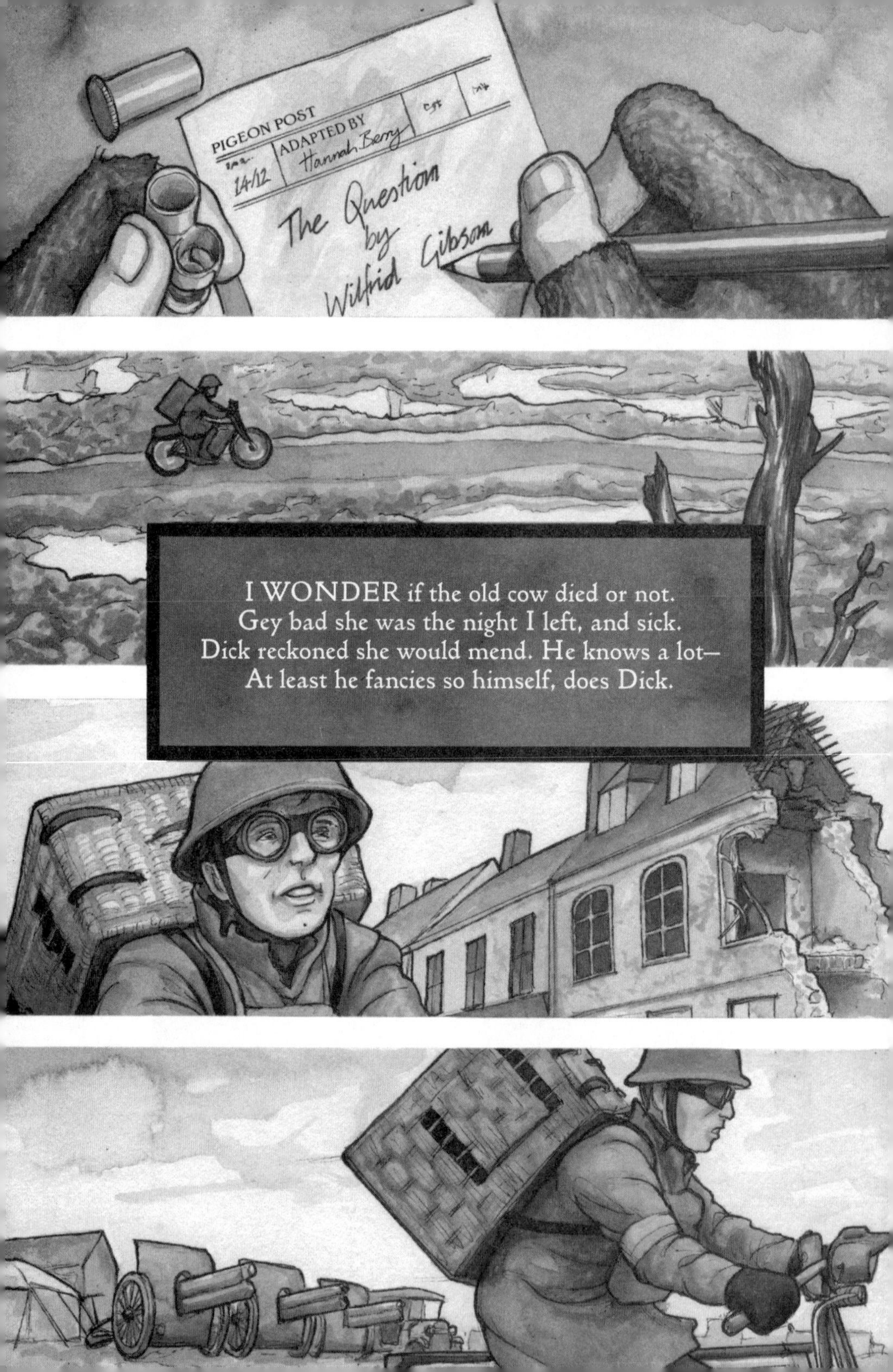
PIGEON POST
ADAPTED BY Hannah Berry
14/12
The Question
by
Wilfrid Gibson
I WONDER if the old cow died or not.
Gey bad she was the night I left, and sick.
Dick reckoned she would mend. He knows a lot—
At least he fancies so himself, does Dick.

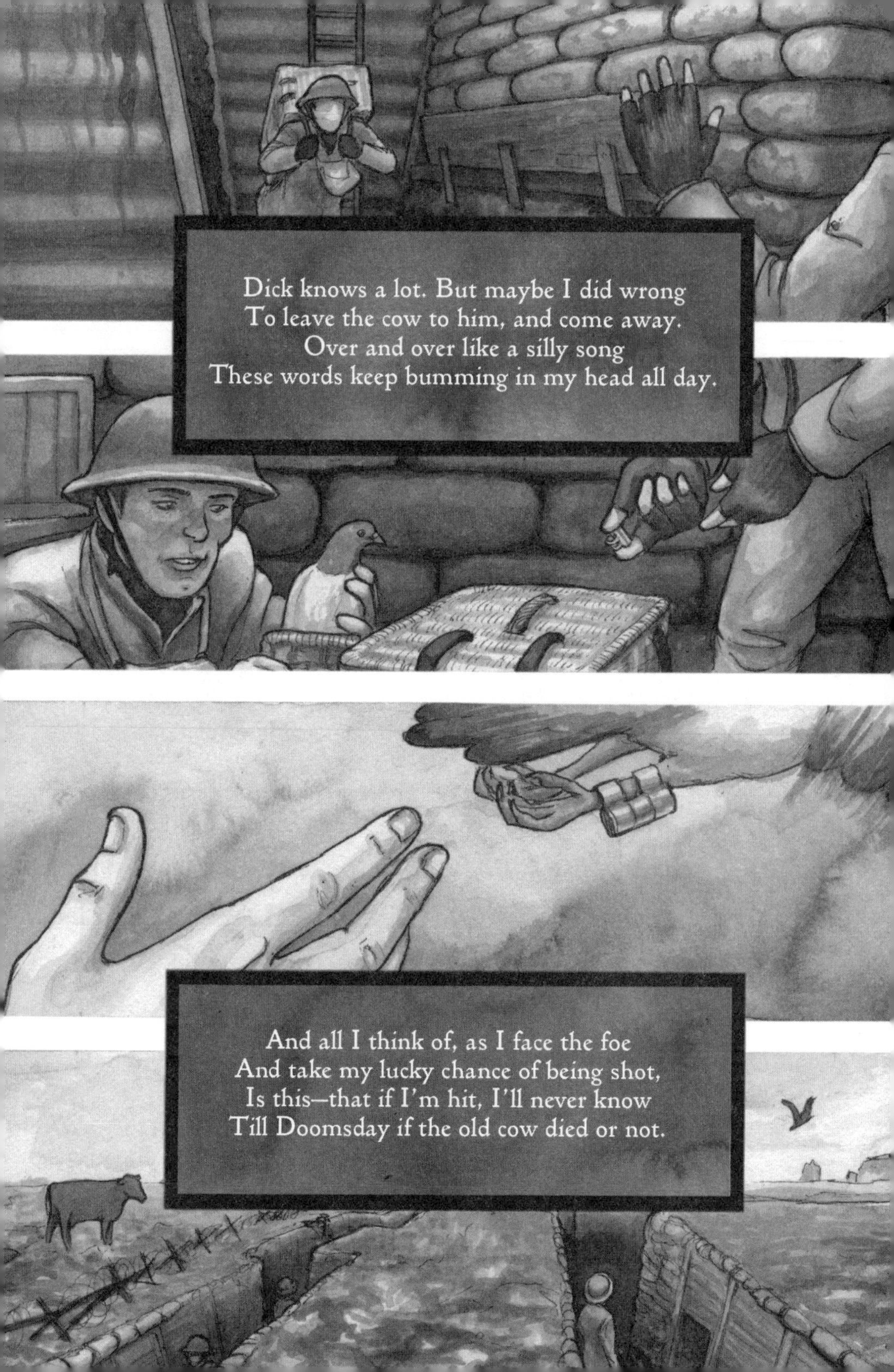
Dick knows a lot. But maybe I did wrong
To leave the cow to him, and come away.
Over and over like a silly song
These words keep bumming in my head all day.
And all I think of, as I face the foe
And take my lucky chance of being shot,
Is this—that if I'm hit, I'll never know
Till Doomsday if the old cow died or not.

SING ME TO SLEEP

SOLDIERS' SONG ADAPTED BY HUNT EMERSON

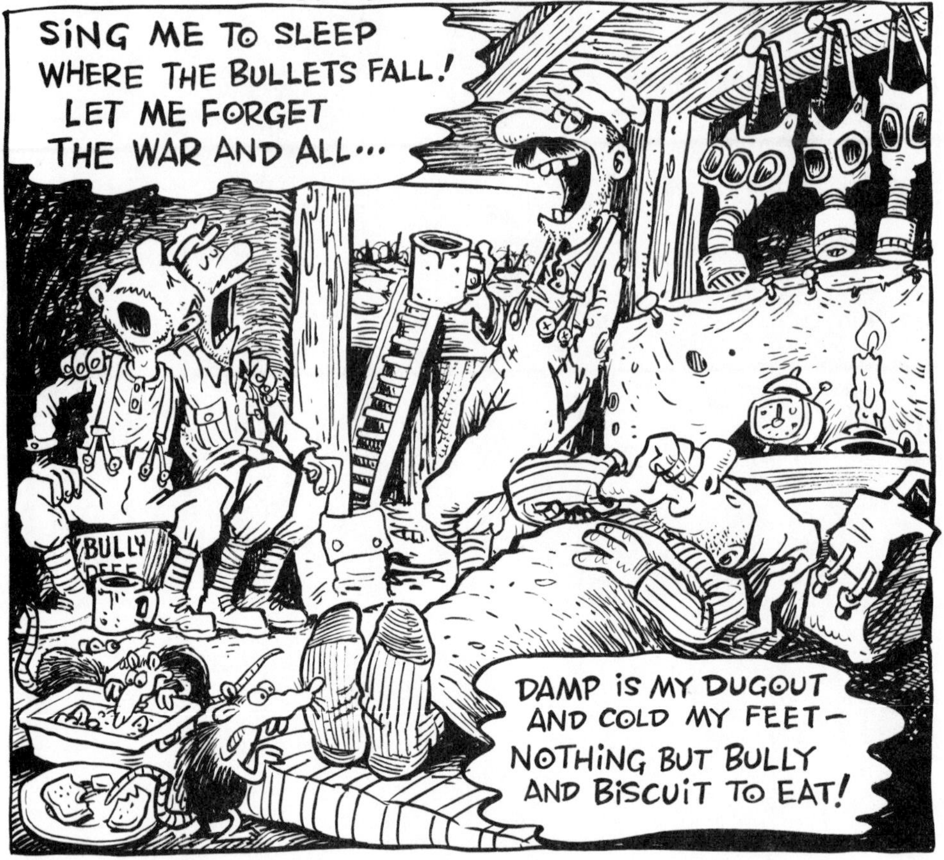
SING ME TO SLEEP WHERE THE BULLETS FALL! LET ME FORGET THE WAR AND ALL...
BULLY
DAMP IS MY DUGOUT AND COLD MY FEET— NOTHING BUT BULLY AND BISCUIT TO EAT!

OVER THE SANDBAGS HELMETS YOU'LL FIND,
CORPSES IN FRONT AND CORPSES BEHIND...

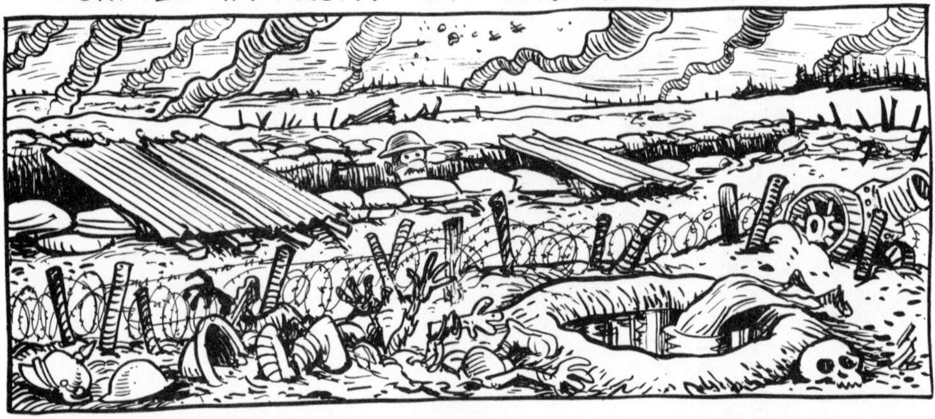

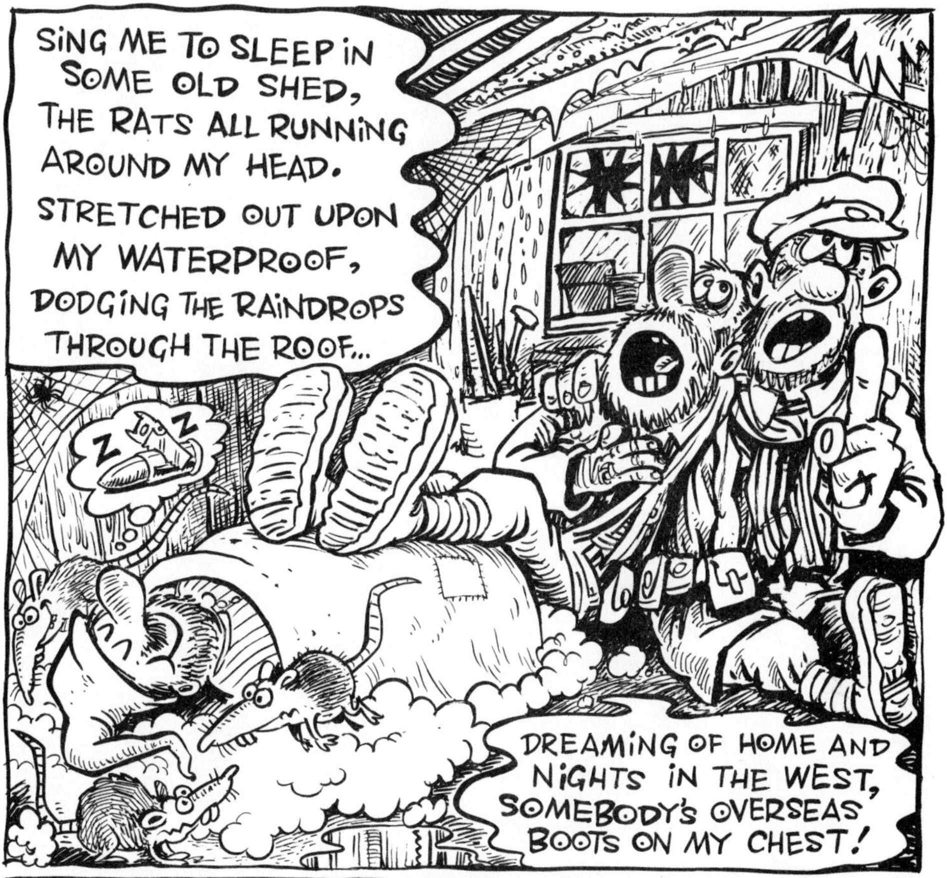
SING ME TO SLEEP IN SOME OLD SHED, THE RATS ALL RUNNING AROUND MY HEAD. STRETCHED OUT UPON MY WATERPROOF, DODGING THE RAINDROPS THROUGH THE ROOF...
Z Z
DREAMING OF HOME AND NIGHTS IN THE WEST, SOMEBODY'S OVERSEAS BOOTS ON MY CHEST!

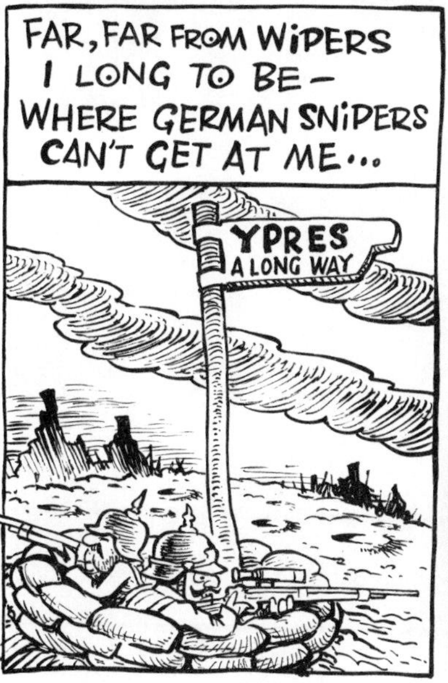
FAR, FAR FROM WIPERS I LONG TO BE— WHERE GERMAN SNIPERS CAN'T GET AT ME...
YPRES
A LONG WAY

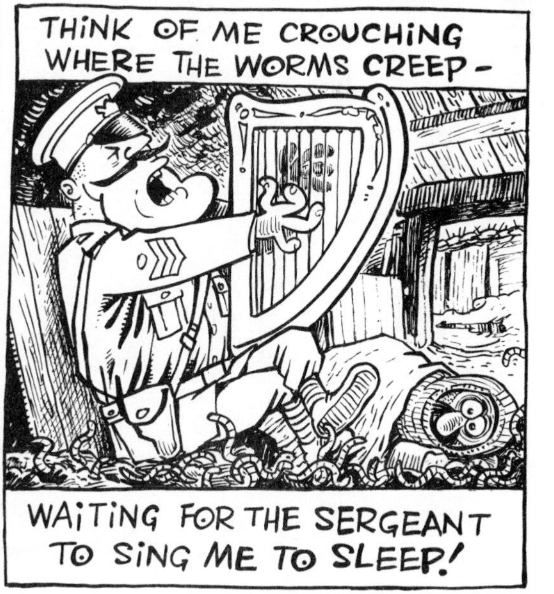
THINK OF ME CROUCHING WHERE THE WORMS CREEP—
WAITING FOR THE SERGEANT TO SING ME TO SLEEP!

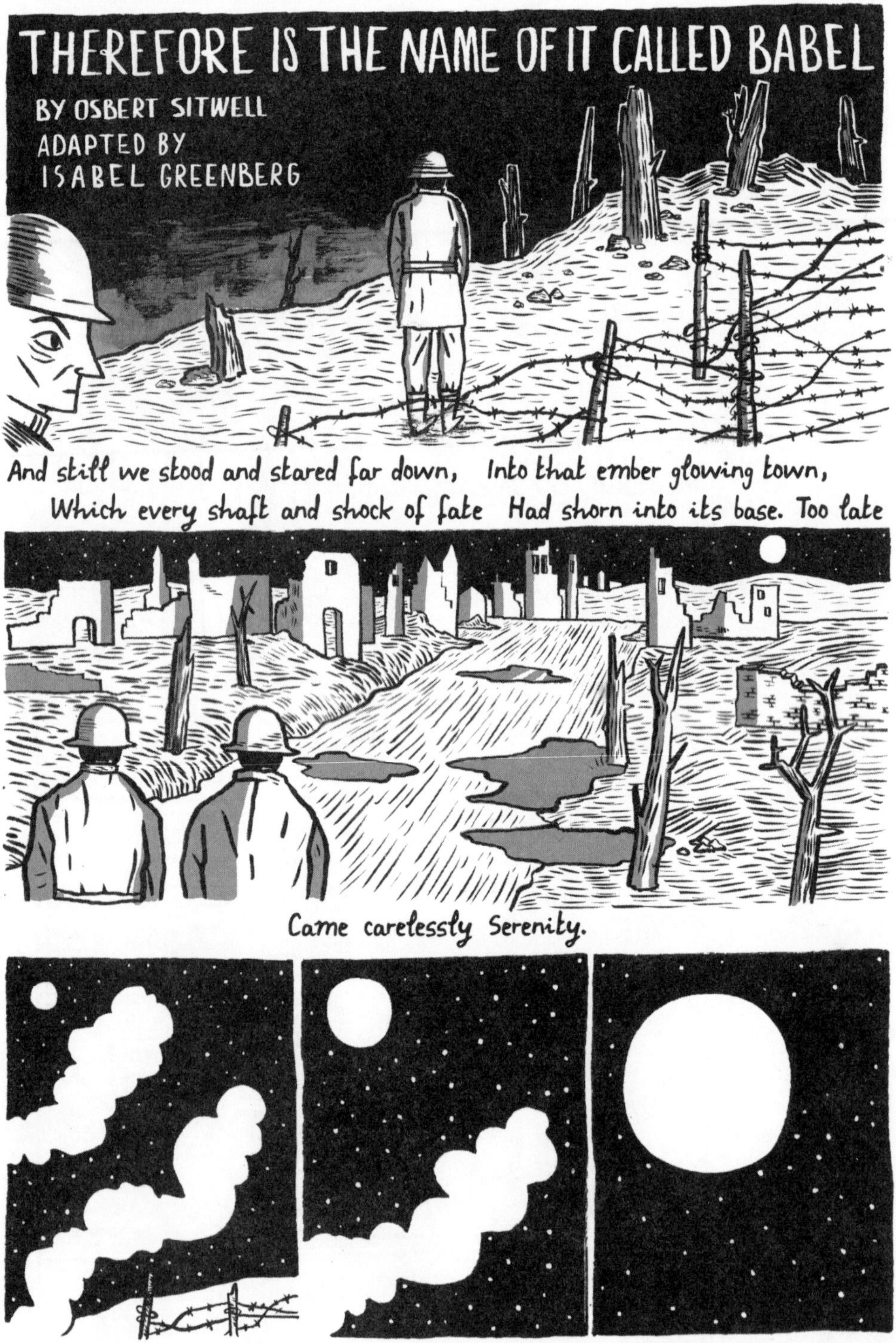
THEREFORE IS THE NAME OF IT CALLED BABEL
BY OSBERT SITWELL
ADAPTED BY
ISABEL GREENBERG
And still we stood and stared far down, Into that ember glowing town,
Which every shaft and shock of fate Had shorn into its base. Too late
Came carelessly Serenity.

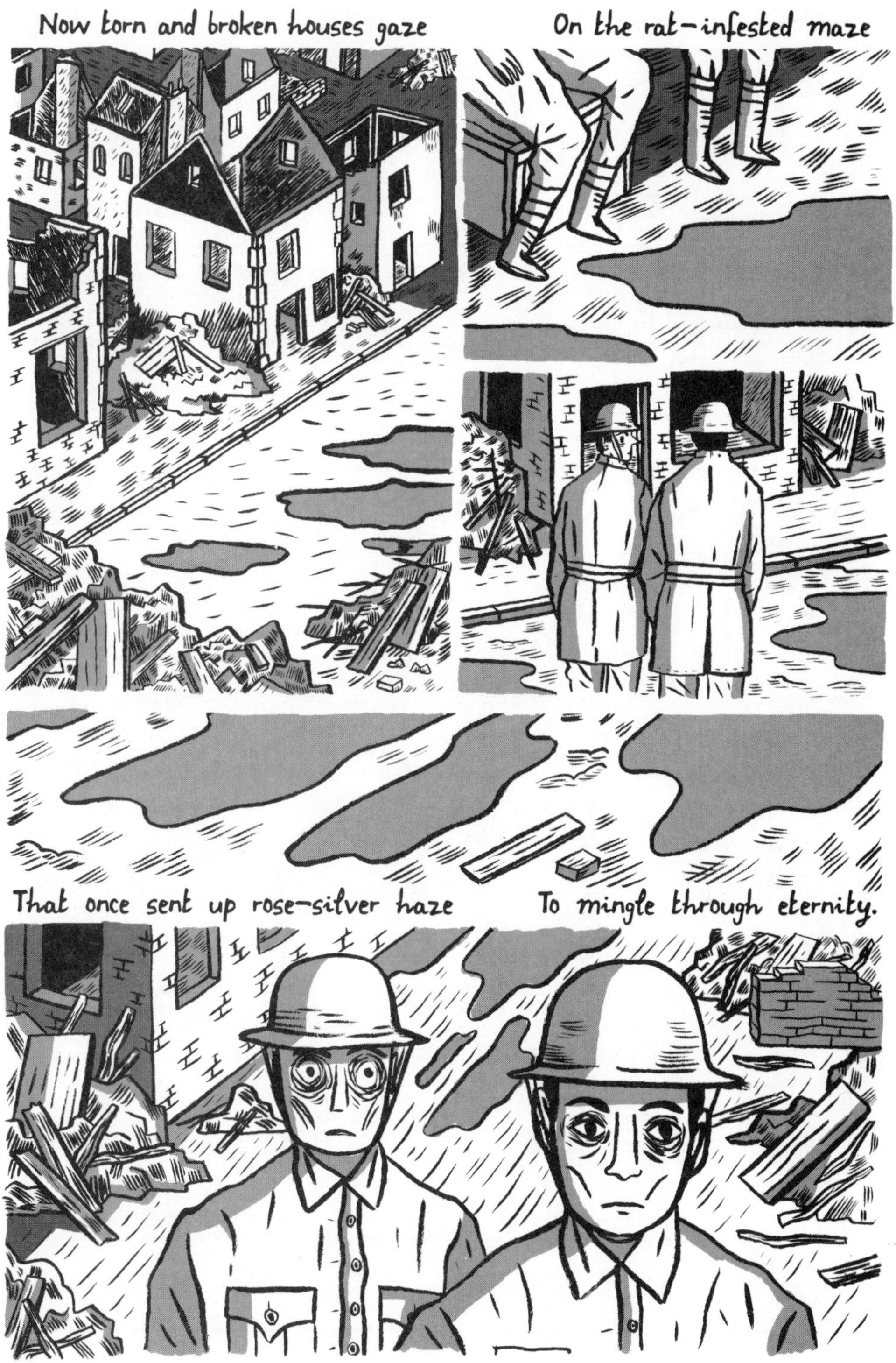
Now torn and broken houses gaze
On the rat-infested maze
That once sent up rose-silver haze
To mingle through eternity.

The outlines, once so strongly wrought, Of city walls, are now a thought

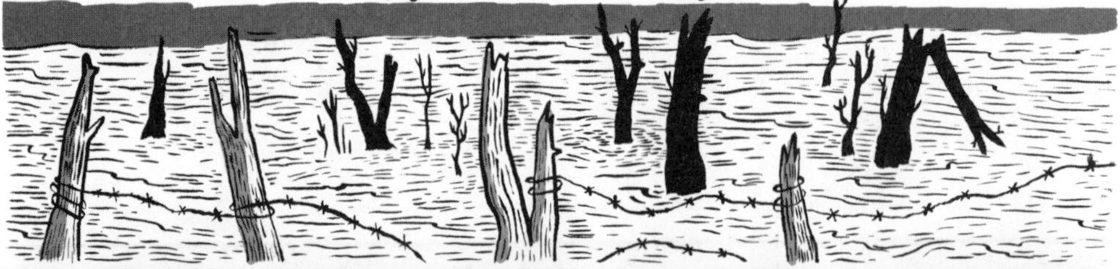

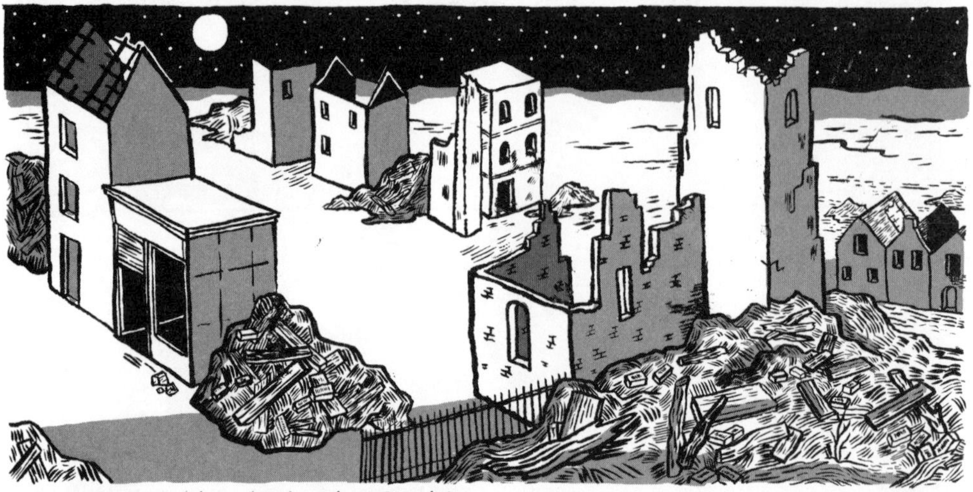

Or jest unto the dead who fought...

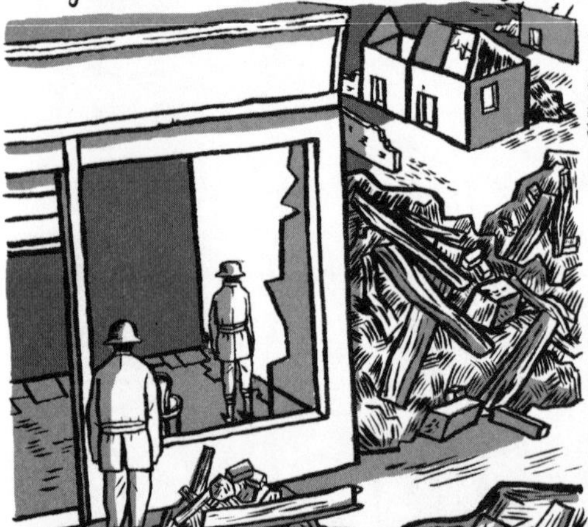

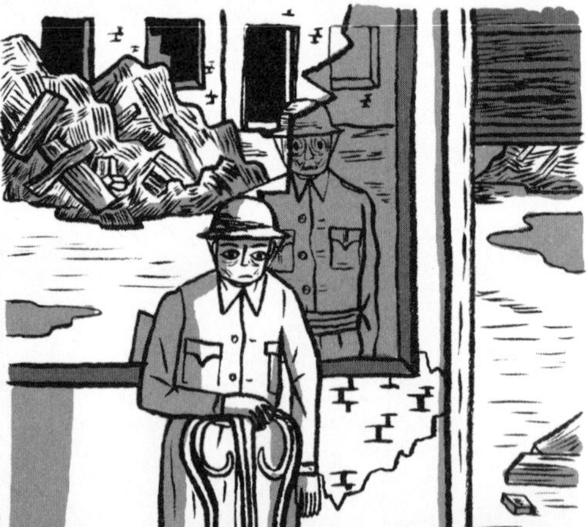

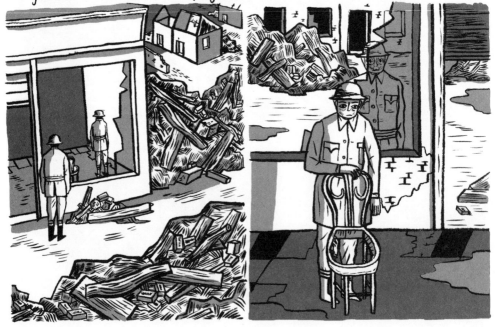

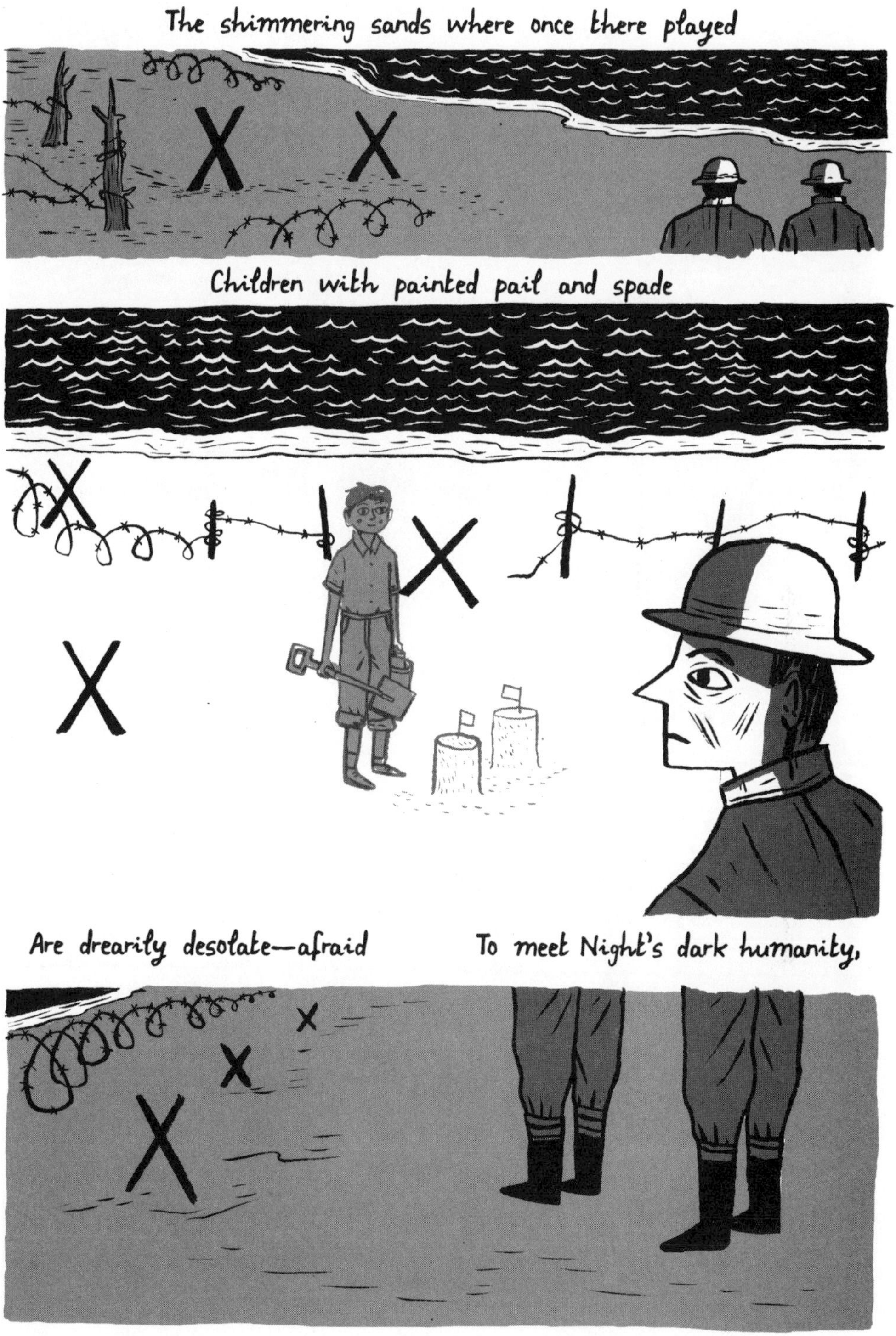
The shimmering sands where once there played
Children with painted pail and spade
Are drearily desolate—afraid
To meet Night's dark humanity,

Whose silver cool remakes the dead, And lays no blame on any head

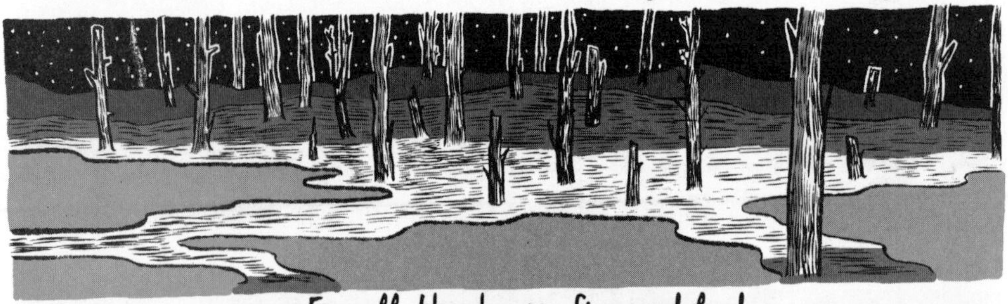

For all the havoc, fire, and lead

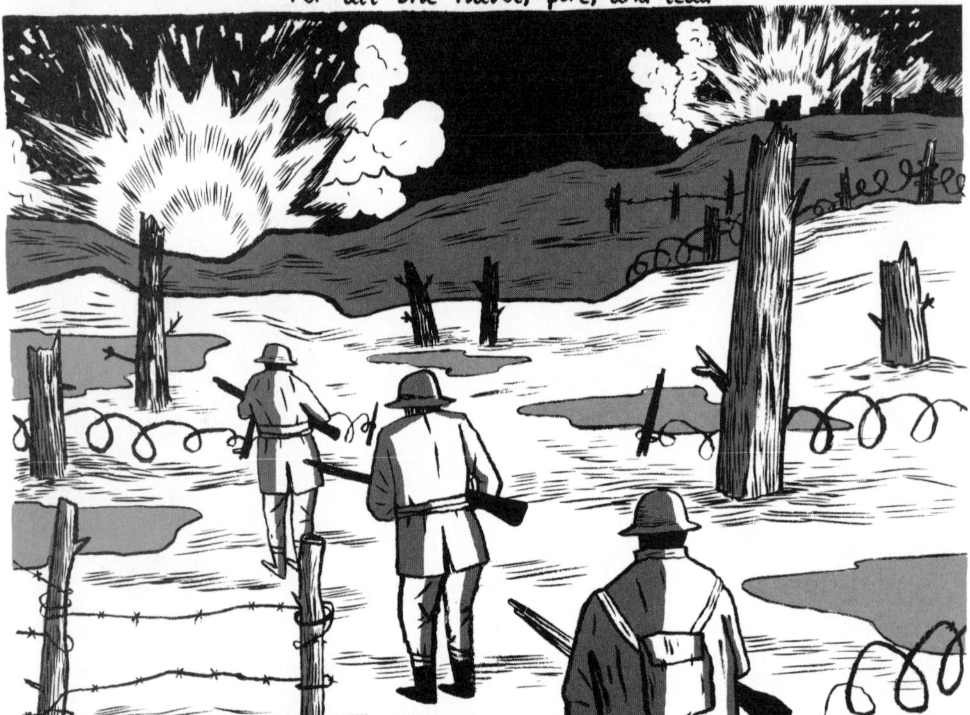

That fell upon us suddenly.

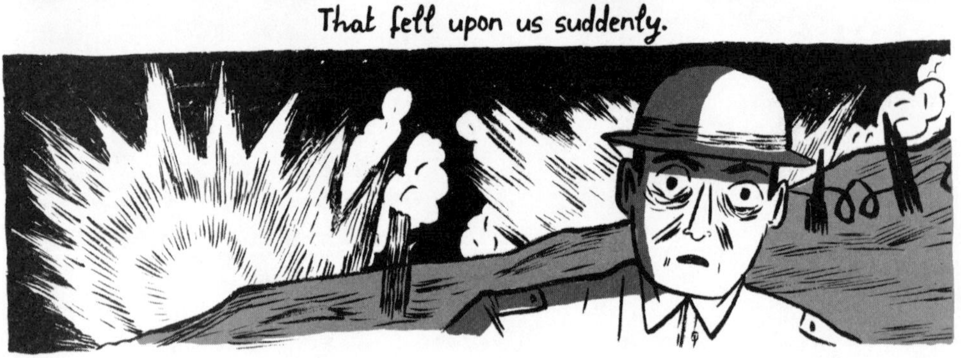

When all we came to know as good Gave way to Evil's fiery flood,

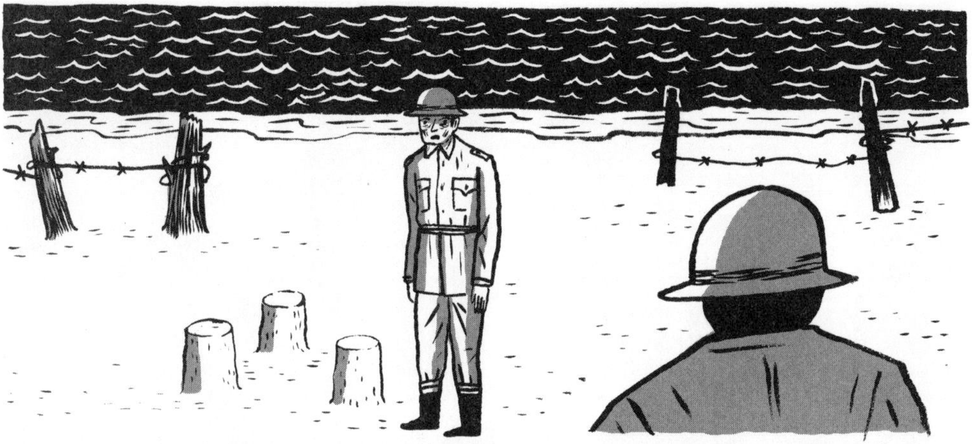

And monstrous myths of iron and blood

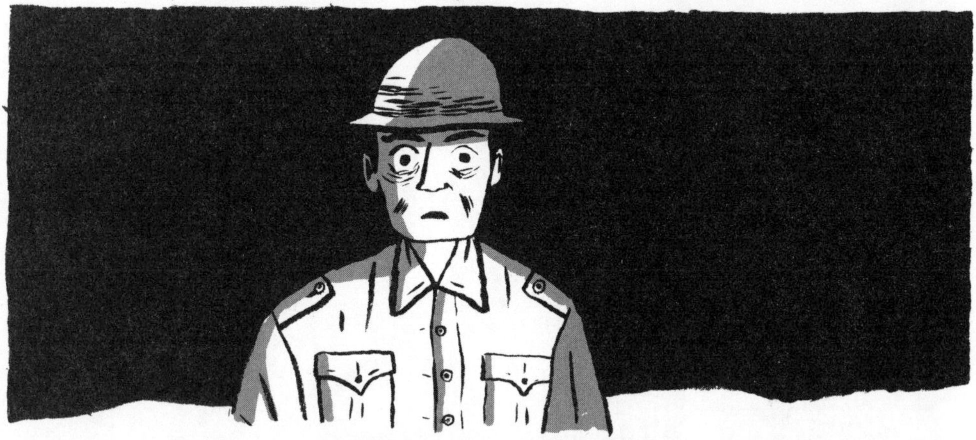

Seem to obscure God's clarity.

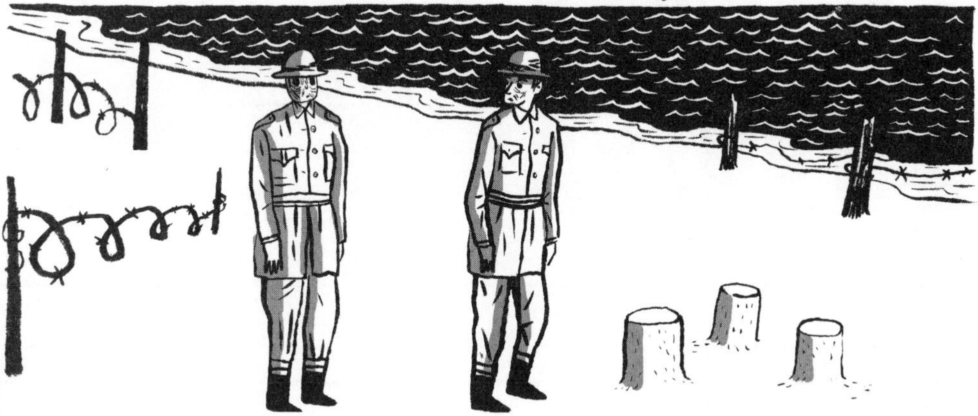

Deep sunk in sin, this tragic star Sinks deeper still, and wages war

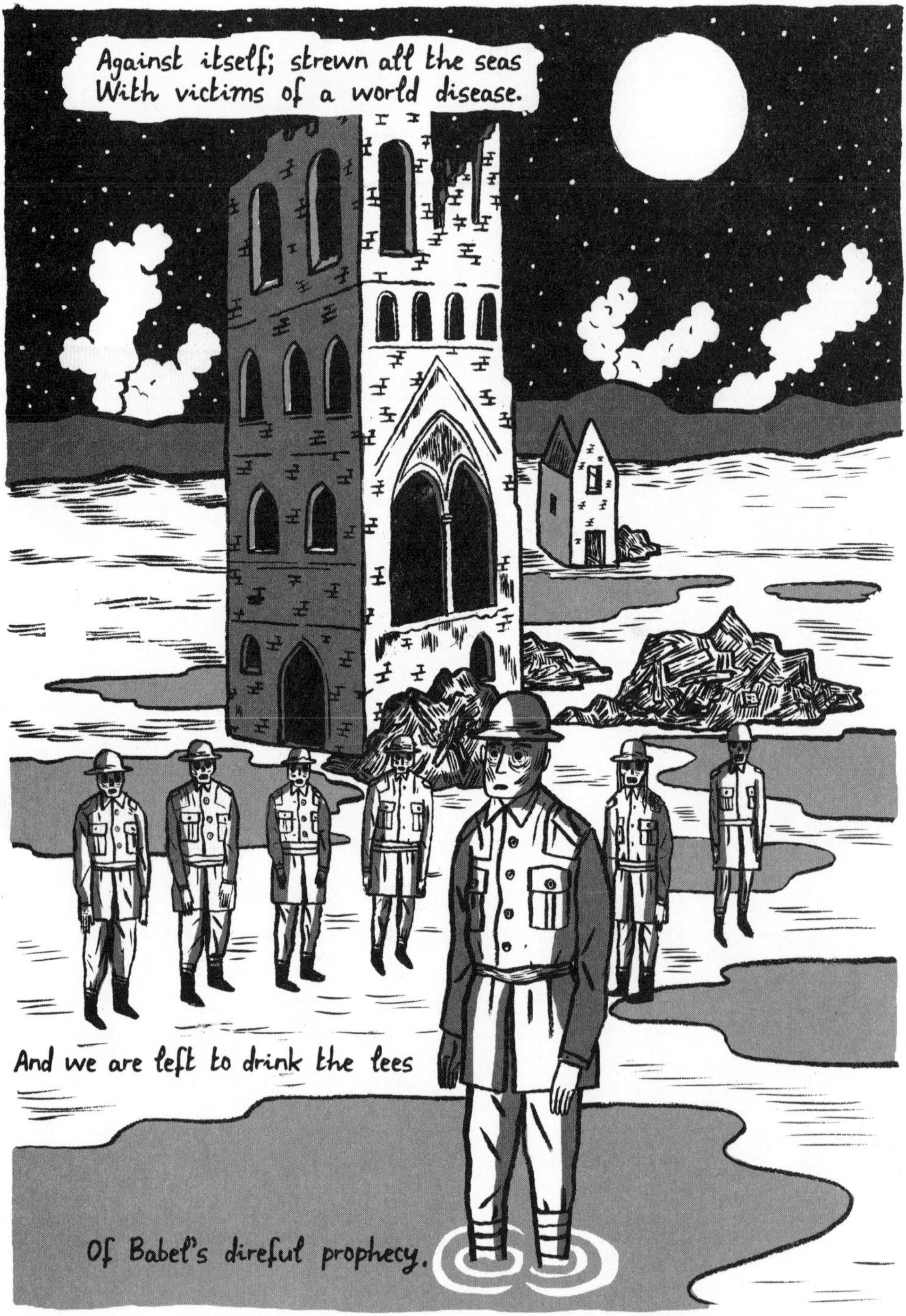
Against itself; strewn all the seas
With victims of a world disease.
And we are left to drink the lees
Of Babel's direful prophecy.

THE GENERAL

by SIEGFRIED SASSOON

"GOOD-MORNING; good-morning!" the General said
When we met him last week on our way to the line.
Now the soldiers he smiled at are most of 'em dead,
And we're cursing his staff for incompetent swine.
"He's a cheery old card," grunted Harry to Jack
As they slogged up to Arras with rifle and pack.

. . . .

But he did for them both by his plan of attack.

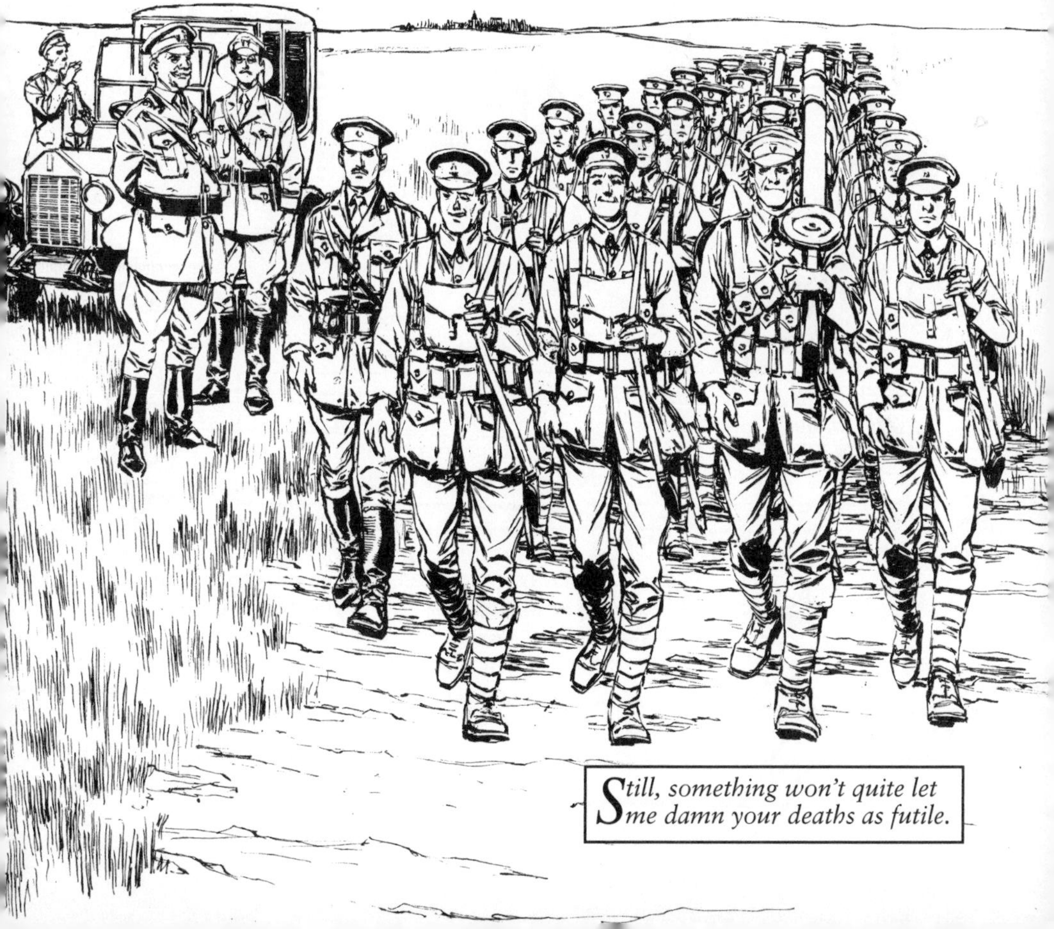
Still, something won't quite let me damn your deaths as futile.

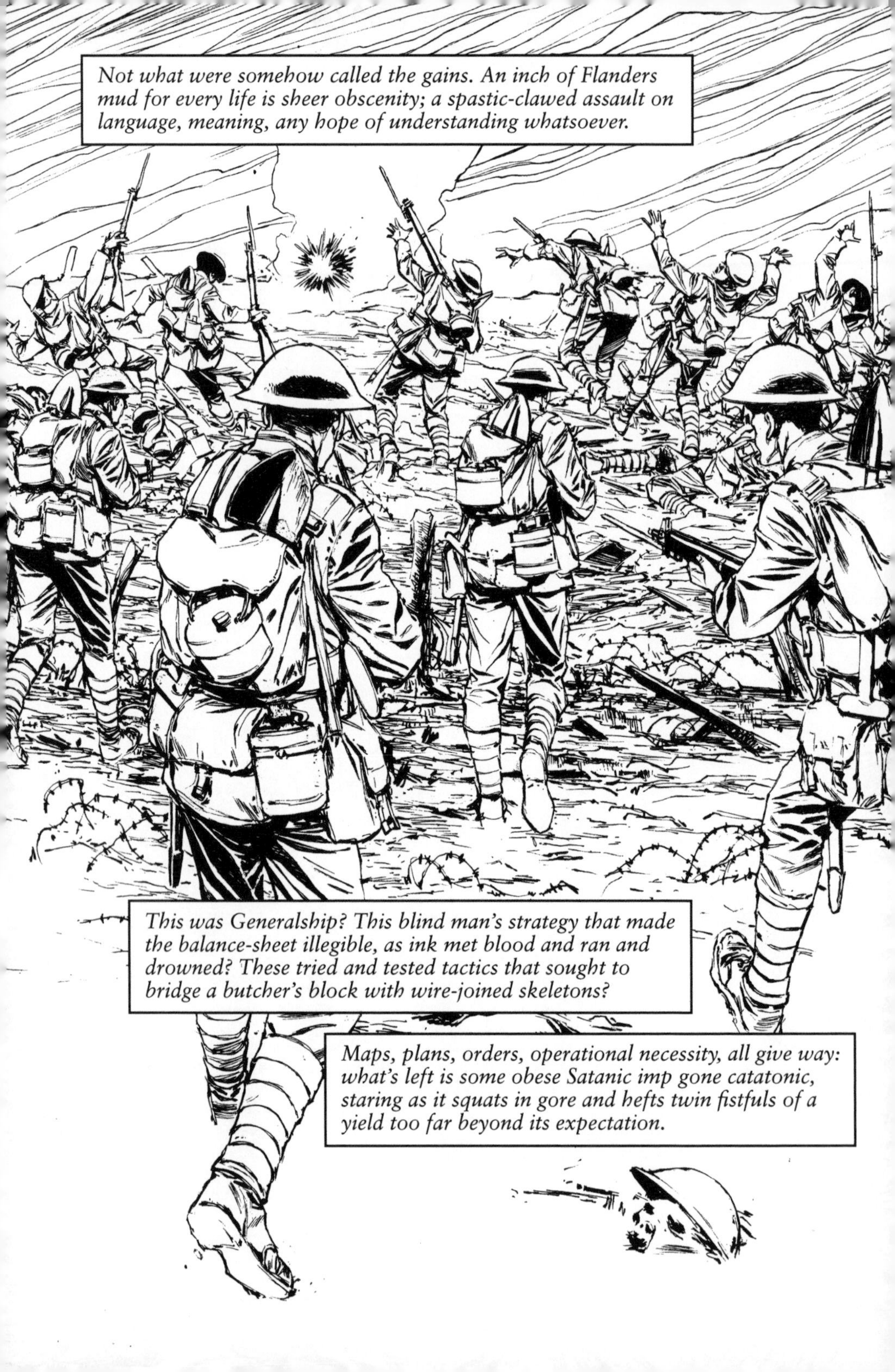
Not what were somehow called the gains. An inch of Flanders mud for every life is sheer obscenity; a spastic-clawed assault on language, meaning, any hope of understanding whatsoever.
This was Generalship? This blind man's strategy that made the balance-sheet illegible, as ink met blood and ran and drowned? These tried and tested tactics that sought to bridge a butcher's block with wire-joined skeletons?
Maps, plans, orders, operational necessity, all give way: what's left is some obese Satanic imp gone catatonic, staring as it squats in gore and hefts twin fistfuls of a yield too far beyond its expectation.

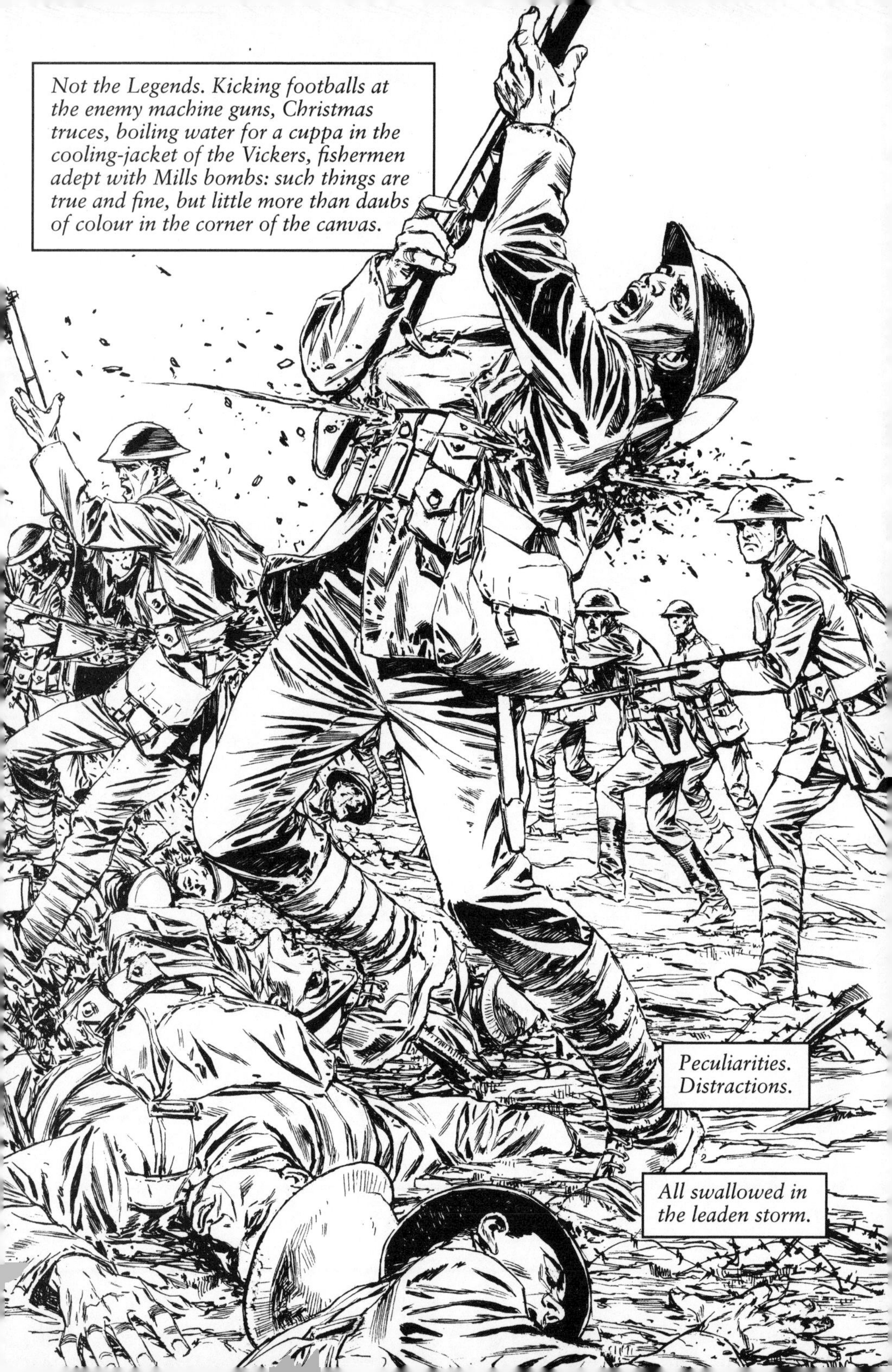
Not the Legends. Kicking footballs at the enemy machine guns, Christmas truces, boiling water for a cuppa in the cooling-jacket of the Vickers, fishermen adept with Mills bombs: such things are true and fine, but little more than daubs of colour in the corner of the canvas.
Peculiarities. Distractions.
All swallowed in the leaden storm.

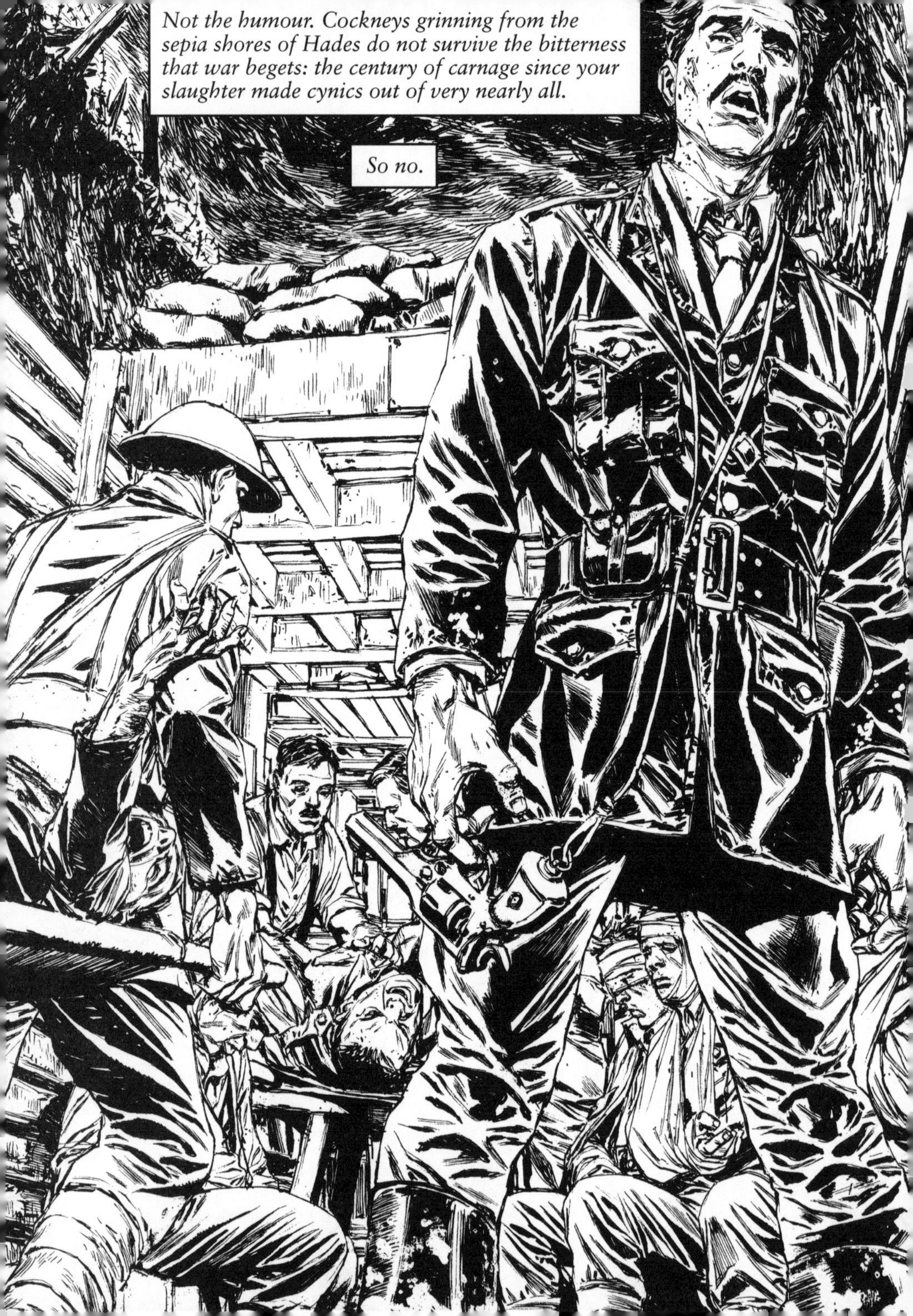
Not the humour. Cockneys grinning from the sepia shores of Hades do not survive the bitterness that war begets: the century of carnage since your slaughter made cynics out of very nearly all.
So no.

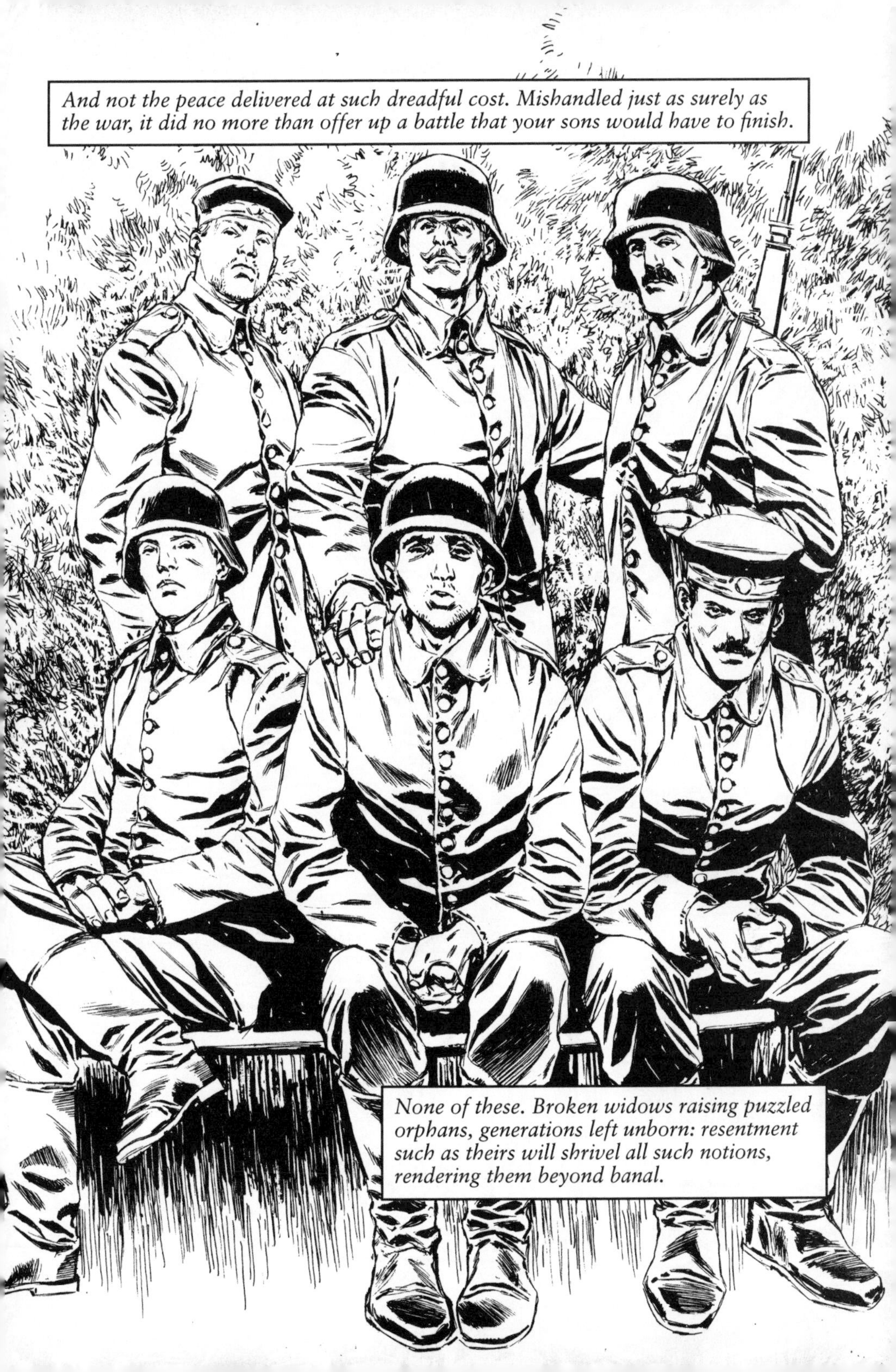
And not the peace delivered at such dreadful cost. Mishandled just as surely as the war, it did no more than offer up a battle that your sons would have to finish.
None of these. Broken widows raising puzzled orphans, generations left unborn: resentment such as theirs will shrivel all such notions, rendering them beyond banal.

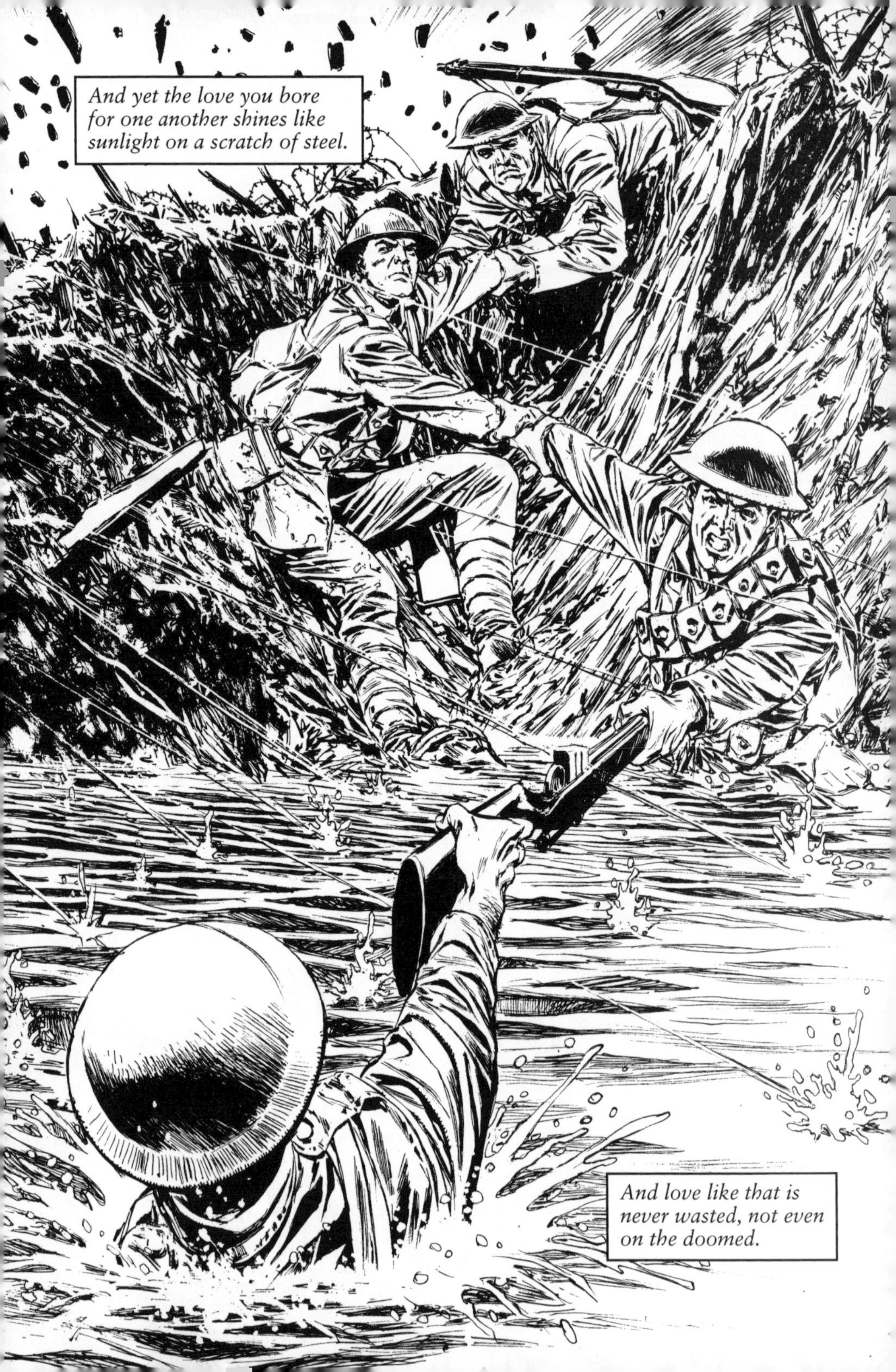
And yet the love you bore for one another shines like sunlight on a scratch of steel.
And love like that is never wasted, not even on the doomed.

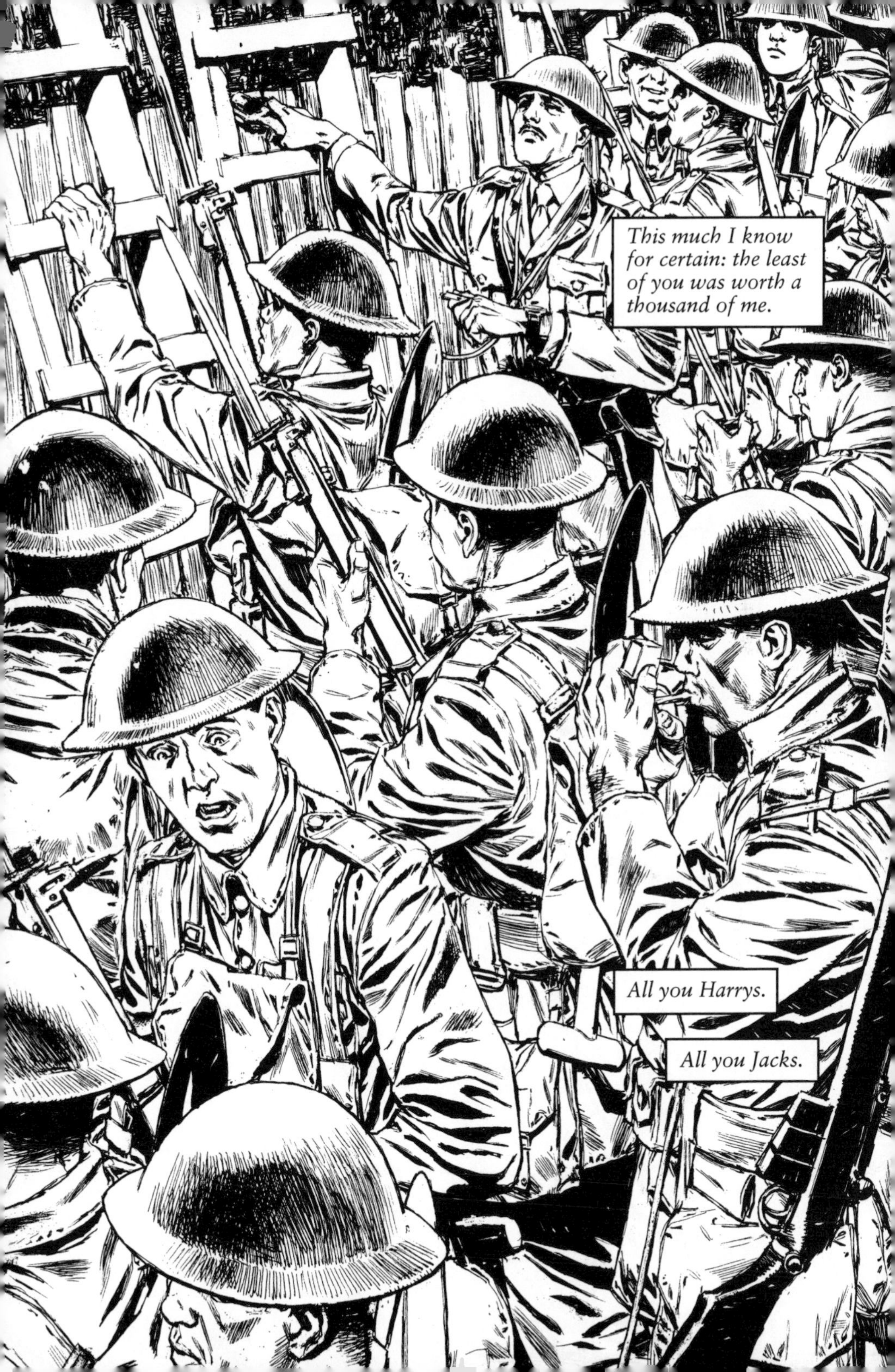
This much I know for certain: the least of you was worth a thousand of me.
All you Harrys.
All you Jacks.

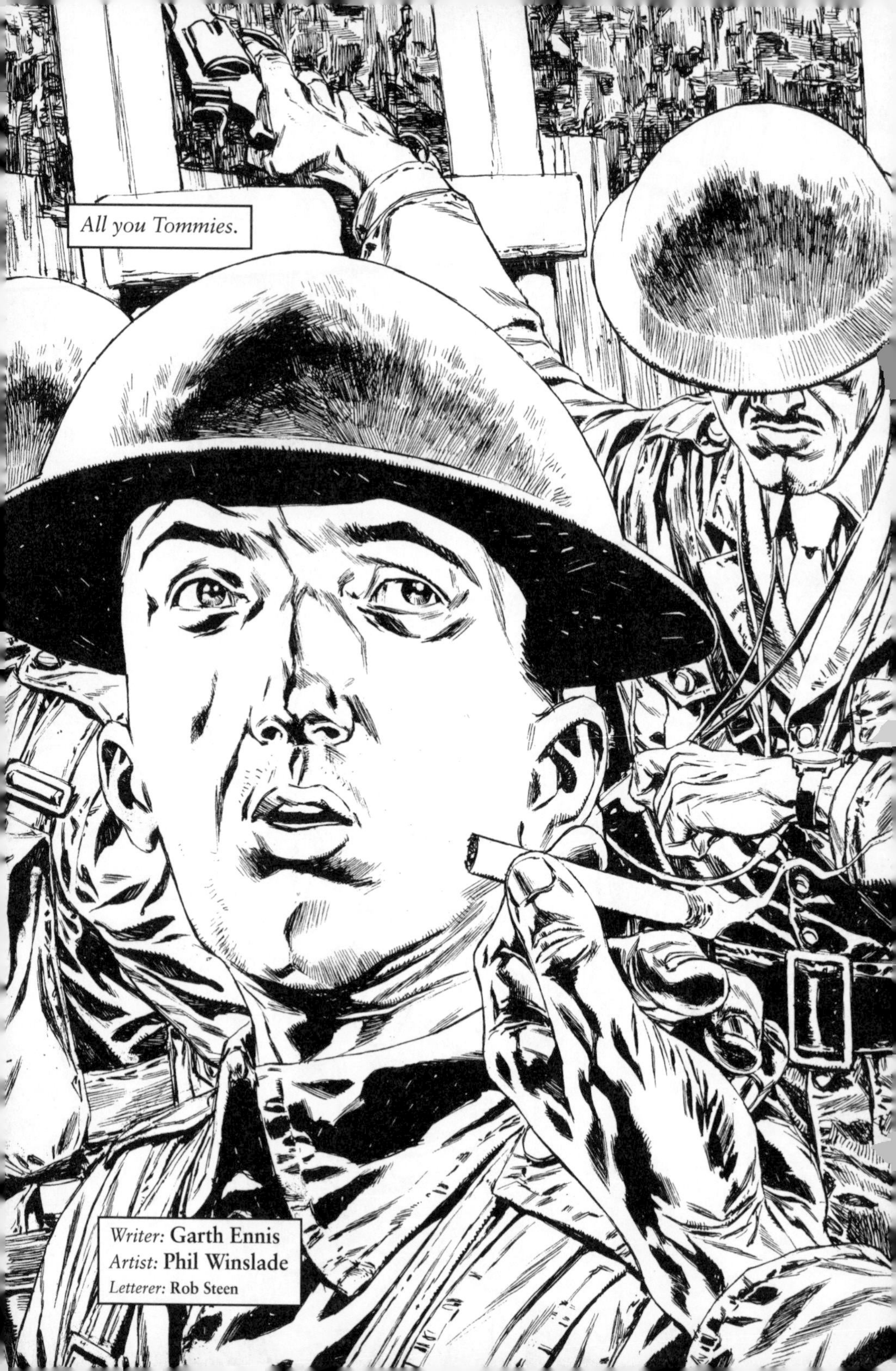
All you Tommies.
Writer: Garth Ennis
Artist: Phil Winslade
Letterer: Rob Steen

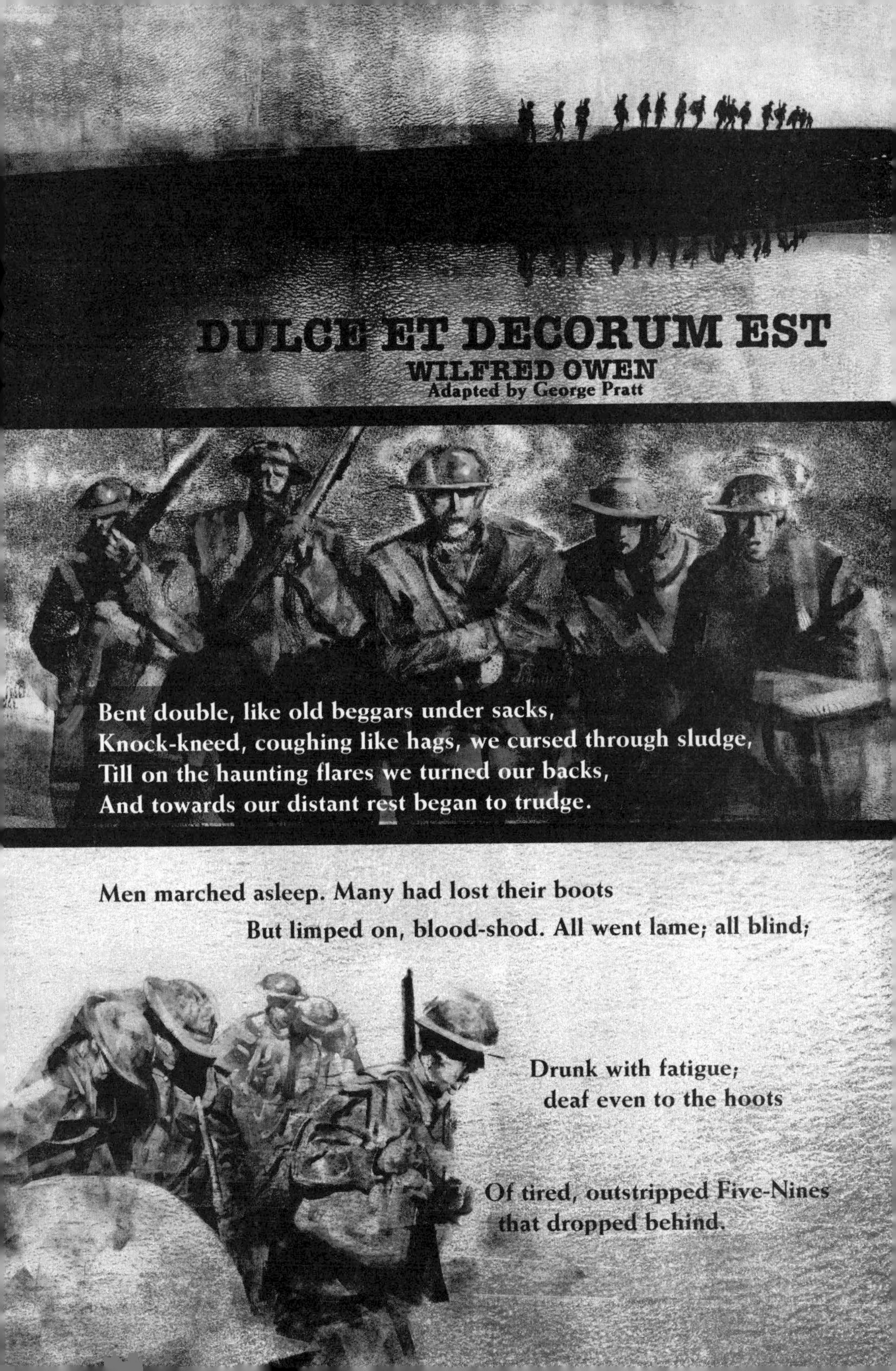
DULCE ET DECORUM EST
WILFRED OWEN
Adapted by George Pratt
Bent double, like old beggars under sacks,
Knock-kneed, coughing like hags, we cursed through sludge,
Till on the haunting flares we turned our backs,
And towards our distant rest began to trudge.
Men marched asleep. Many had lost their boots
But limped on, blood-shod. All went lame; all blind;
Drunk with fatigue; deaf even to the hoots
Of tired, outstripped Five-Nines that dropped behind.

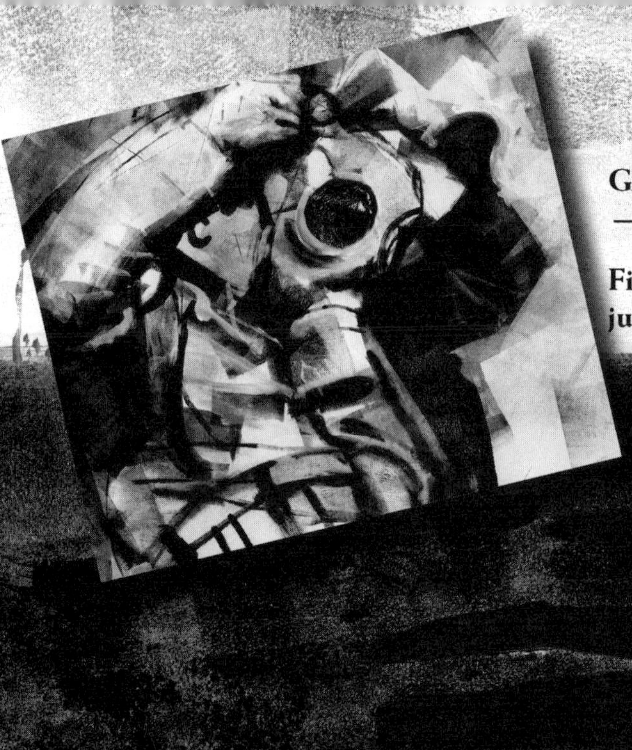

Gas! GAS! Quick, boys!
—An ecstasy of fumbling,

Fitting the clumsy helmets
just in time;

But someone still was yelling out and stumbling,
And flound'ring like a man in fire or lime...

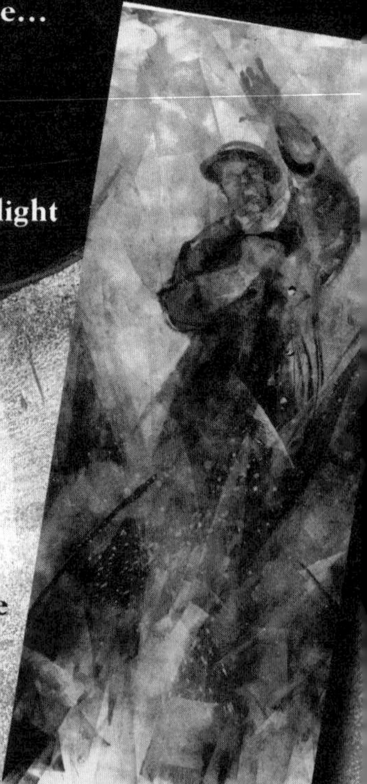

Dim, through the misty panes and thick green light
As under a green sea, I saw him drowning.

In all my dreams, before my helpless sight,
He plunges at me, guttering, choking, drowning.

If in some smothering dreams you too could pace
Behind the wagon that we flung him in,
And watch the white eyes writhing in his face,
His hanging face, like a devil's sick of sin;

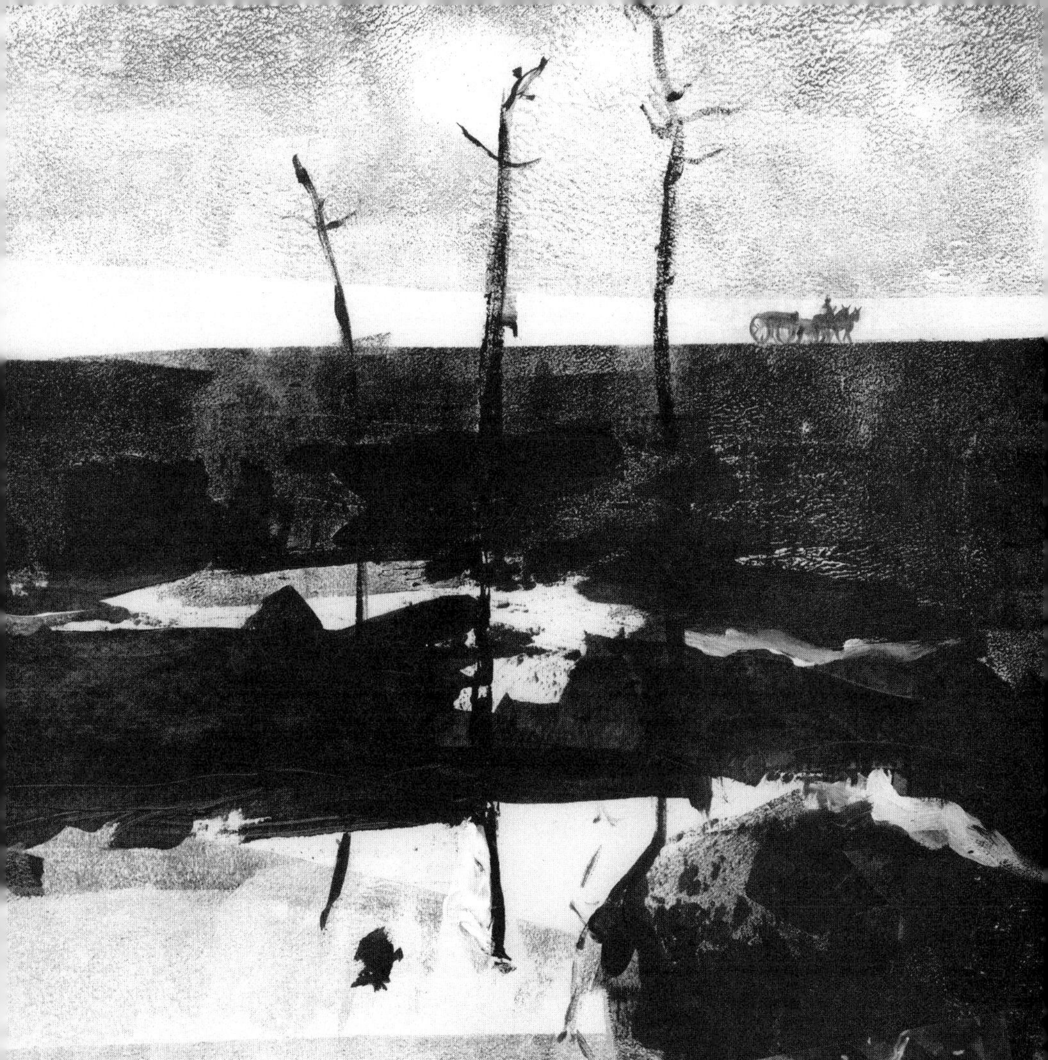

If you could hear, at every jolt, the blood
Come gargling from the froth-corrupted lungs,
Obscene as cancer, bitter as the cud
Of vile, incurable sores on innocent tongues,

My friend, you would not tell with such high zest
To children ardent for some desperate glory,
The old Lie; Dulce et decorum est
Pro patria mori.

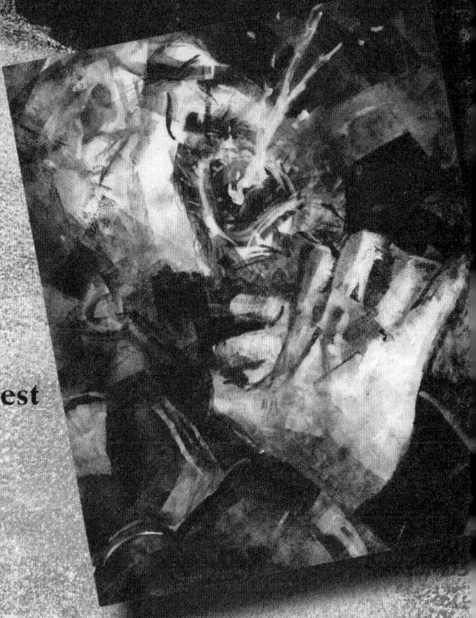

A PRIVATE
by Edward Thomas

Adapted by
Hannah Berry

This ploughman dead in battle
slept out of doors
Many a frozen night,

and merrily
Answered staid drinkers,

good bedmen,

and all bores:

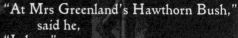

"At Mrs Greenland's Hawthorn Bush,"
said he,
"I slept."

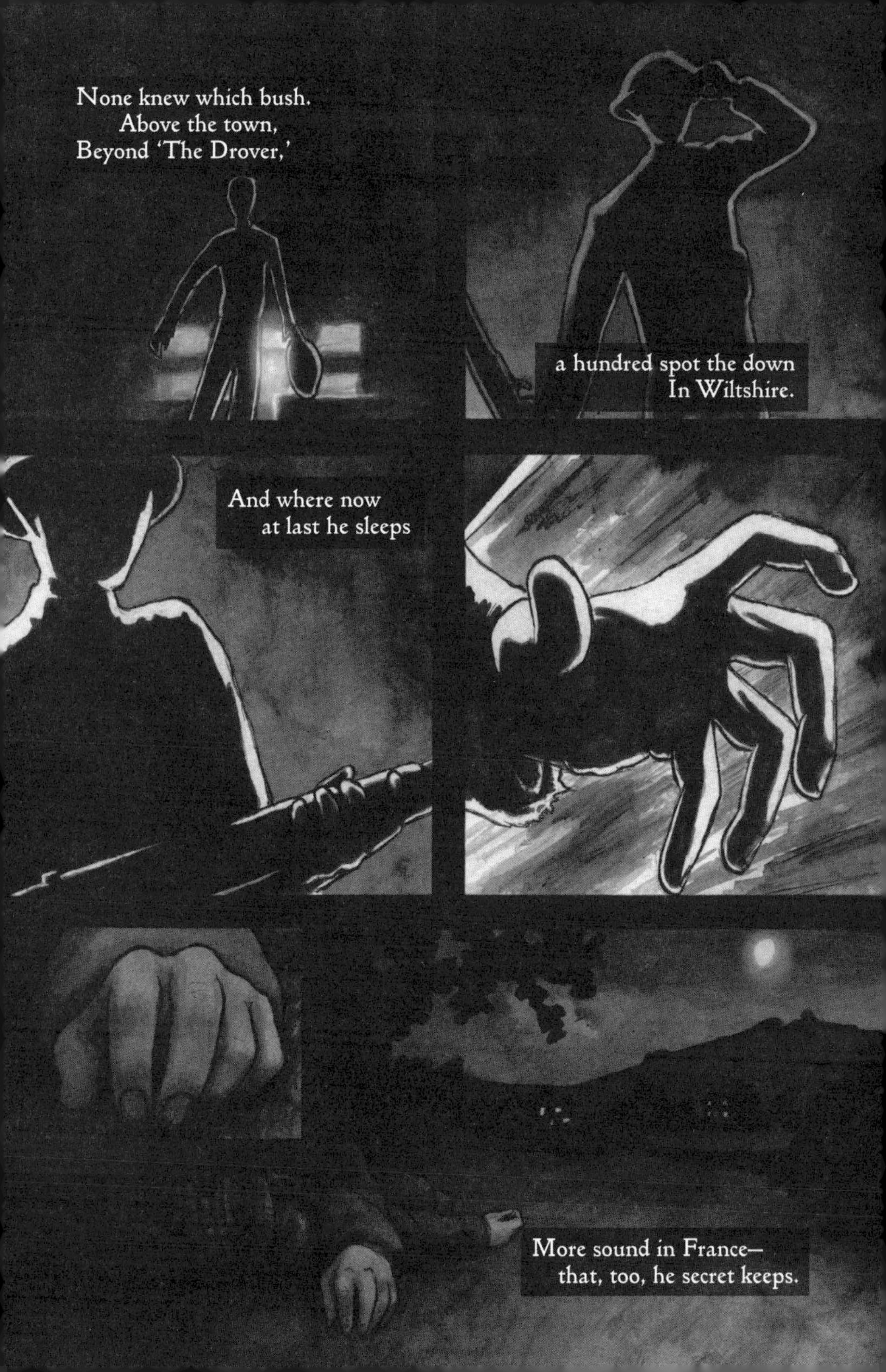
None knew which bush.
Above the town,
Beyond 'The Drover,'
a hundred spot the down
In Wiltshire.
And where now
at last he sleeps
More sound in France—
that, too, he secret keeps.

WHEN THIS BLOODY WAR IS OVER

SOLDIERS' SONG ADAPTED BY HUNT EMERSON

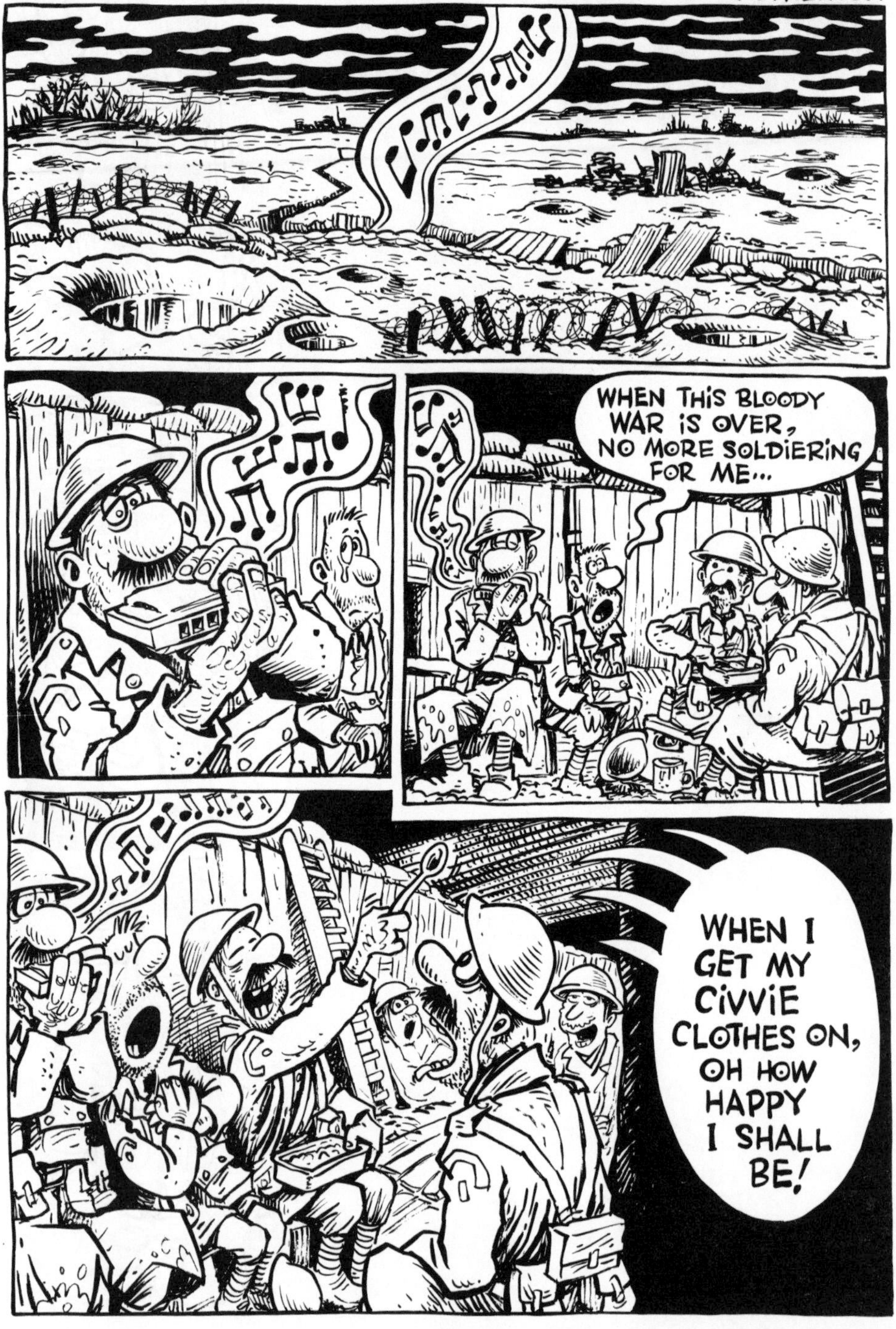
WHEN THIS BLOODY WAR IS OVER, NO MORE SOLDIERING FOR ME...
WHEN I GET MY CIVVIE CLOTHES ON, OH HOW HAPPY I SHALL BE!

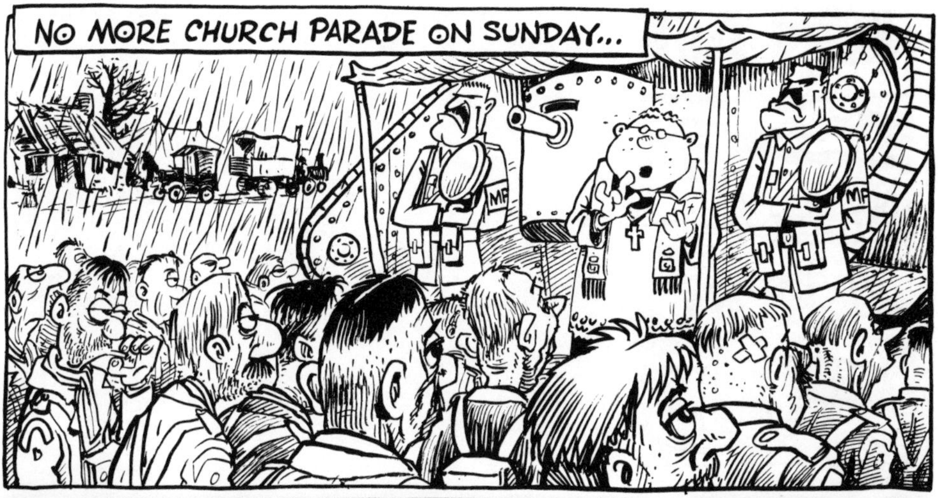
NO MORE CHURCH PARADE ON SUNDAY...
MP
MP

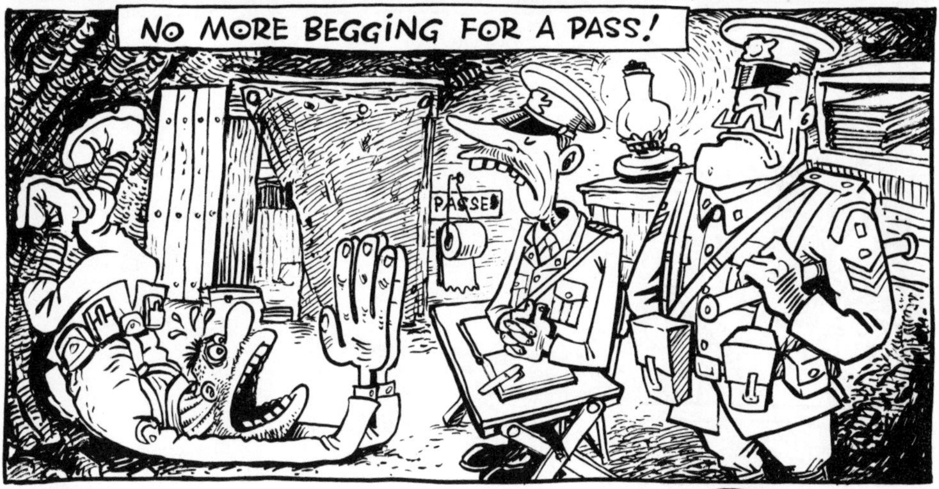
NO MORE BEGGING FOR A PASS!
PASSES

YOU CAN TELL THE SERGEANT-MAJOR

TO STICK HIS PASSES UP HIS ARSE!

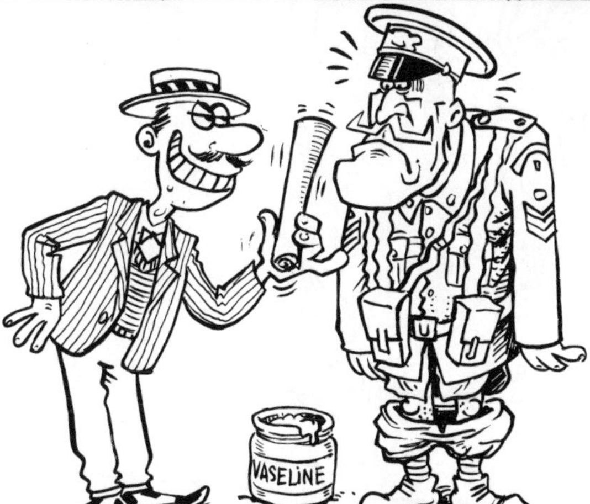
VASELINE

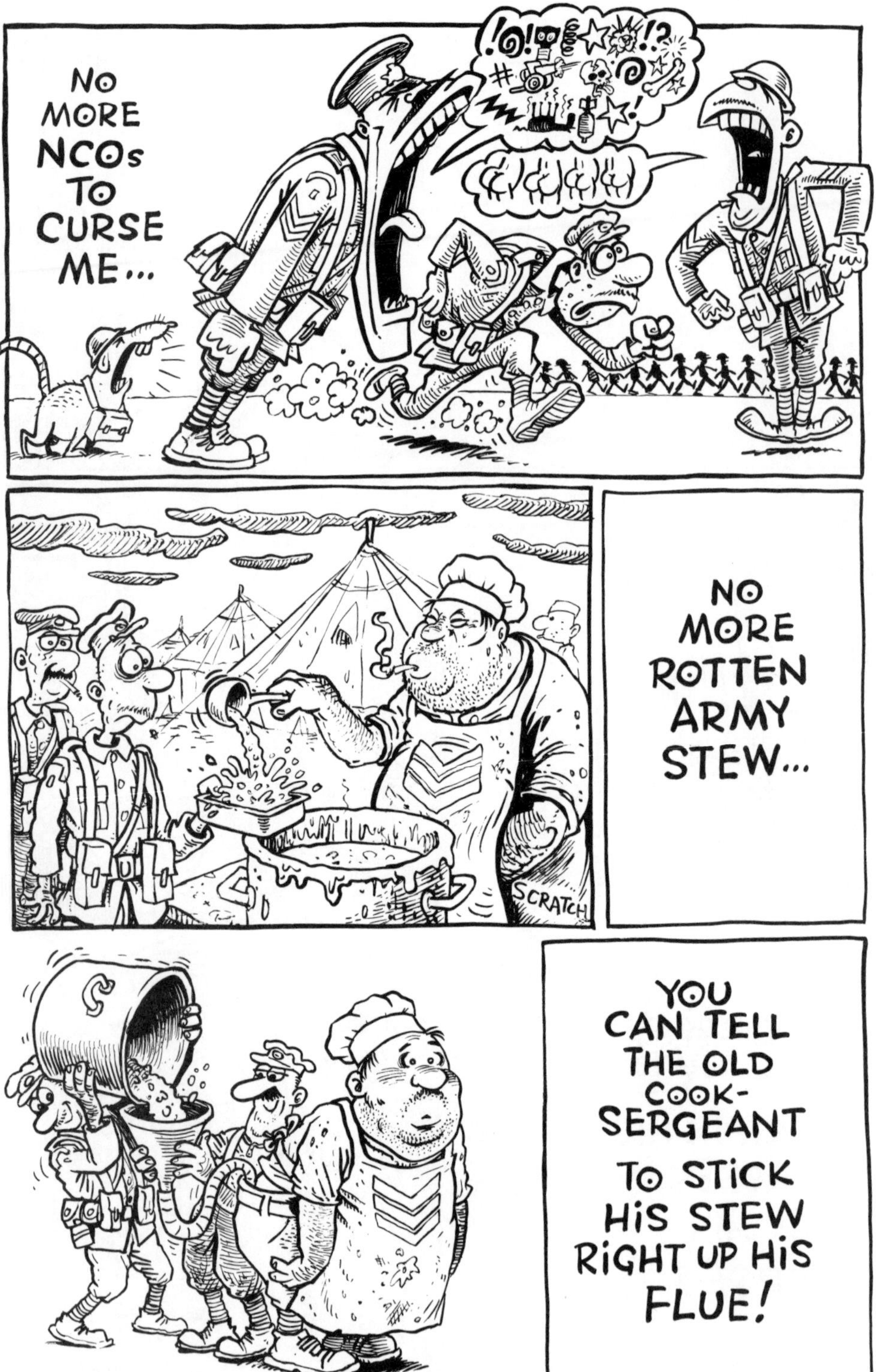
NO MORE NCOs TO CURSE ME...
SCRATCH
NO MORE ROTTEN ARMY STEW...
YOU CAN TELL THE OLD COOK-SERGEANT
TO STICK HIS STEW RIGHT UP HIS FLUE!

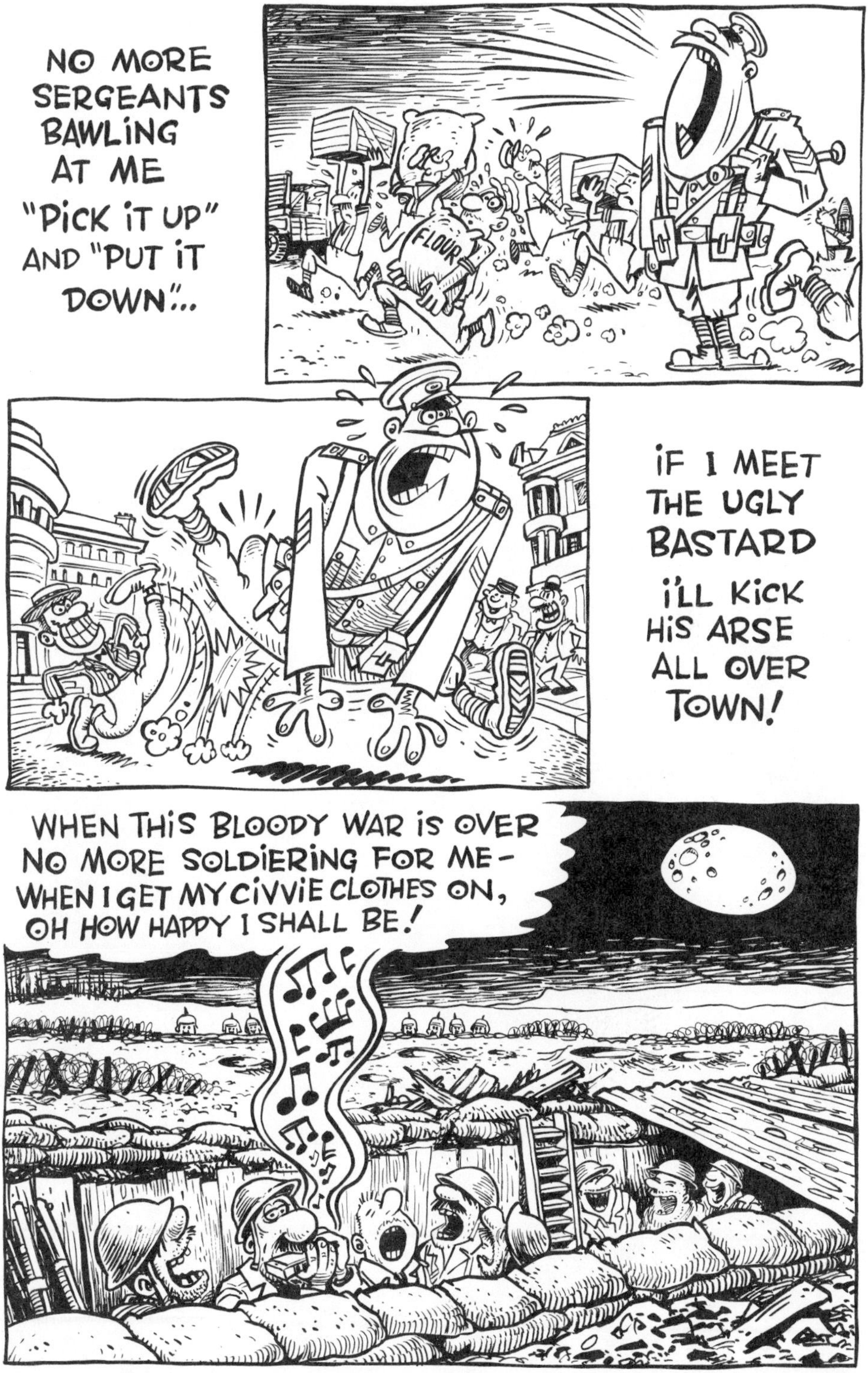
NO MORE SERGEANTS BAWLING AT ME "PICK IT UP" AND "PUT IT DOWN"...
FLOUR
IF I MEET THE UGLY BASTARD
I'LL KICK HIS ARSE ALL OVER TOWN!
WHEN THIS BLOODY WAR IS OVER NO MORE SOLDIERING FOR ME- WHEN I GET MY CIVVIE CLOTHES ON, OH HOW HAPPY I SHALL BE!

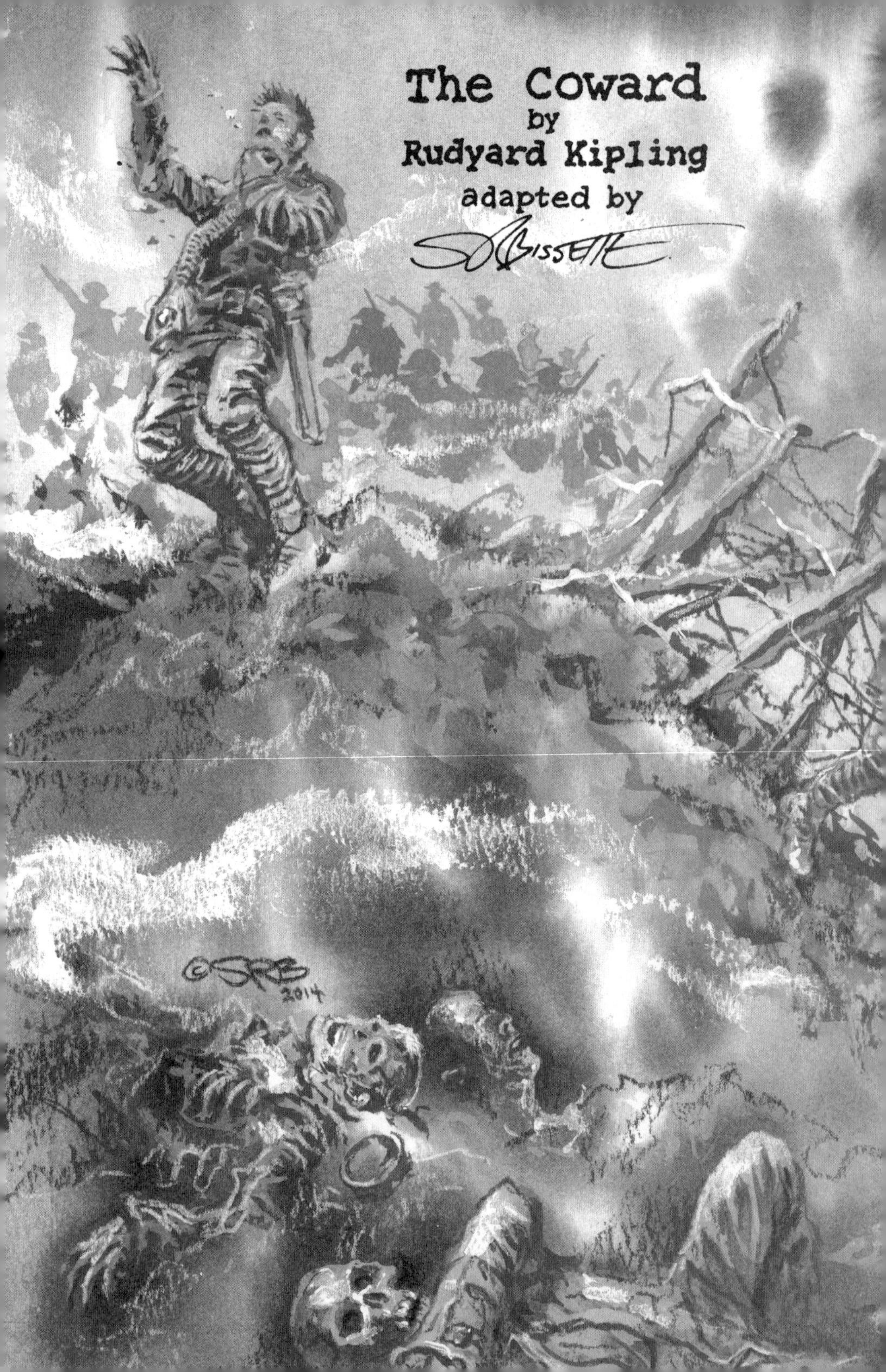
The Coward
by
Rudyard Kipling
adapted by
SRBissette
©SRB
2014

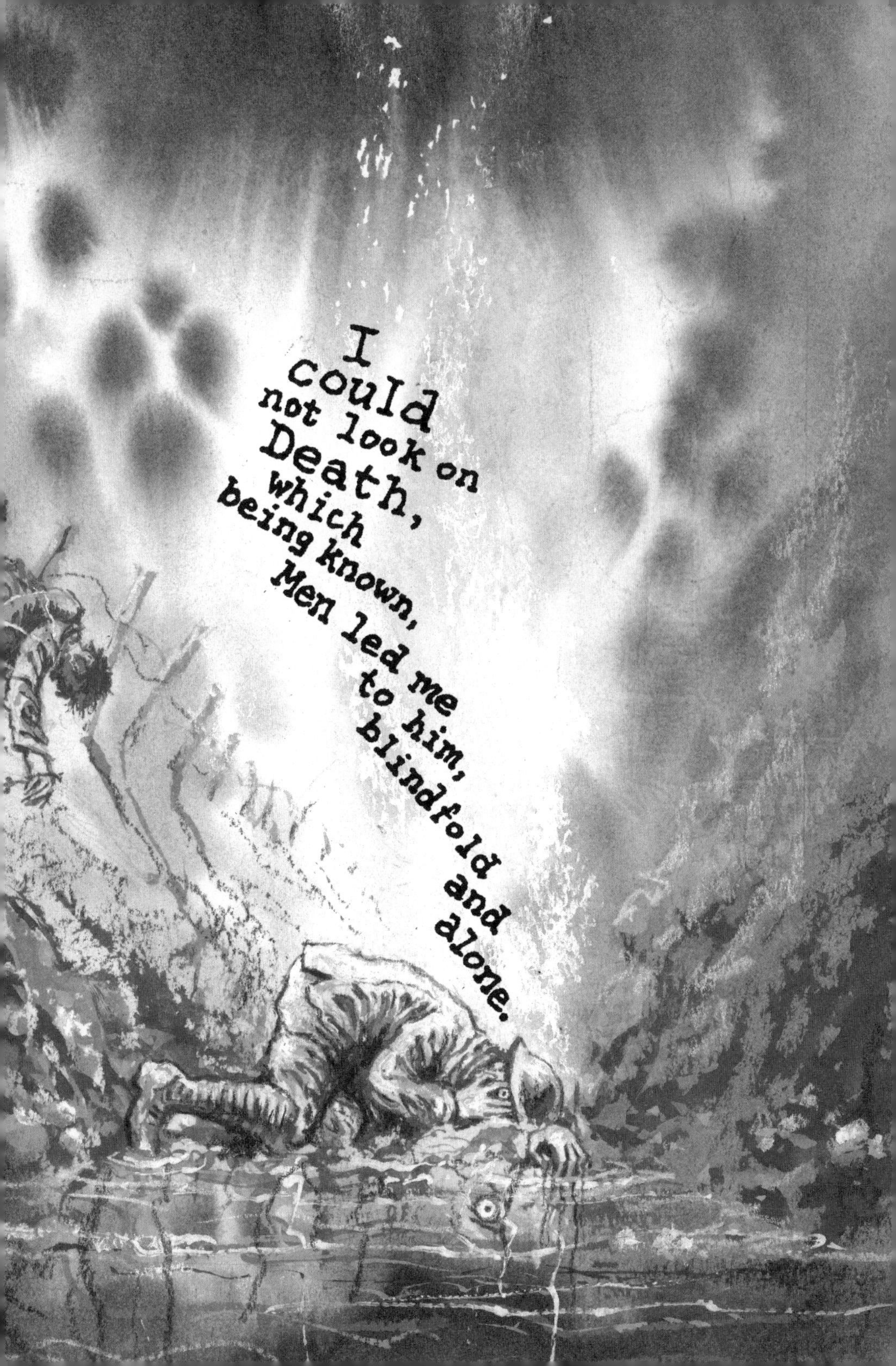
I could not look on Death, which being known, Men led me to him, blindfold and alone.

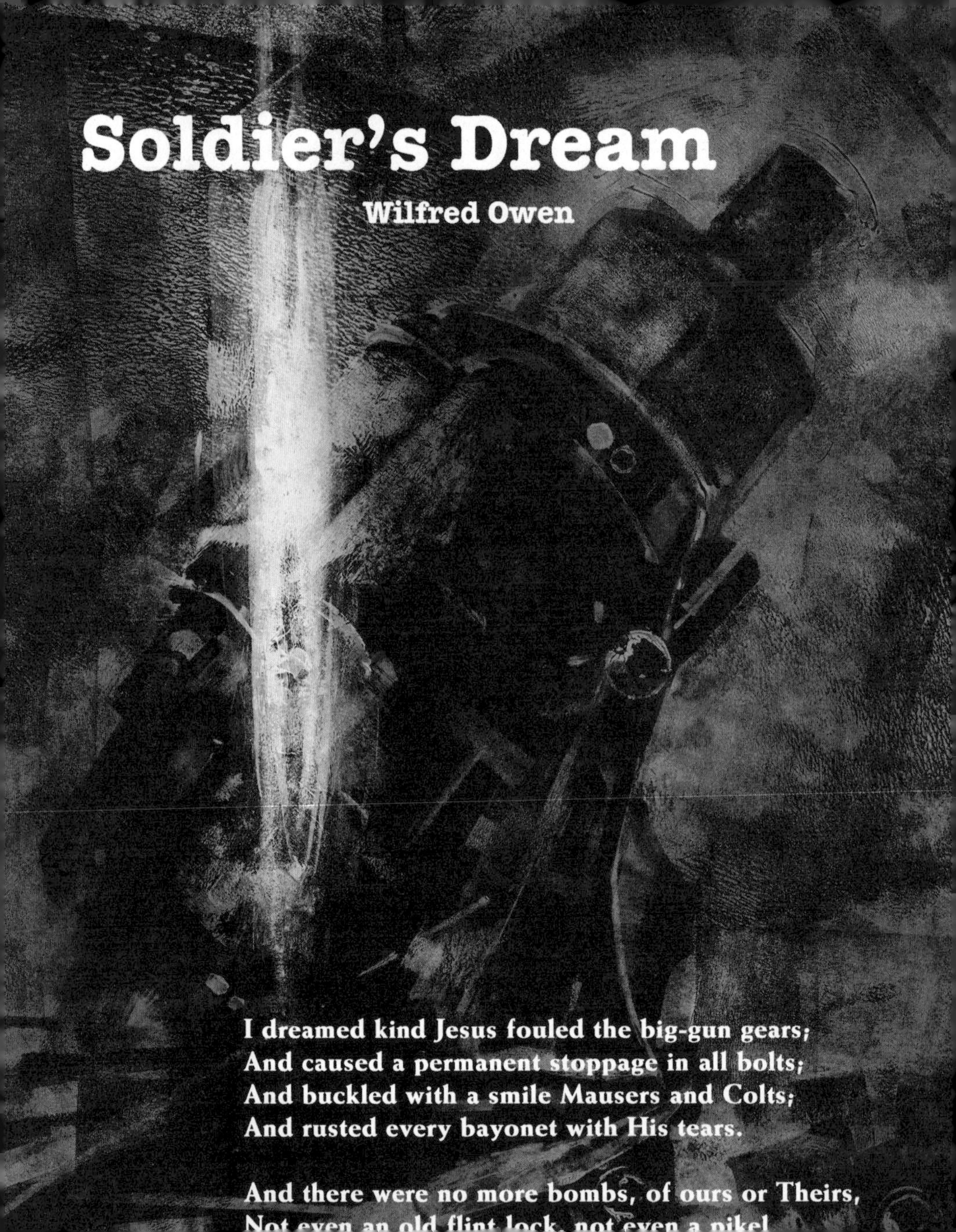

Soldier's Dream

Wilfred Owen

I dreamed kind Jesus fouled the big-gun gears;
And caused a permanent stoppage in all bolts;
And buckled with a smile Mausers and Colts;
And rusted every bayonet with His tears.

And there were no more bombs, of ours or Theirs,
Not even an old flint lock, not even a pike!

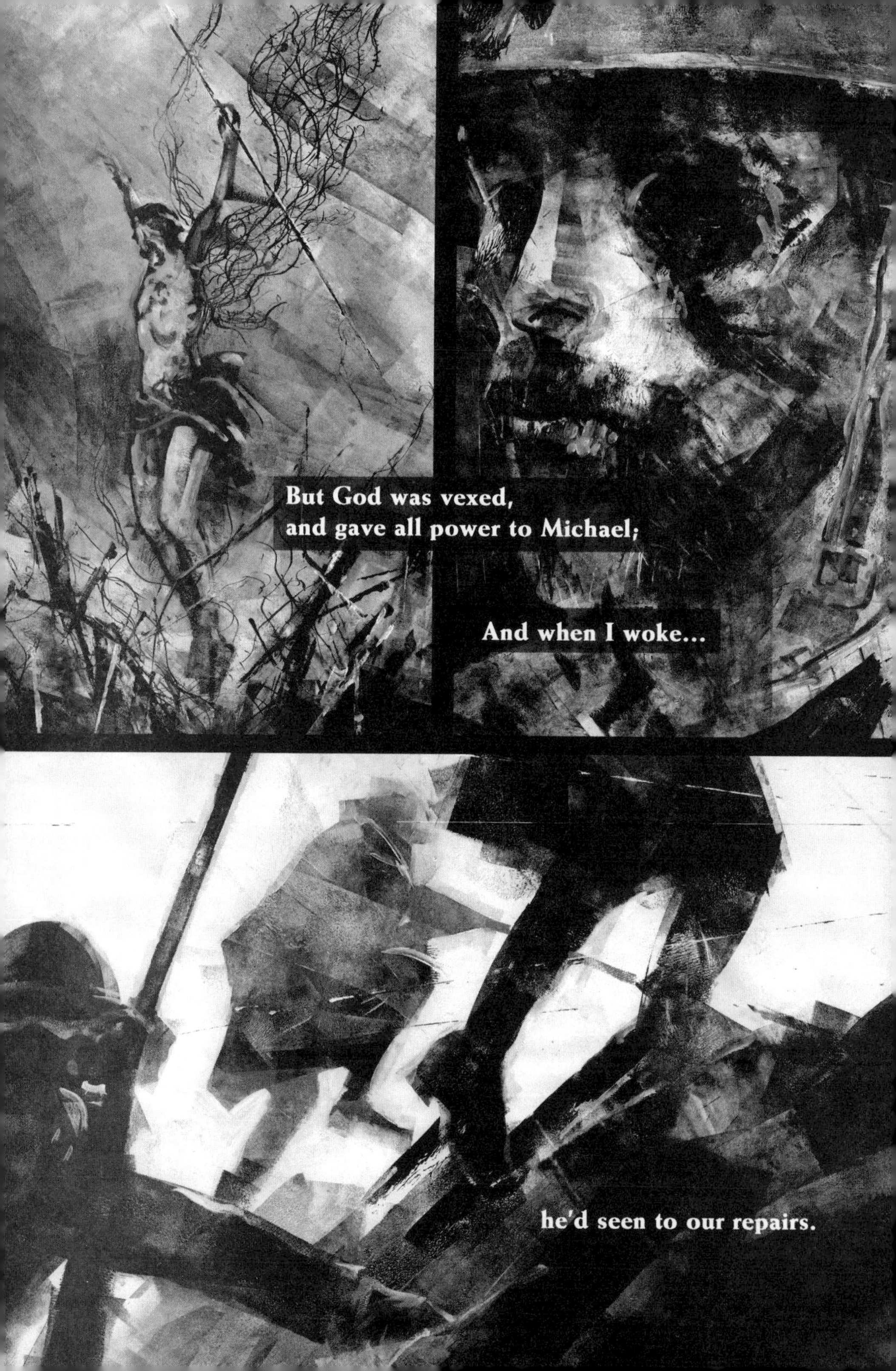
But God was vexed,
and gave all power to Michael;
And when I woke...
he'd seen to our repairs.

"BREAK OF DAY IN THE TRENCHES" BY ISAAC ROSENBERG

ADAPTED BY SARAH GLIDDEN

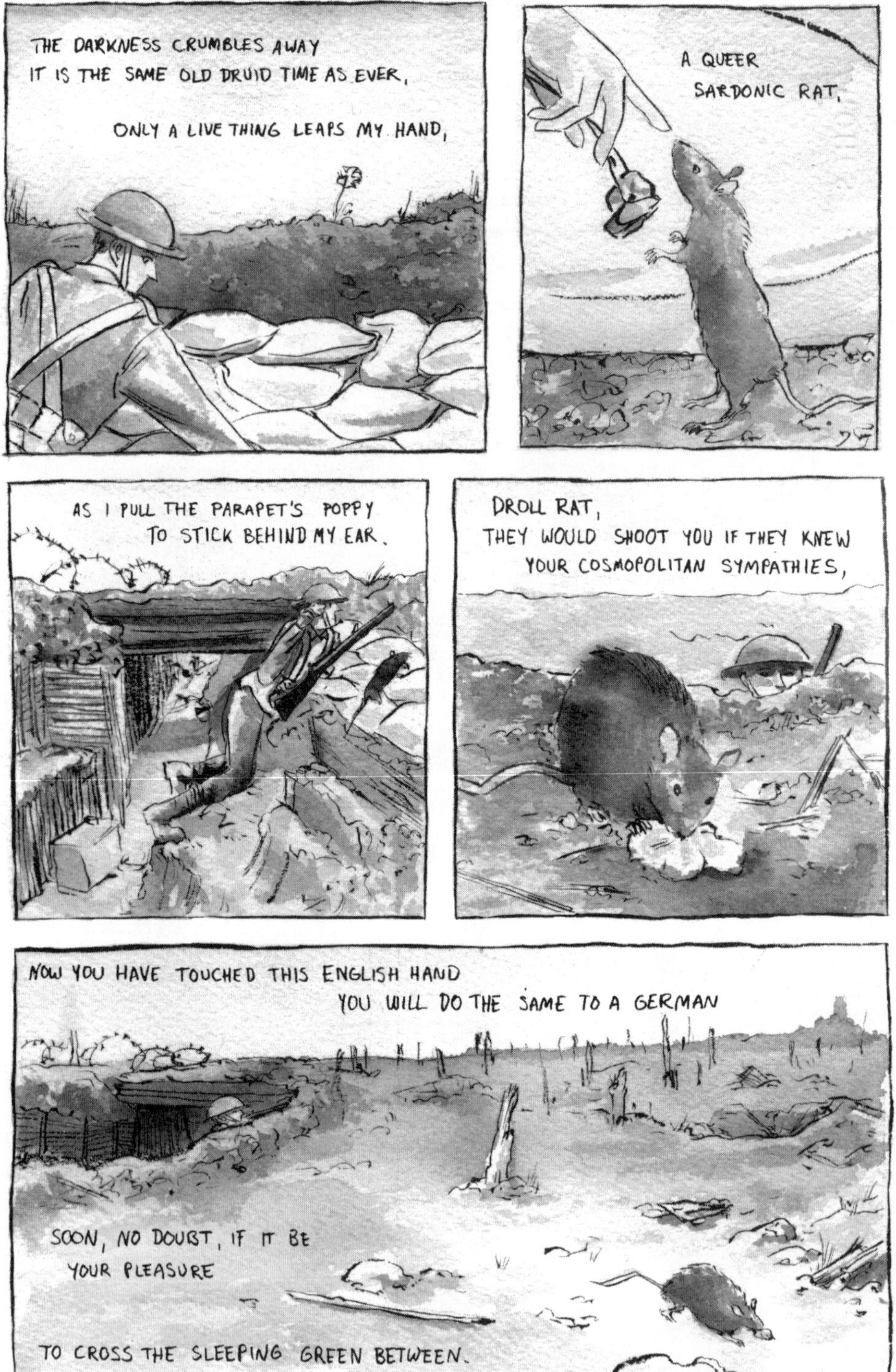
THE DARKNESS CRUMBLES AWAY
IT IS THE SAME OLD DRUID TIME AS EVER,
ONLY A LIVE THING LEAPS MY HAND,
A QUEER SARDONIC RAT,
AS I PULL THE PARAPET'S POPPY
TO STICK BEHIND MY EAR.
DROLL RAT,
THEY WOULD SHOOT YOU IF THEY KNEW
YOUR COSMOPOLITAN SYMPATHIES,
NOW YOU HAVE TOUCHED THIS ENGLISH HAND
YOU WILL DO THE SAME TO A GERMAN
SOON, NO DOUBT, IF IT BE
YOUR PLEASURE
TO CROSS THE SLEEPING GREEN BETWEEN.

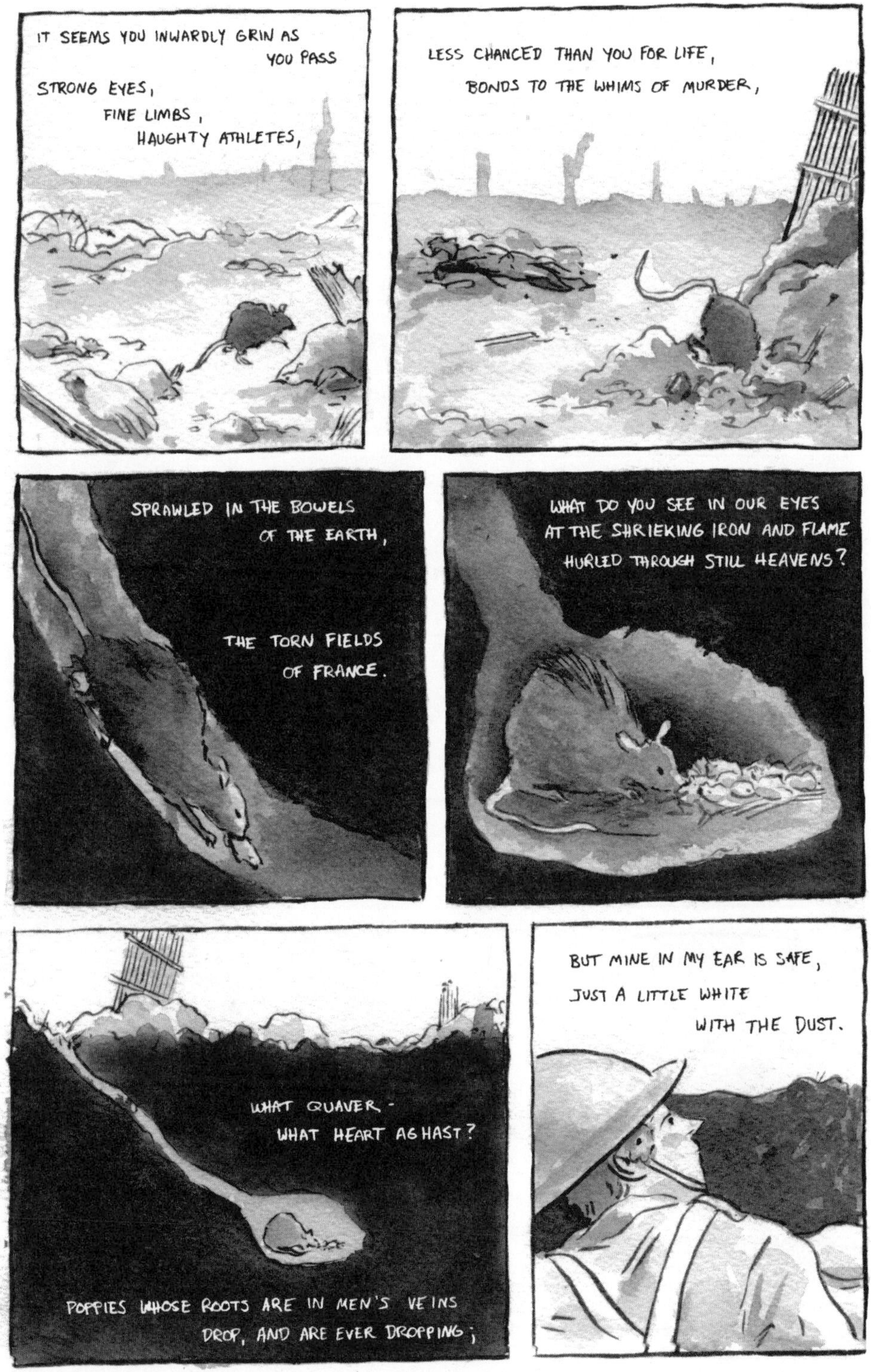
IT SEEMS YOU INWARDLY GRIN AS YOU PASS
STRONG EYES,
FINE LIMBS,
HAUGHTY ATHLETES,
LESS CHANCED THAN YOU FOR LIFE,
BONDS TO THE WHIMS OF MURDER,
SPRAWLED IN THE BOWELS OF THE EARTH,
THE TORN FIELDS OF FRANCE.
WHAT DO YOU SEE IN OUR EYES
AT THE SHRIEKING IRON AND FLAME
HURLED THROUGH STILL HEAVENS?
WHAT QUAVER -
WHAT HEART AGHAST?
POPPIES WHOSE ROOTS ARE IN MEN'S VEINS
DROP, AND ARE EVER DROPPING;
BUT MINE IN MY EAR IS SAFE,
JUST A LITTLE WHITE
WITH THE DUST.

I LOOKED UP FROM MY WRITING *by Thomas Hardy*

adapted by Kathryn Immonen & Stuart Immonen

I looked up from my writing.

And gave a start to see,

As if rapt in my inditing.

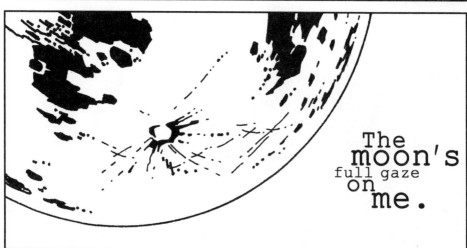

The moon's full gaze on me.

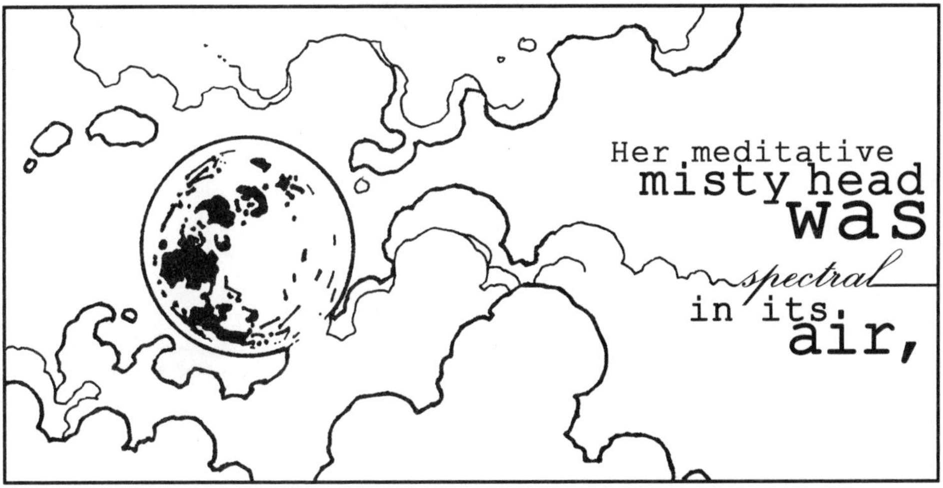
Her meditative misty head was spectral in its air,

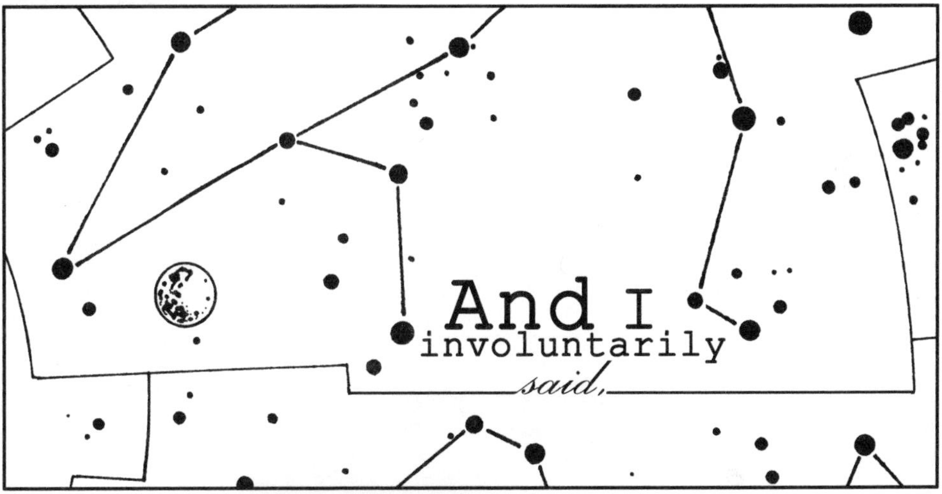
And I involuntarily said,

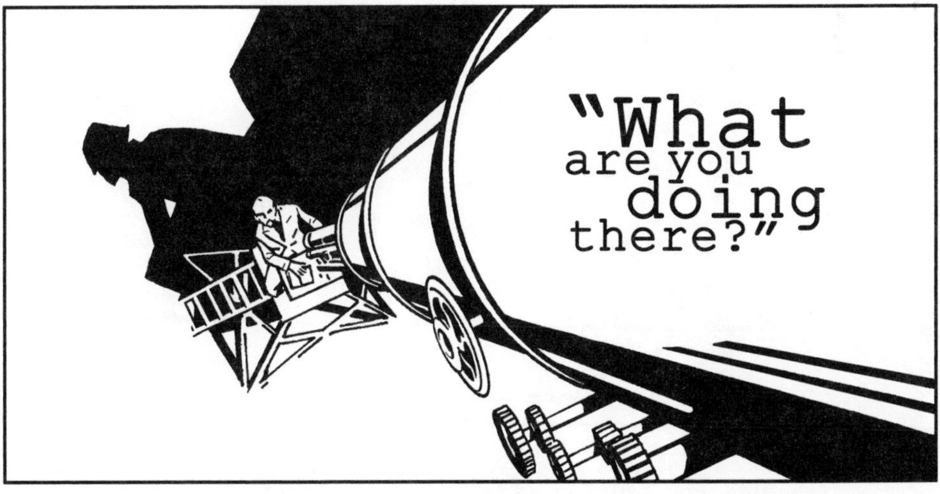
"What are you doing there?"

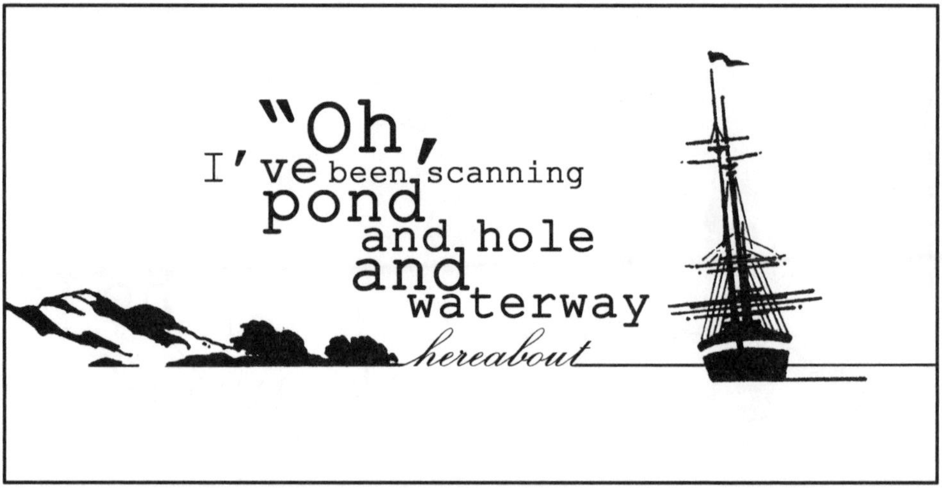
"Oh, I've been scanning pond and hole and waterway hereabout

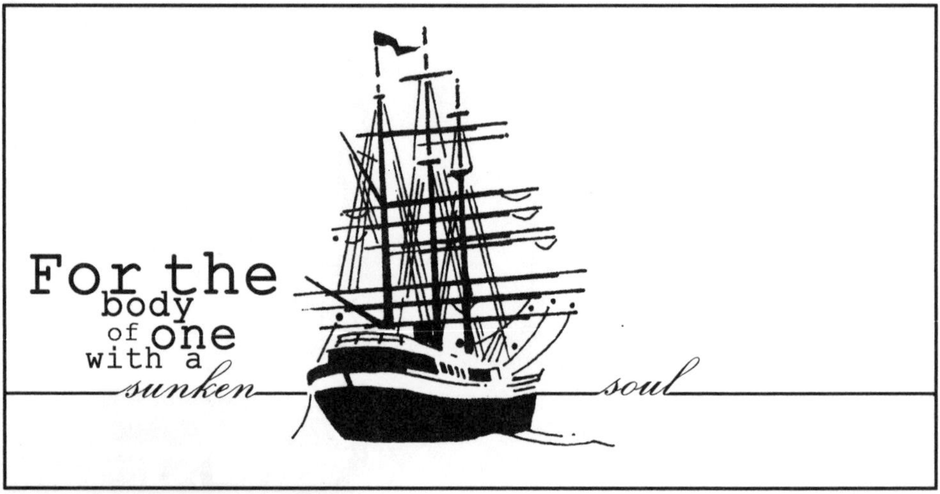
For the body of one with a sunken soul

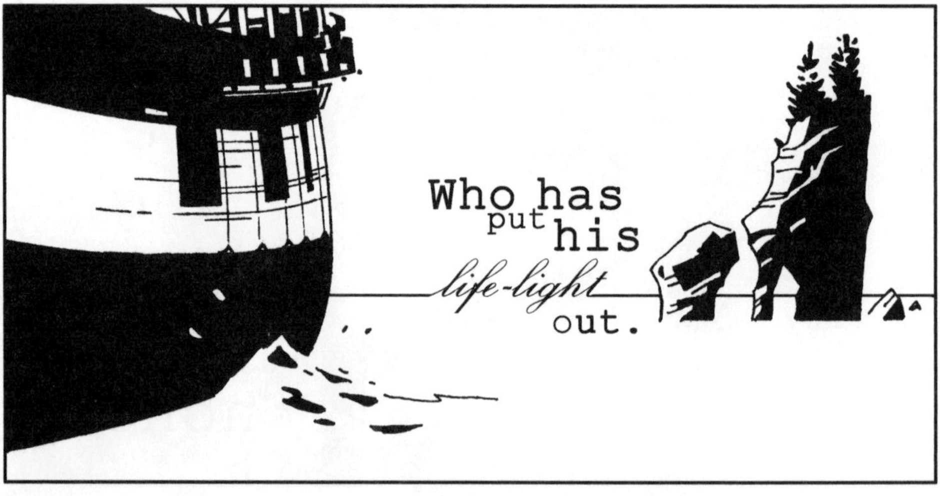
Who has put his life-light out.

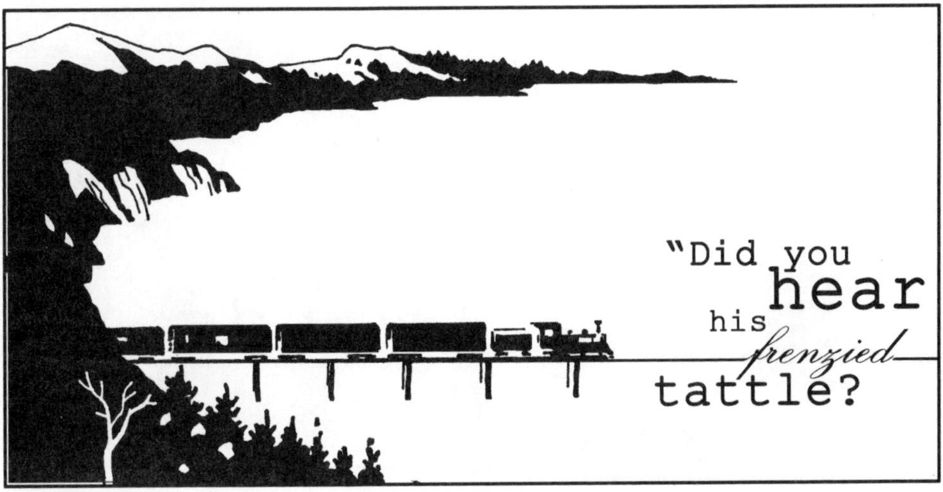
"Did you hear his frenzied tattle?

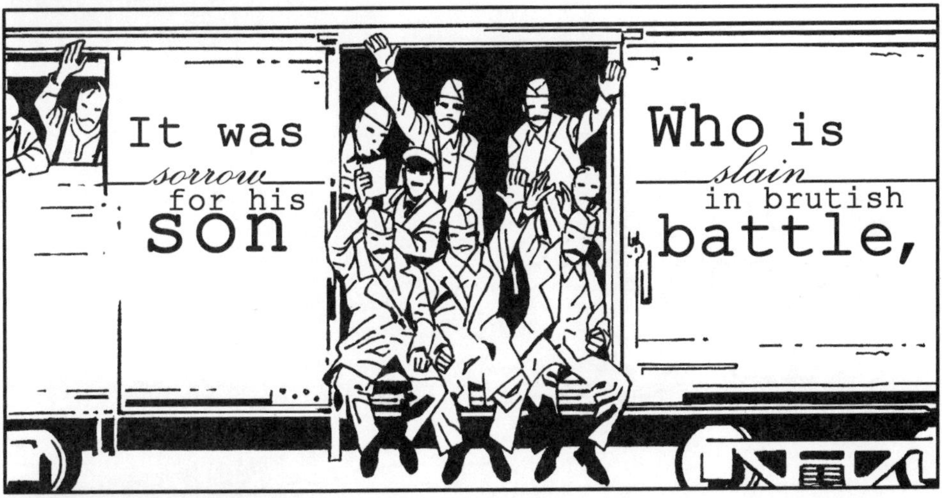
It was sorrow for his son
Who is slain in brutish battle,

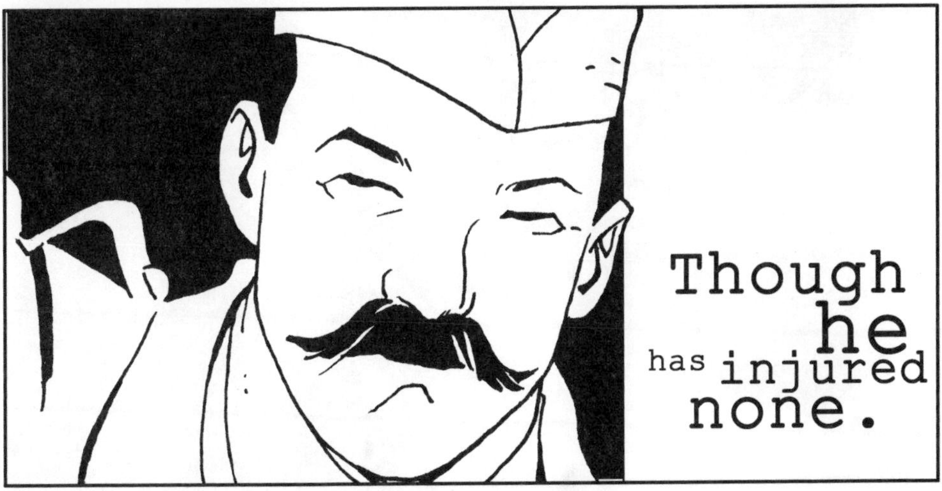
Though he has injured none.

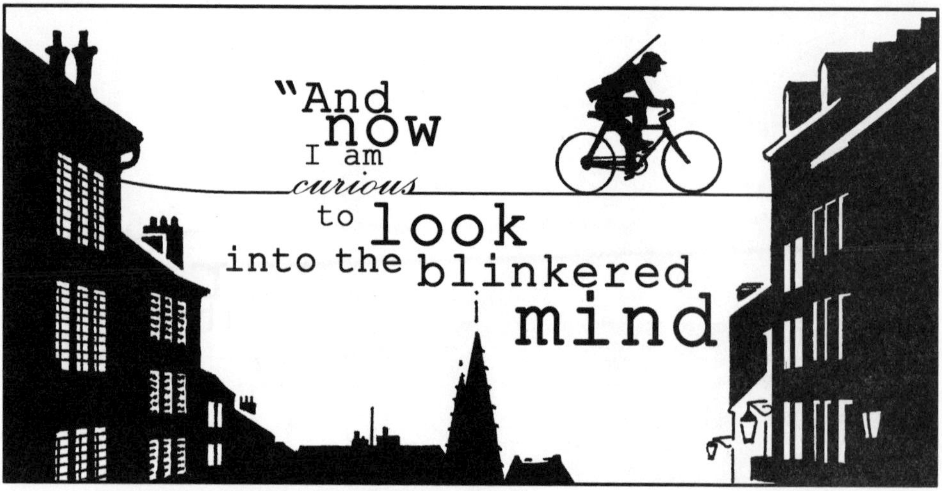
"And now I am *curious* to look into the blinkered mind

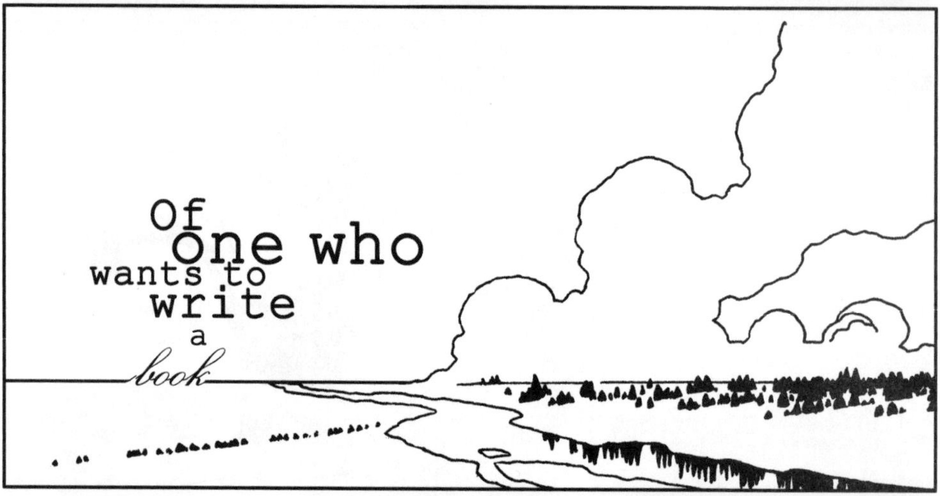
Of one who wants to write a *book*

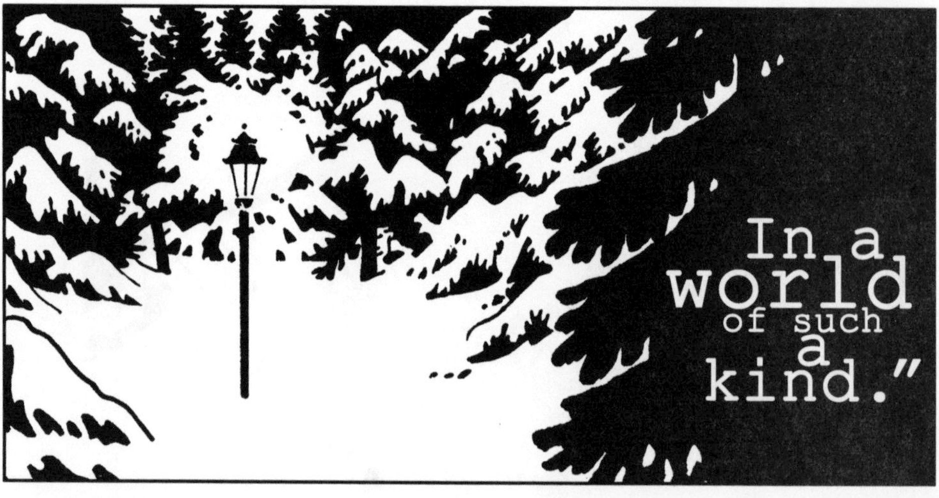
In a world of such a kind."

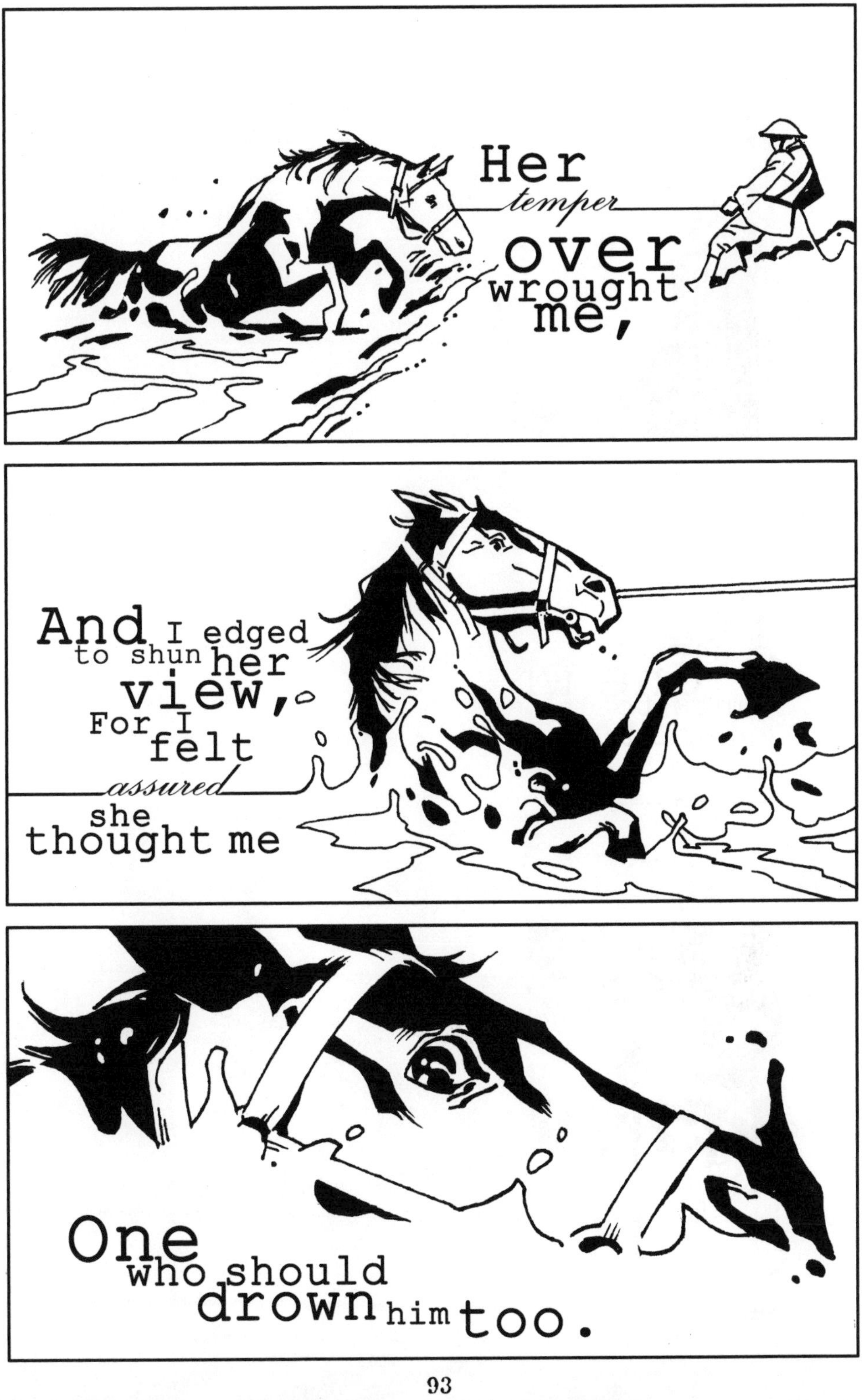
Her temper over wrought me,
And I edged to shun her view, For I felt assured she thought me
One who should drown him too.

By Wilfrid Wilson Gibson

THE DANCERS

Adapted by Lilli Carré

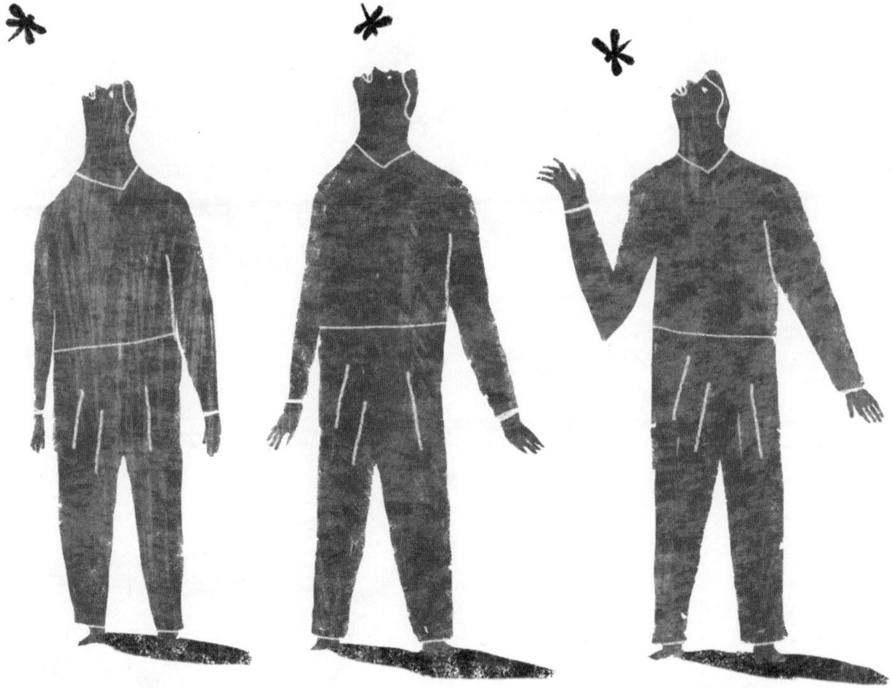

All day beneath the hurtling shells
Before my burning eyes
Hover the dainty demoiselles—
The peacock dragonflies.

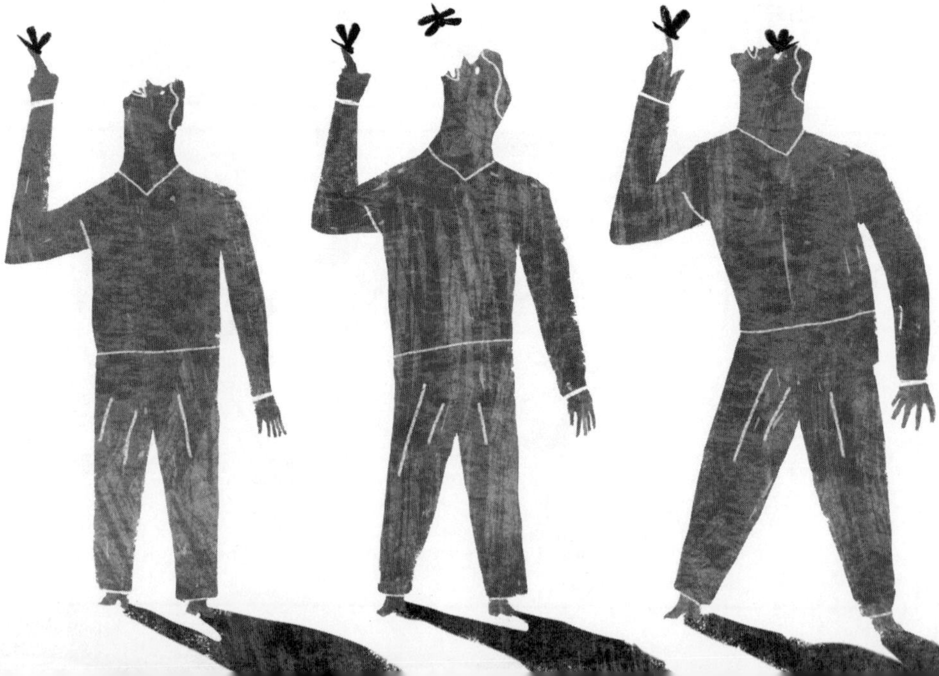

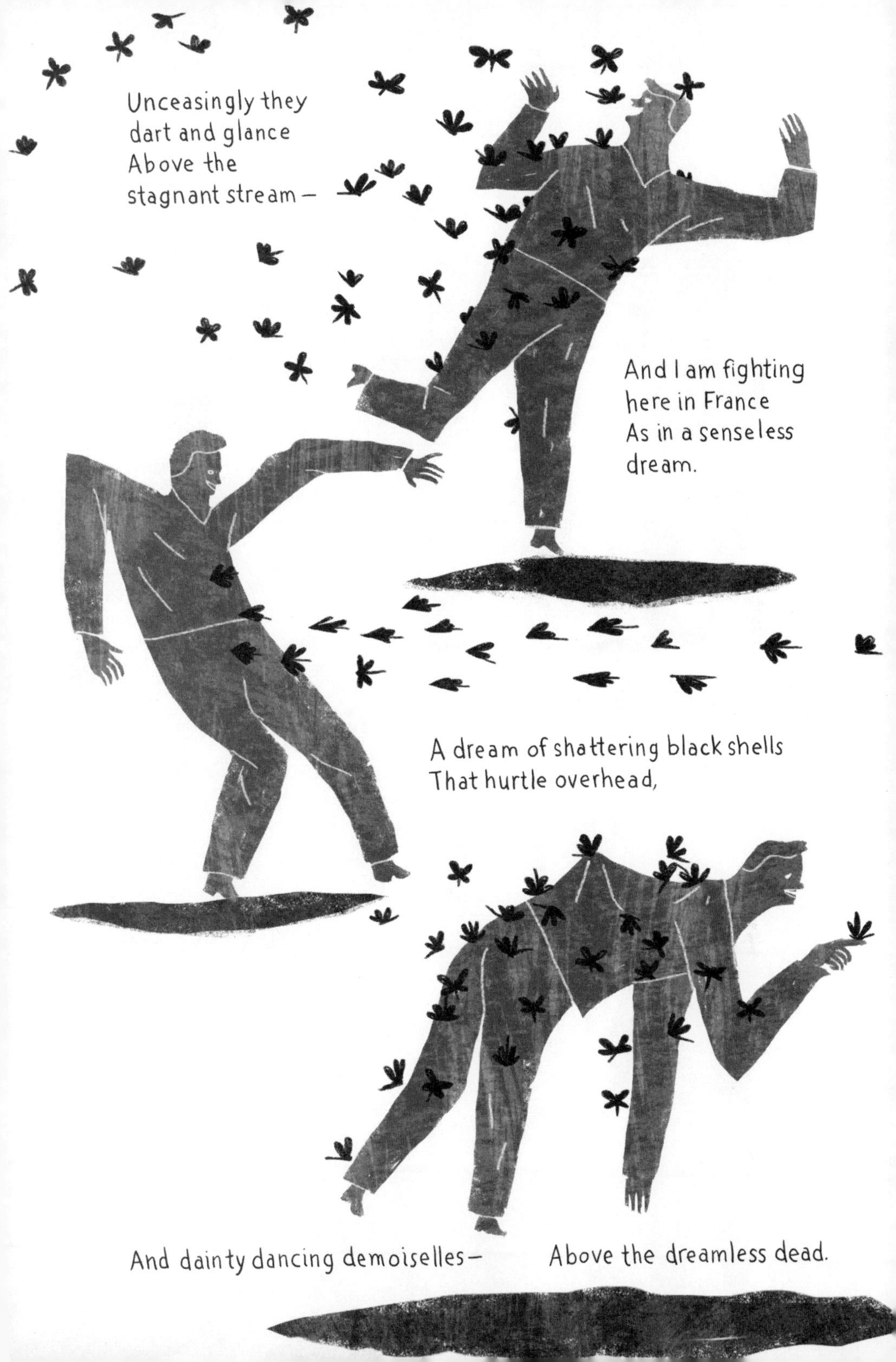
Unceasingly they
dart and glance
Above the
stagnant stream—
And I am fighting
here in France
As in a senseless
dream.
A dream of shattering black shells
That hurtle overhead,
And dainty dancing demoiselles—
Above the dreamless dead.

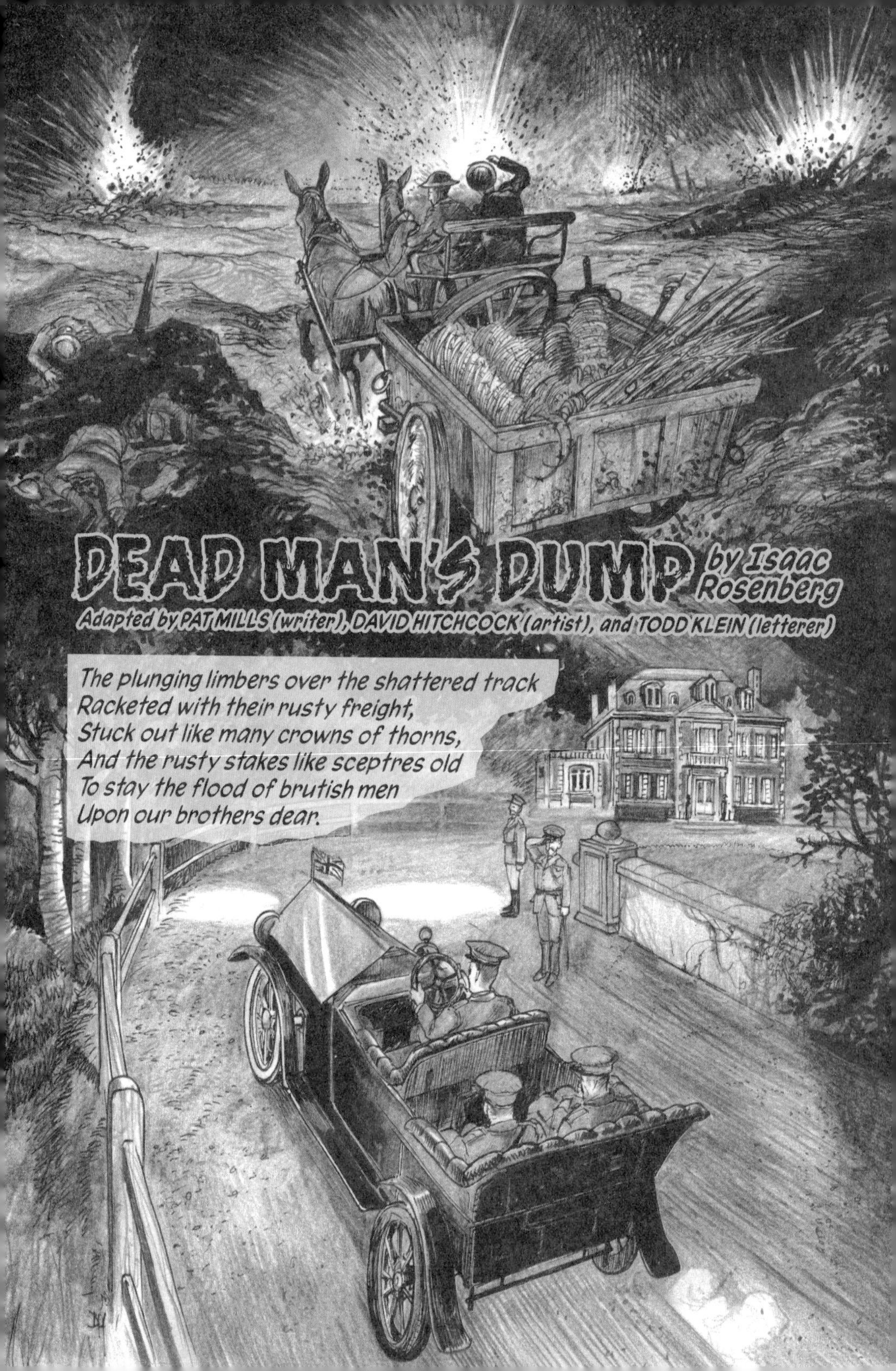
DEAD MAN'S DUMP by Isaac Rosenberg
Adapted by PAT MILLS (writer), DAVID HITCHCOCK (artist), and TODD KLEIN (letterer)
The plunging limbers over the shattered track
Racketed with their rusty freight,
Stuck out like many crowns of thorns,
And the rusty stakes like sceptres old
To stay the flood of brutish men
Upon our brothers dear.

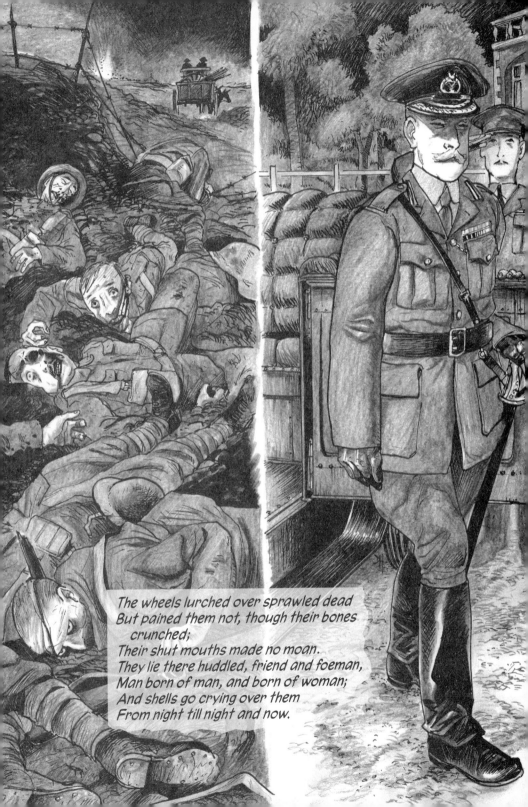

The wheels lurched over sprawled dead
But pained them not, though their bones
    crunched;
Their shut mouths made no moan.
They lie there huddled, friend and foeman,
Man born of man, and born of woman;
And shells go crying over them
From night till night and now.

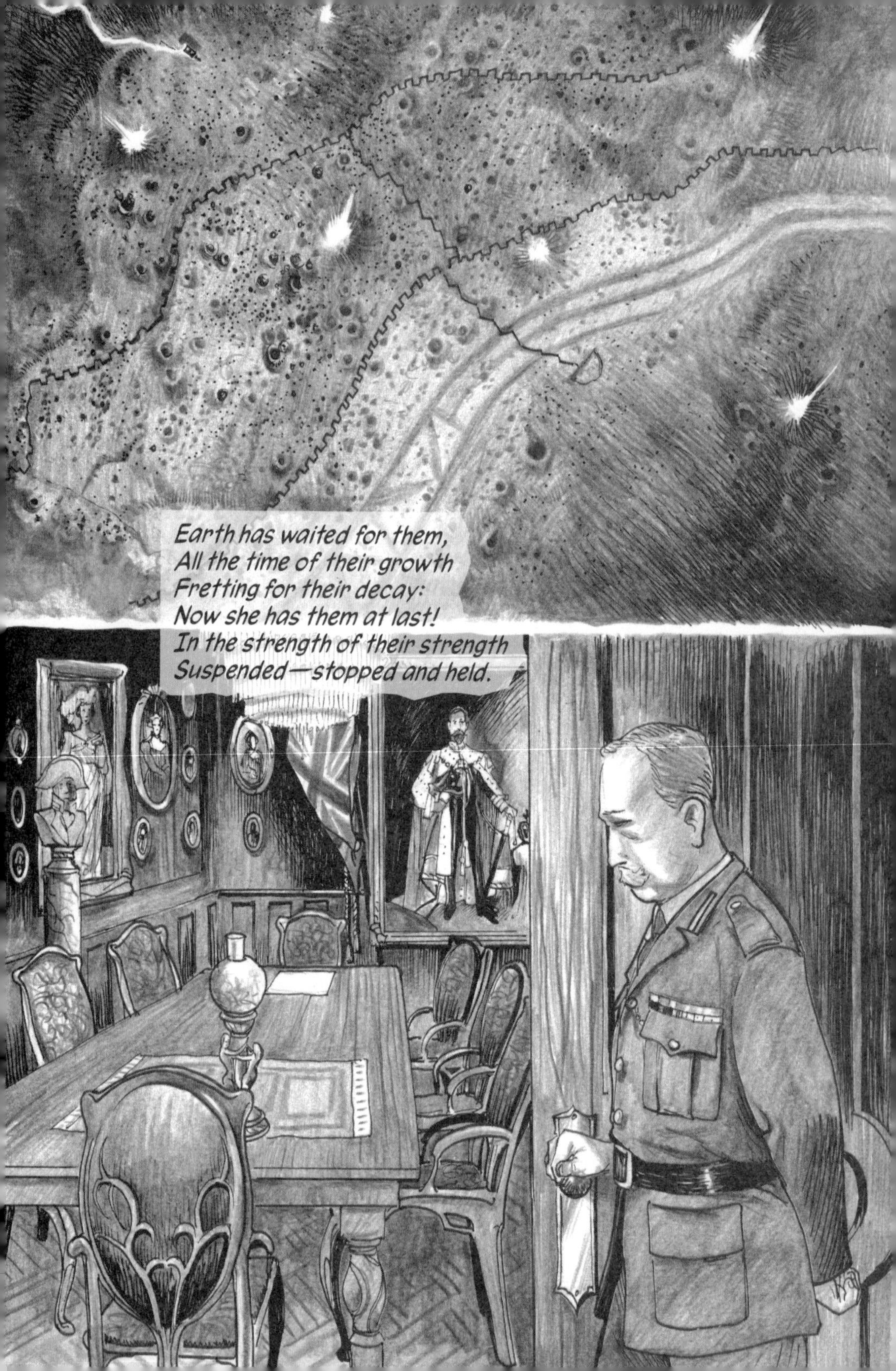
Earth has waited for them,
All the time of their growth
Fretting for their decay:
Now she has them at last!
In the strength of their strength
Suspended—stopped and held.

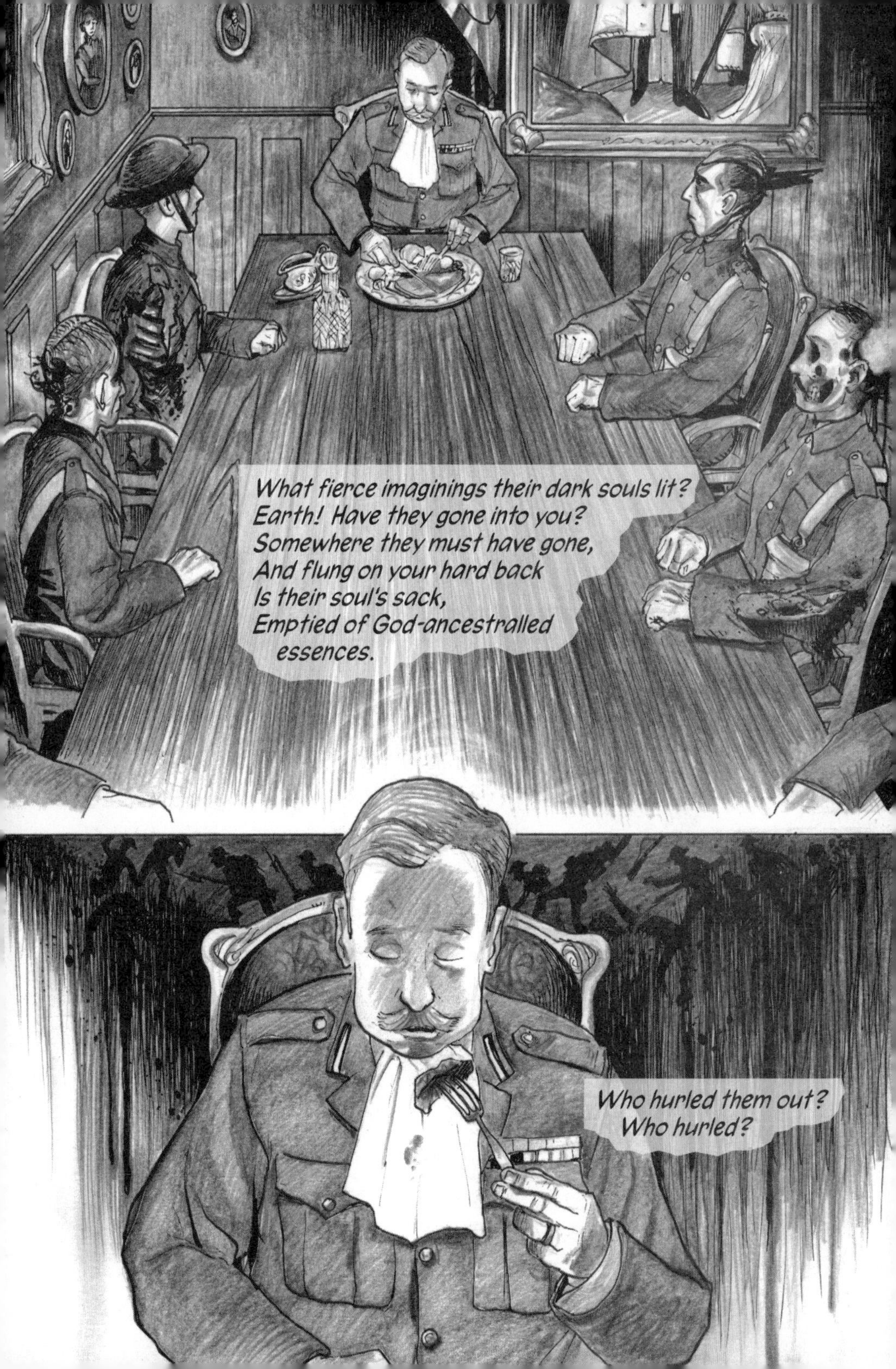
What fierce imaginings their dark souls lit?
Earth! Have they gone into you?
Somewhere they must have gone,
And flung on your hard back
Is their soul's sack,
Emptied of God-ancestralled
essences.
Who hurled them out?
Who hurled?

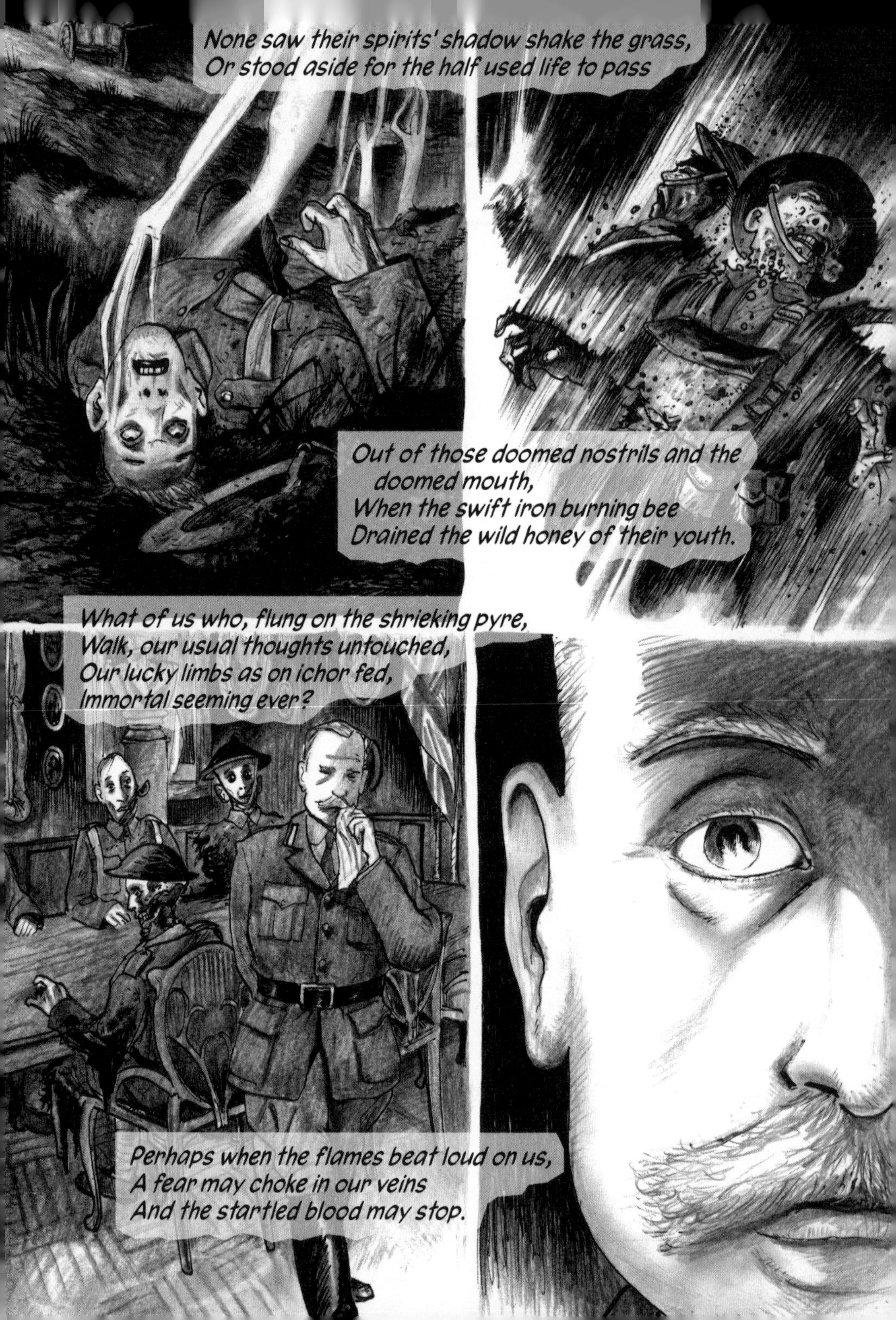
None saw their spirits' shadow shake the grass,
Or stood aside for the half used life to pass
Out of those doomed nostrils and the doomed mouth,
When the swift iron burning bee
Drained the wild honey of their youth.
What of us who, flung on the shrieking pyre,
Walk, our usual thoughts untouched,
Our lucky limbs as on ichor fed,
Immortal seeming ever?
Perhaps when the flames beat loud on us,
A fear may choke in our veins
And the startled blood may stop.

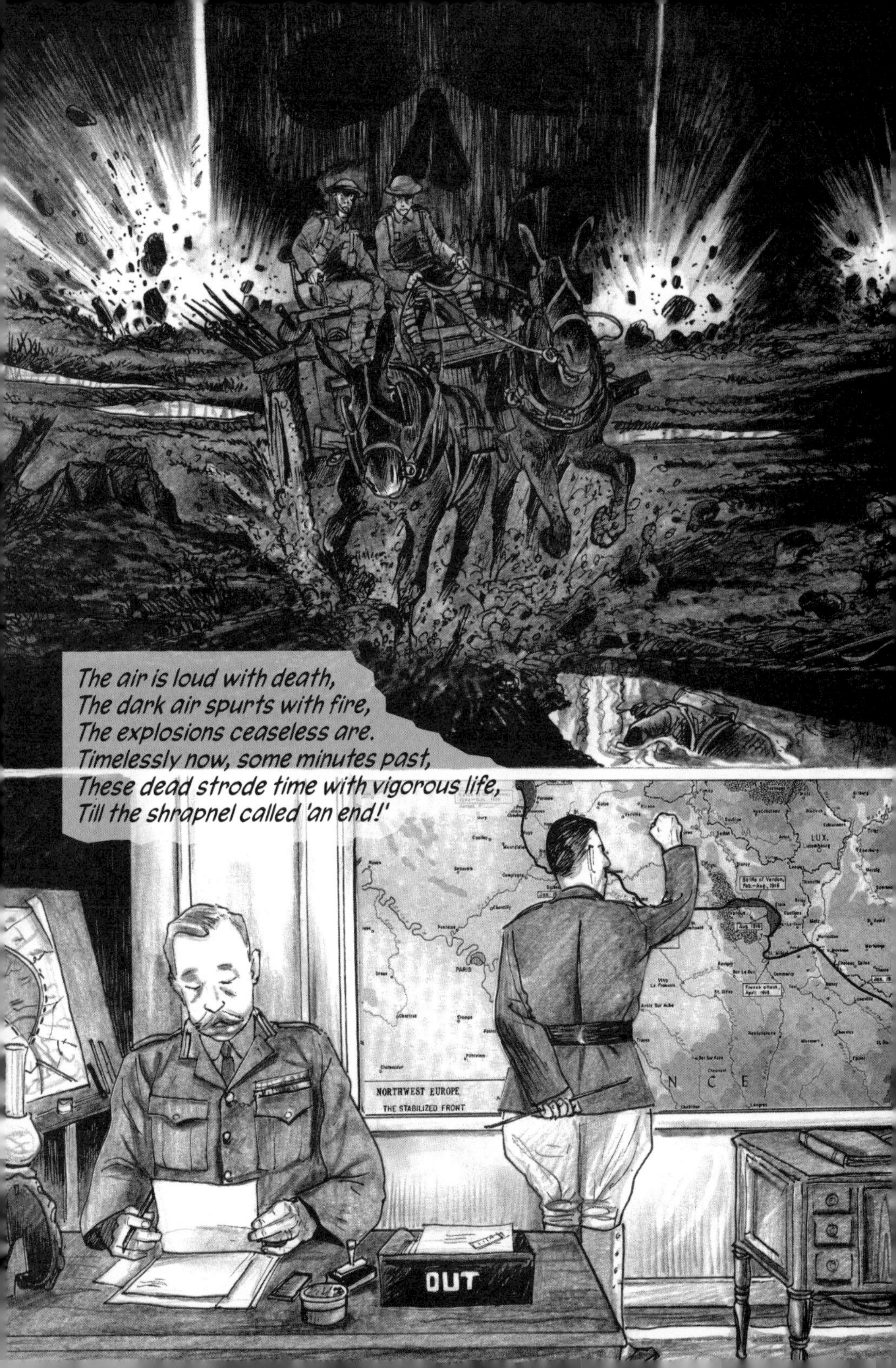
The air is loud with death,
The dark air spurts with fire,
The explosions ceaseless are.
Timelessly now, some minutes past,
These dead strode time with vigorous life,
Till the shrapnel called 'an end!'
LUX.
PARIS
NORTHWEST EUROPE
THE STABILIZED FRONT
OUT

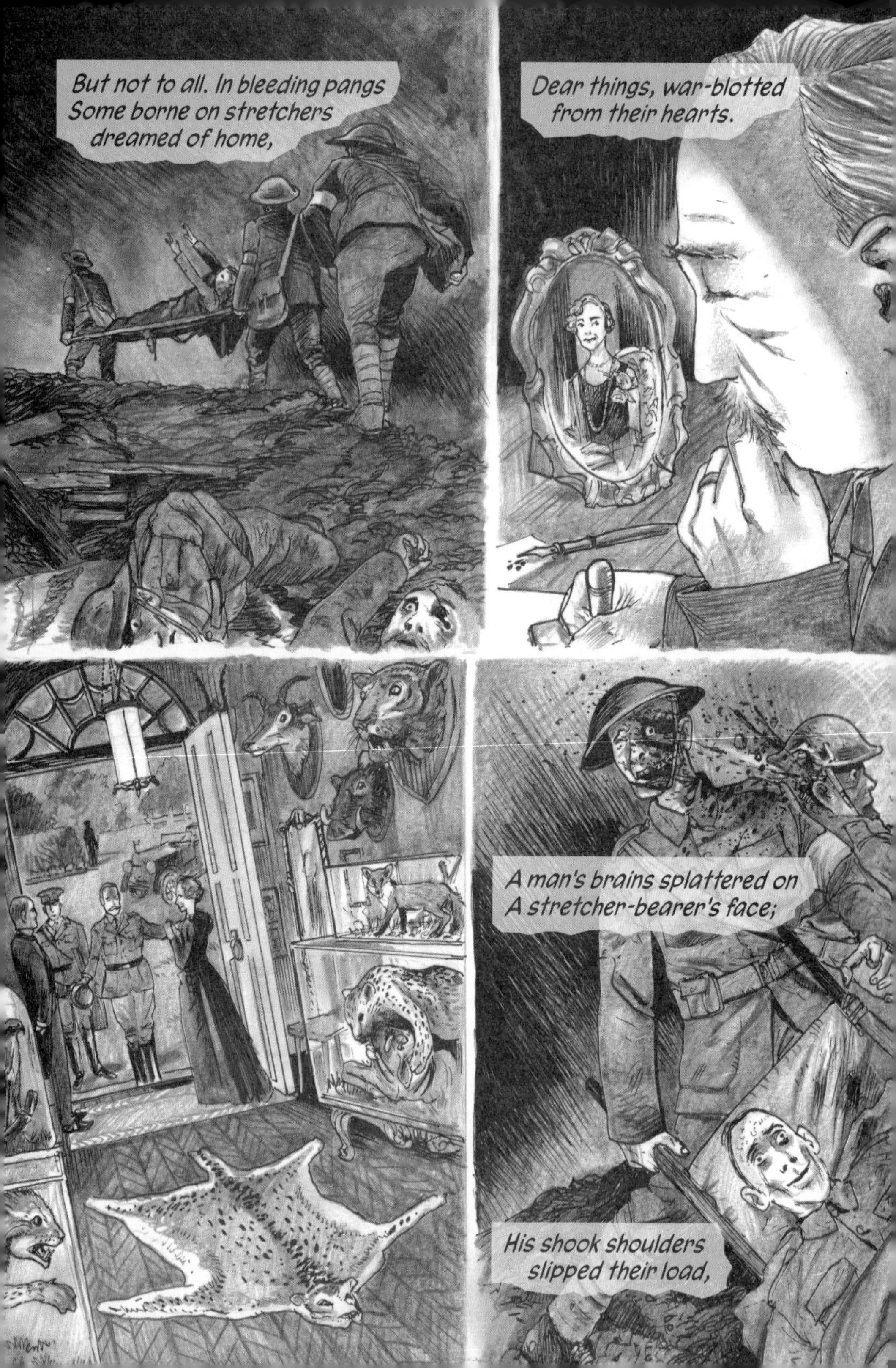
But not to all. In bleeding pangs
Some borne on stretchers
dreamed of home,
Dear things, war-blotted
from their hearts.
A man's brains splattered on
A stretcher-bearer's face;
His shook shoulders
slipped their load,

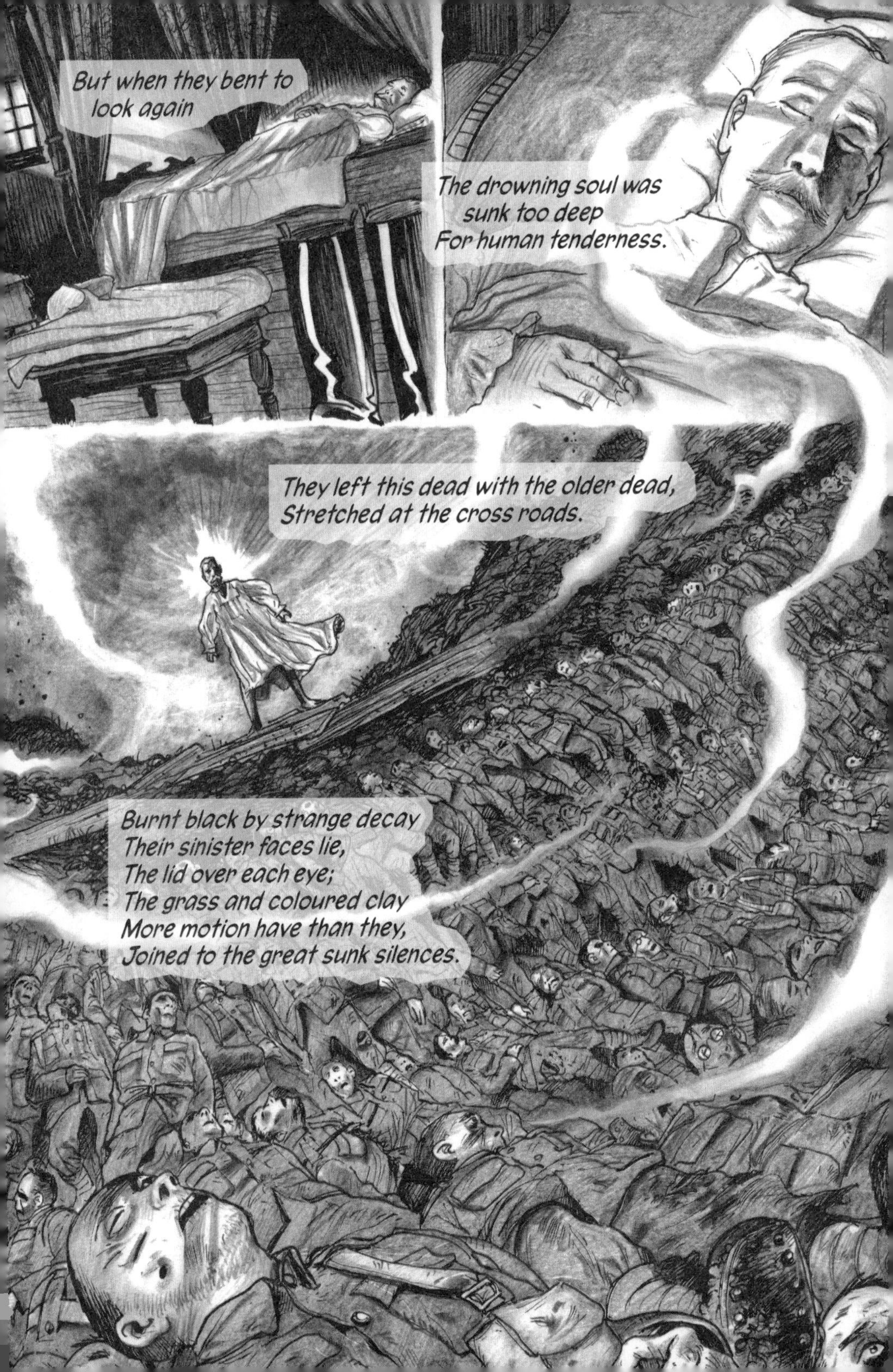
But when they bent to look again
The drowning soul was sunk too deep
For human tenderness.
They left this dead with the older dead,
Stretched at the cross roads.
Burnt black by strange decay
Their sinister faces lie,
The lid over each eye;
The grass and coloured clay
More motion have than they,
Joined to the great sunk silences.

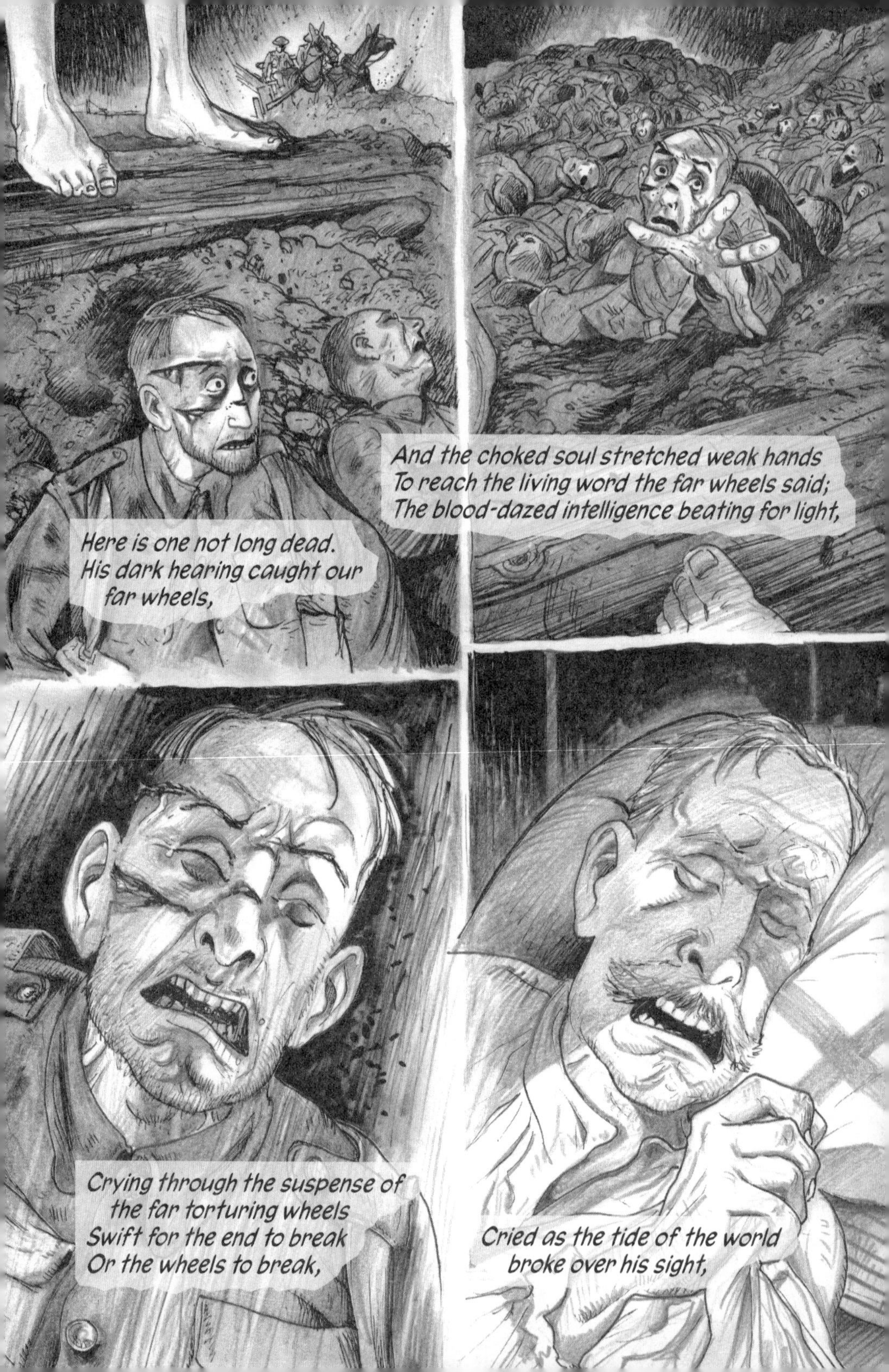
Here is one not long dead.
His dark hearing caught our
far wheels,
And the choked soul stretched weak hands
To reach the living word the far wheels said;
The blood-dazed intelligence beating for light,
Crying through the suspense of
the far torturing wheels
Swift for the end to break
Or the wheels to break,
Cried as the tide of the world
broke over his sight,

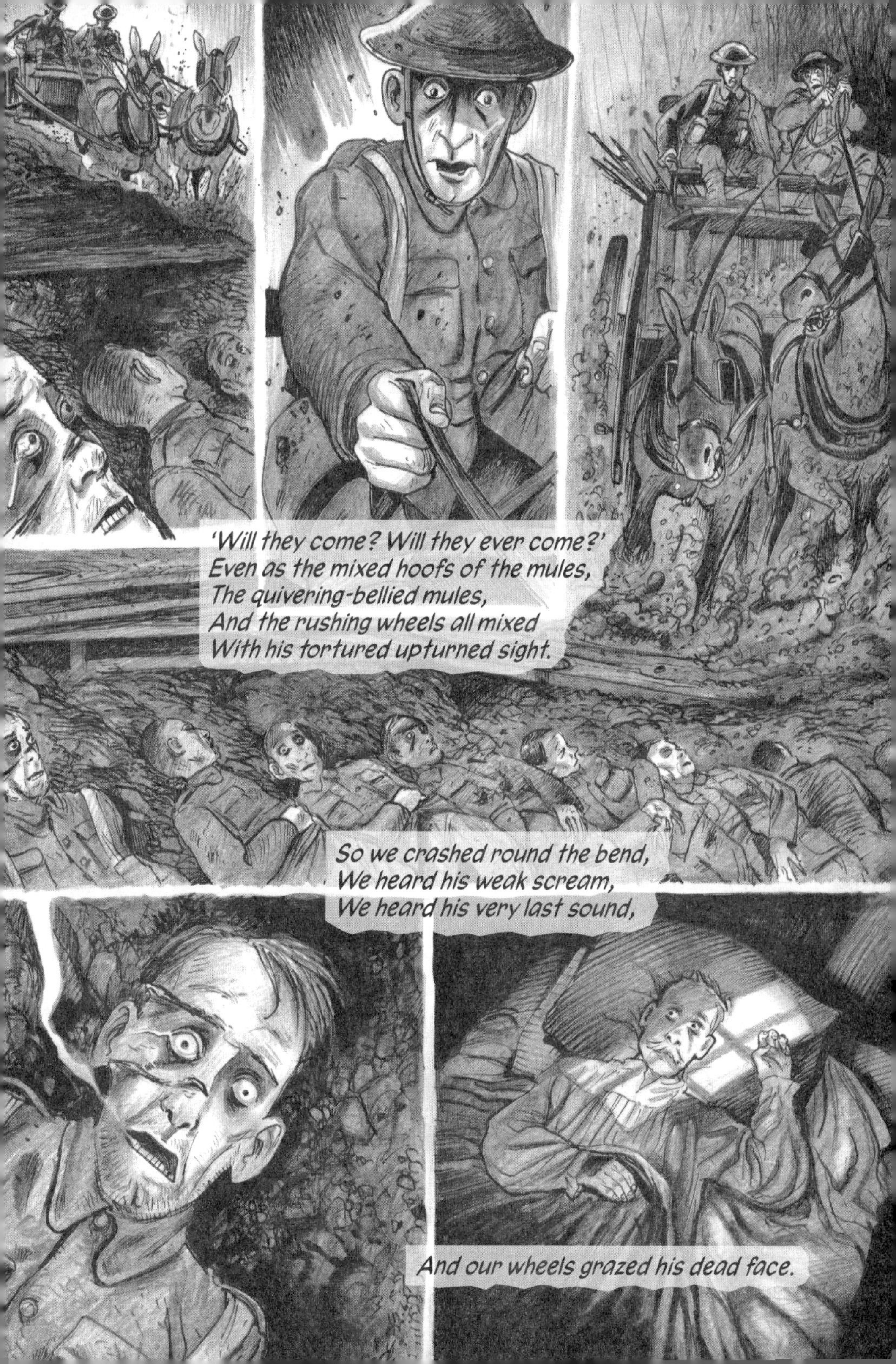
'Will they come? Will they ever come?'
Even as the mixed hoofs of the mules,
The quivering-bellied mules,
And the rushing wheels all mixed
With his tortured upturned sight.
So we crashed round the bend,
We heard his weak scream,
We heard his very last sound,
And our wheels grazed his dead face.

EVERYONE SANG

By Siegfried Sassoon - Adapted by Isabel Greenberg

Everyone suddenly burst out singing;
And I was filled with such delight
As prisoned birds must find in freedom,
Winging wildly across the white

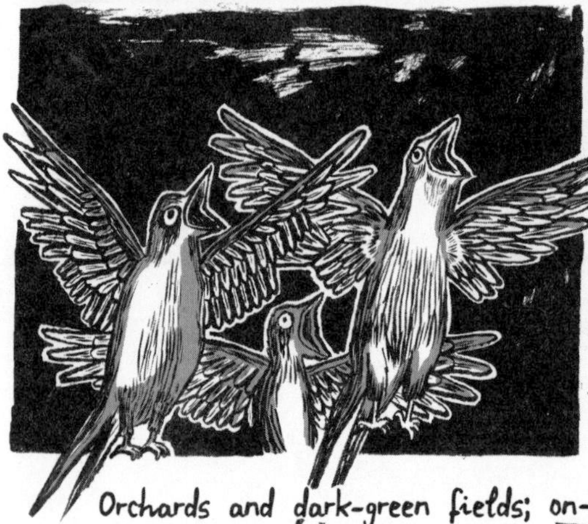

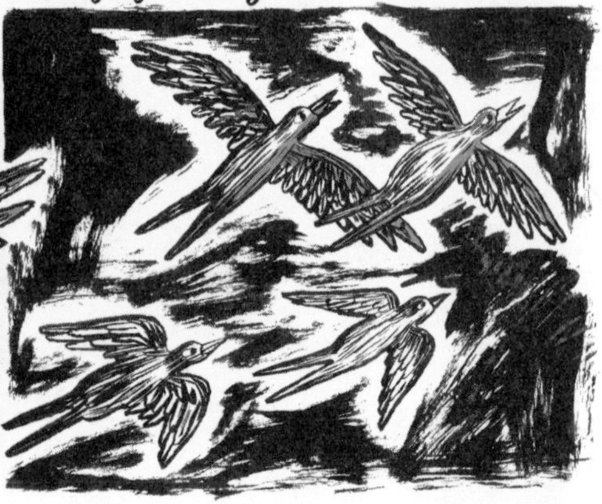

Orchards and dark-green fields; on—on—and out of sight.

Everyone's voice was suddenly lifted;

And beauty came like the setting sun:

My heart was shaken with tears; and horror

Drifted away...O, but Everyone

Was a bird; and the song was wordless;

the singing will never be done.

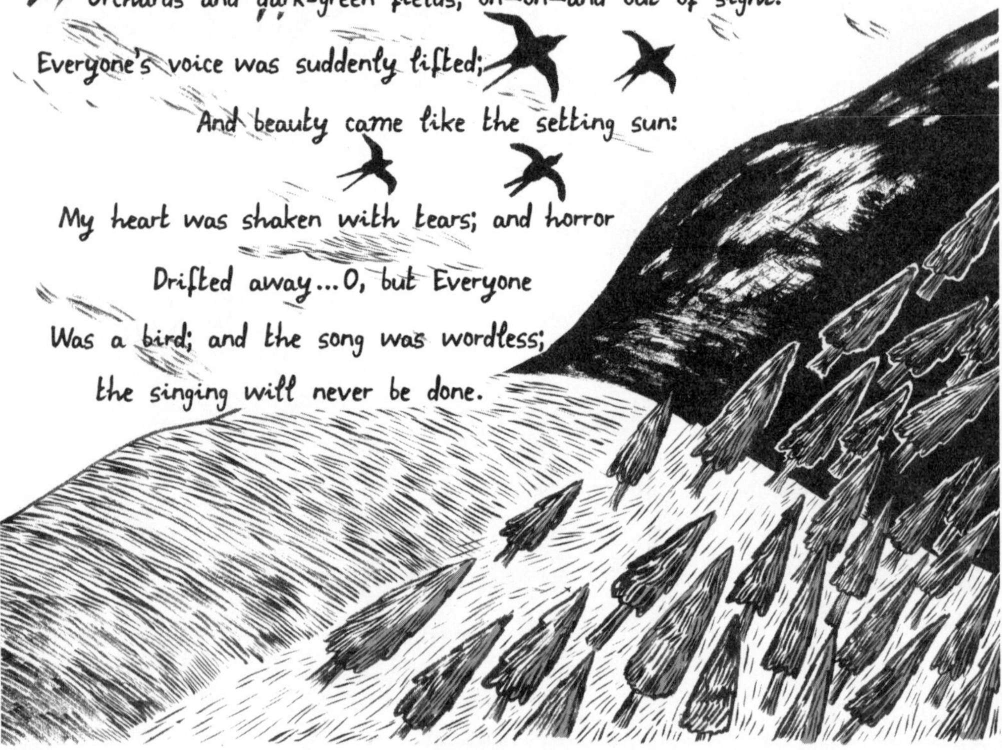

ANCIENT HISTORY BY SIEGFRIED SASSOON
ADAPTED BY LIESBETH DE STERCKE

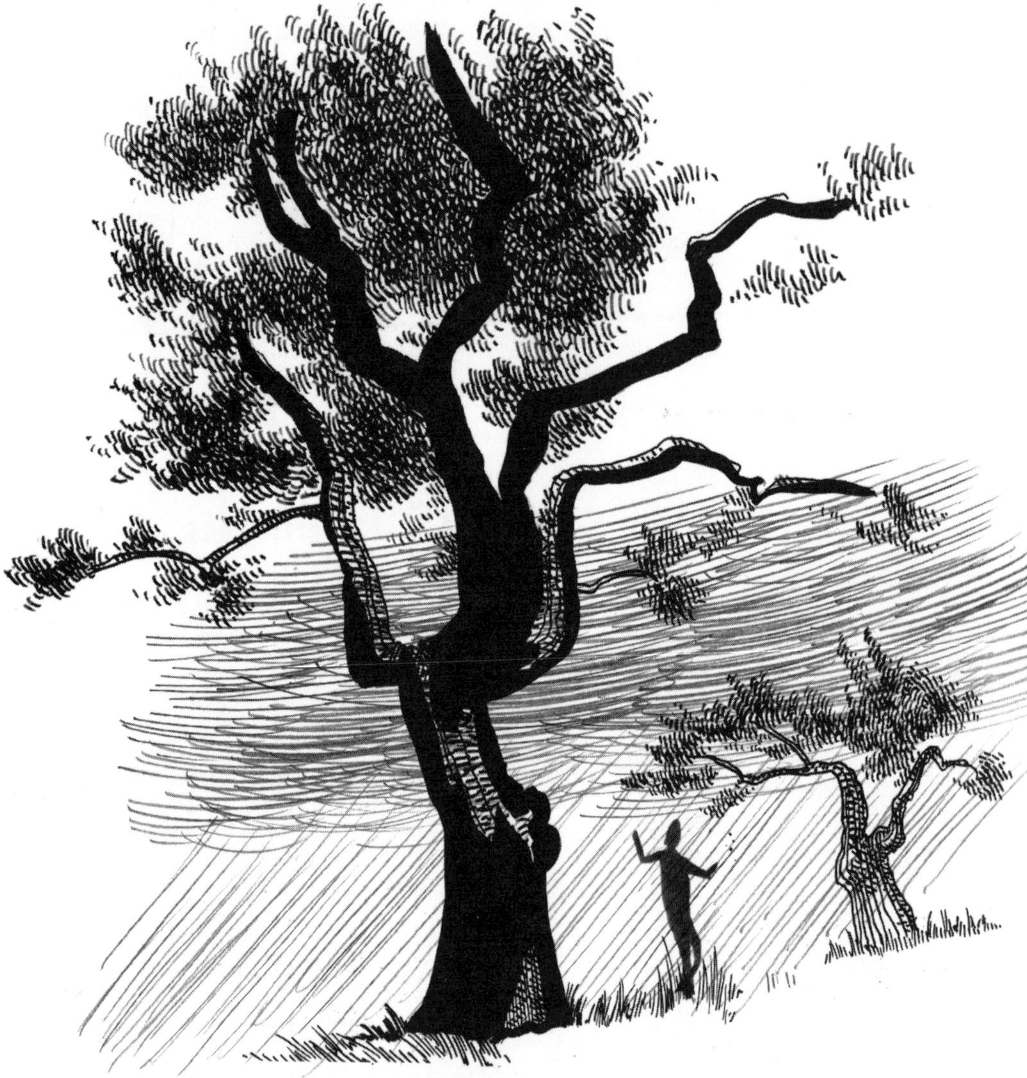

ADAM, A BROWN OLD VULTURE IN THE RAIN,
SHIVERED BELOW HIS WIND-WHIPPED OLIVE-TREES;
HUDDLING SHARP CHIN ON SCARRED AND SCRAGGY KNEES,
HE MOANED AND MUMBLED TO HIS DARKENING BRAIN;

'HE WAS THE GRANDEST OF THEM ALL - WAS CAIN!
'A LION LAIRED IN THE HILLS, THAT NONE COULD TIRE;
'SWIFT AS A STAG; A STALLION OF THE PLAIN,
'HUNGRY AND FIERCE WITH DEEDS OF HUGE DESIRE.'

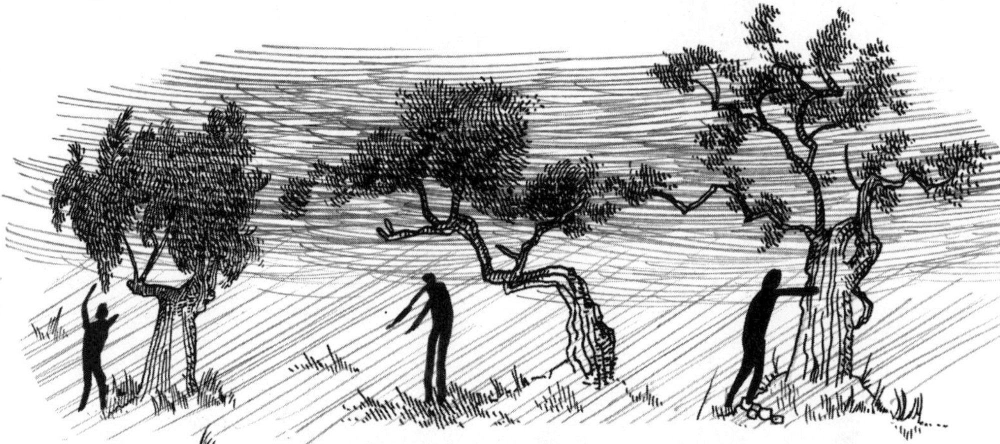

GRIMLY HE THOUGHT OF ABEL, SOFT AND FAIR-
A LOVER WITH DISASTER IN HIS FACE,
AND SCARLET BLOSSOM TWISTED IN BRIGHT HAIR.

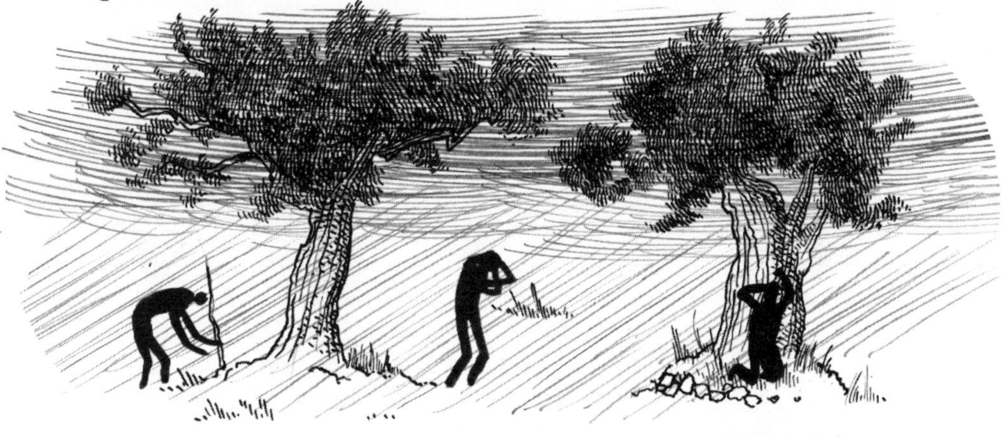

'AFRAID TO FIGHT; WAS MURDER MORE DISGRACE?...
'GOD ALWAYS HATED CAIN'... HE BOWED HIS HEAD-
THE GAUNT WILD MAN WHOSE LOVELY SONS WERE DEAD.

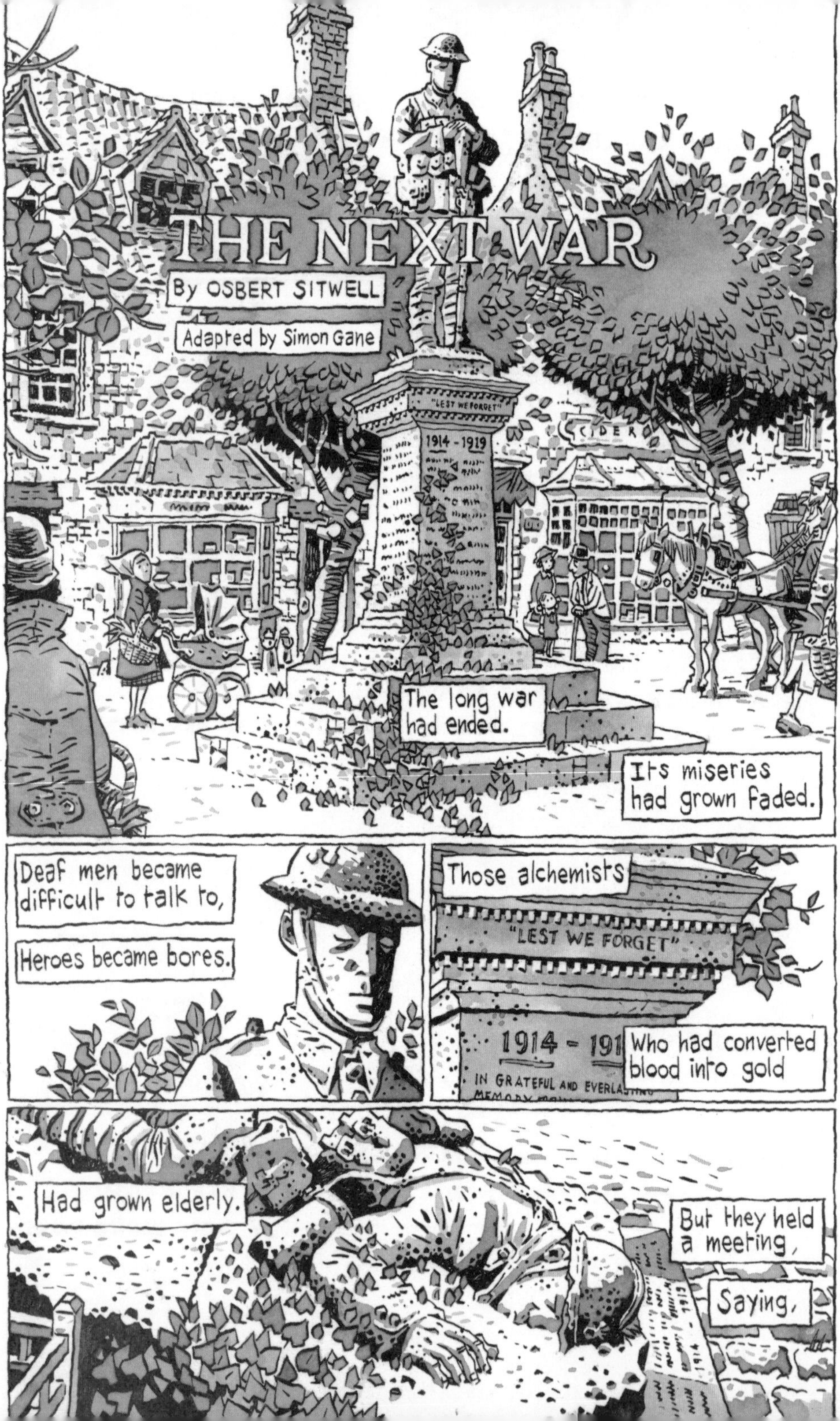

THE NEXT WAR
By OSBERT SITWELL
Adapted by Simon Gane
"LEST WE FORGET"
1914 - 1919
CIDER
The long war had ended.
Its miseries had grown faded.
Deaf men became difficult to talk to,
Heroes became bores.
Those alchemists
"LEST WE FORGET"
1914 - 191
IN GRATEFUL AND EVERLASTING
Who had converted blood into gold
Had grown elderly.
But they held a meeting,
Saying,

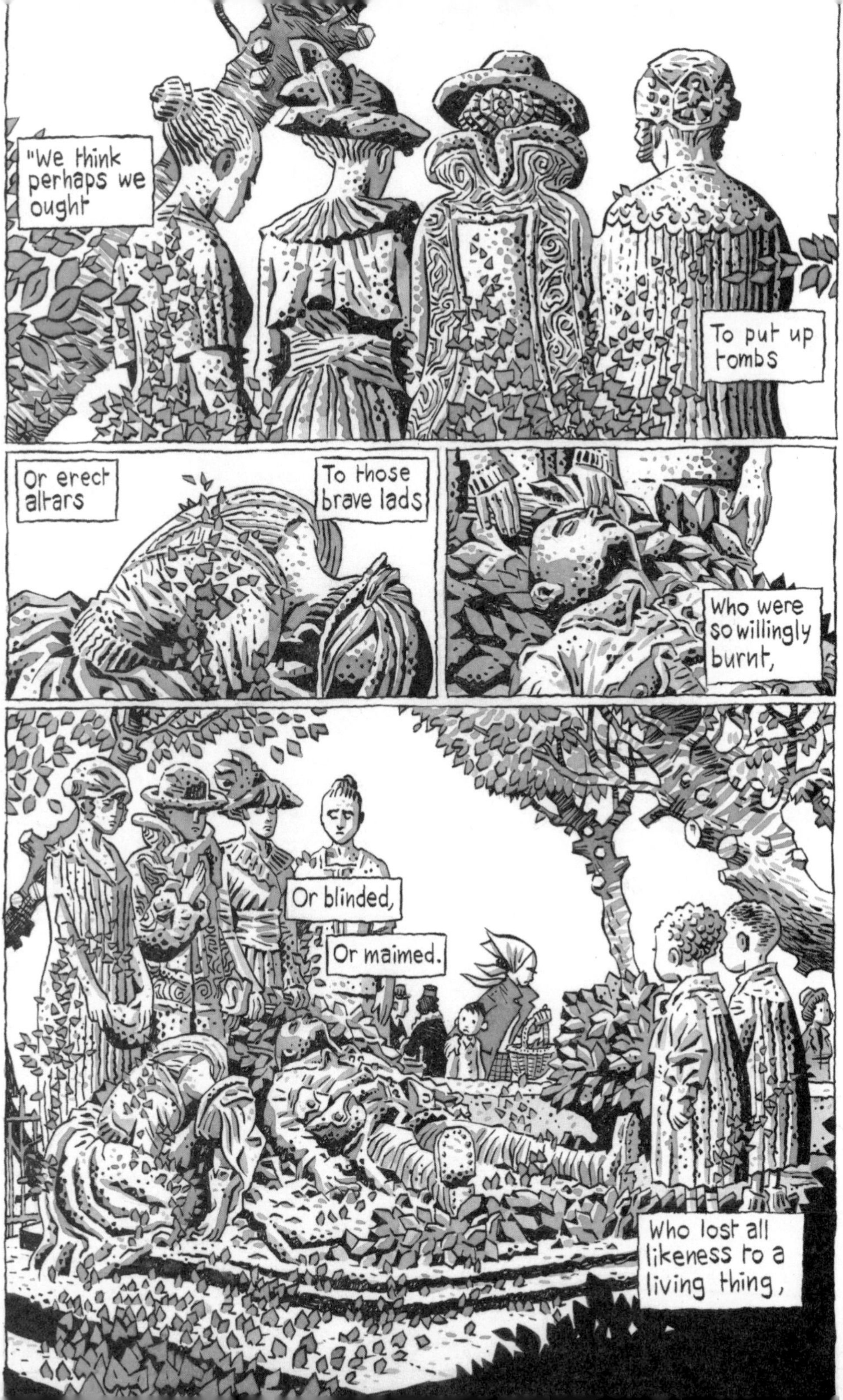

"We think perhaps we ought
To put up tombs
Or erect altars
To those brave lads
Who were so willingly burnt,
Or blinded,
Or maimed.
Who lost all likeness to a living thing,

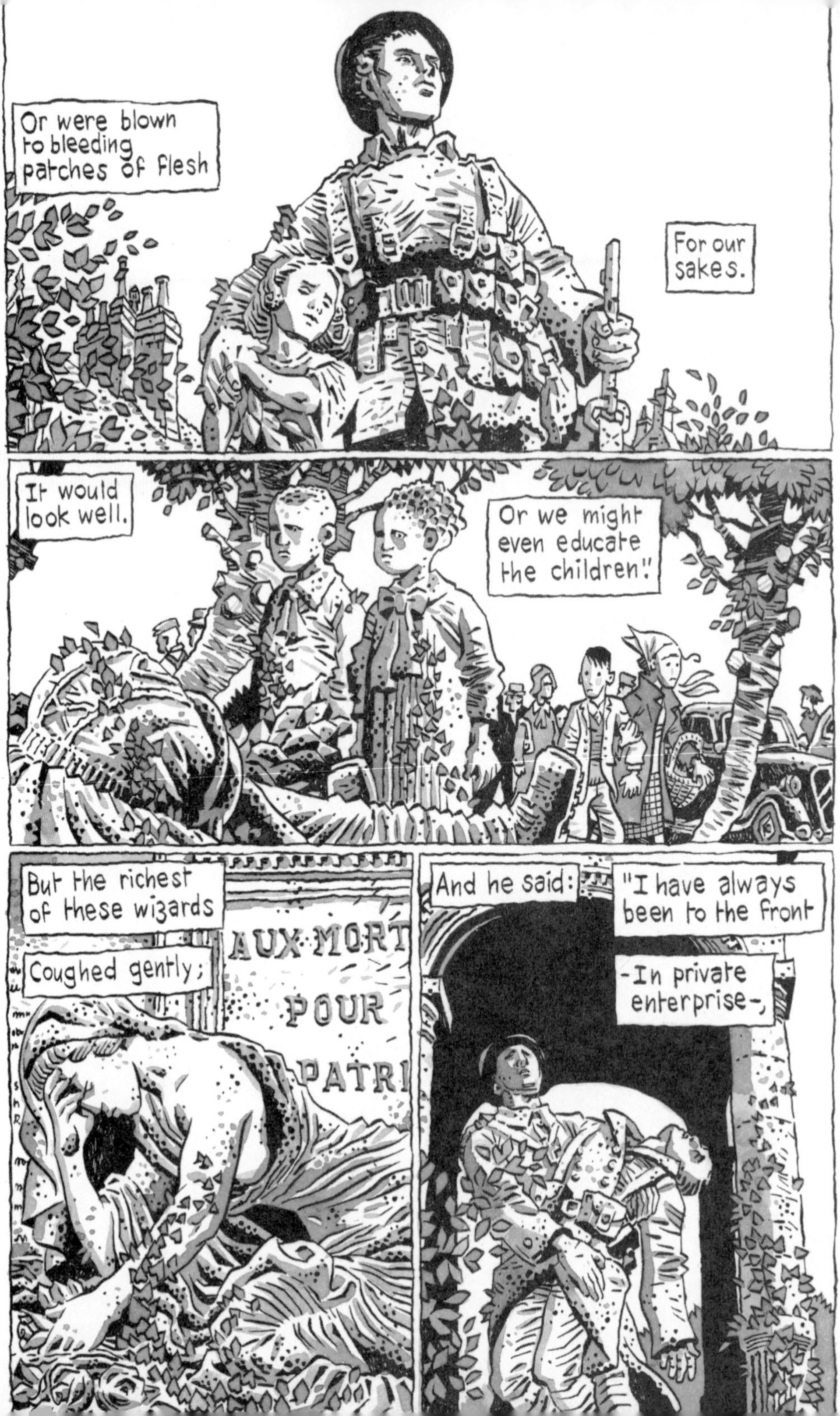

Or were blown to bleeding patches of flesh
For our sakes.
It would look well.
Or we might even educate the children!"
But the richest of these wizards
Coughed gently;
AUX MORT
POUR
PATRI
And he said:
"I have always been to the front
-In private enterprise-,

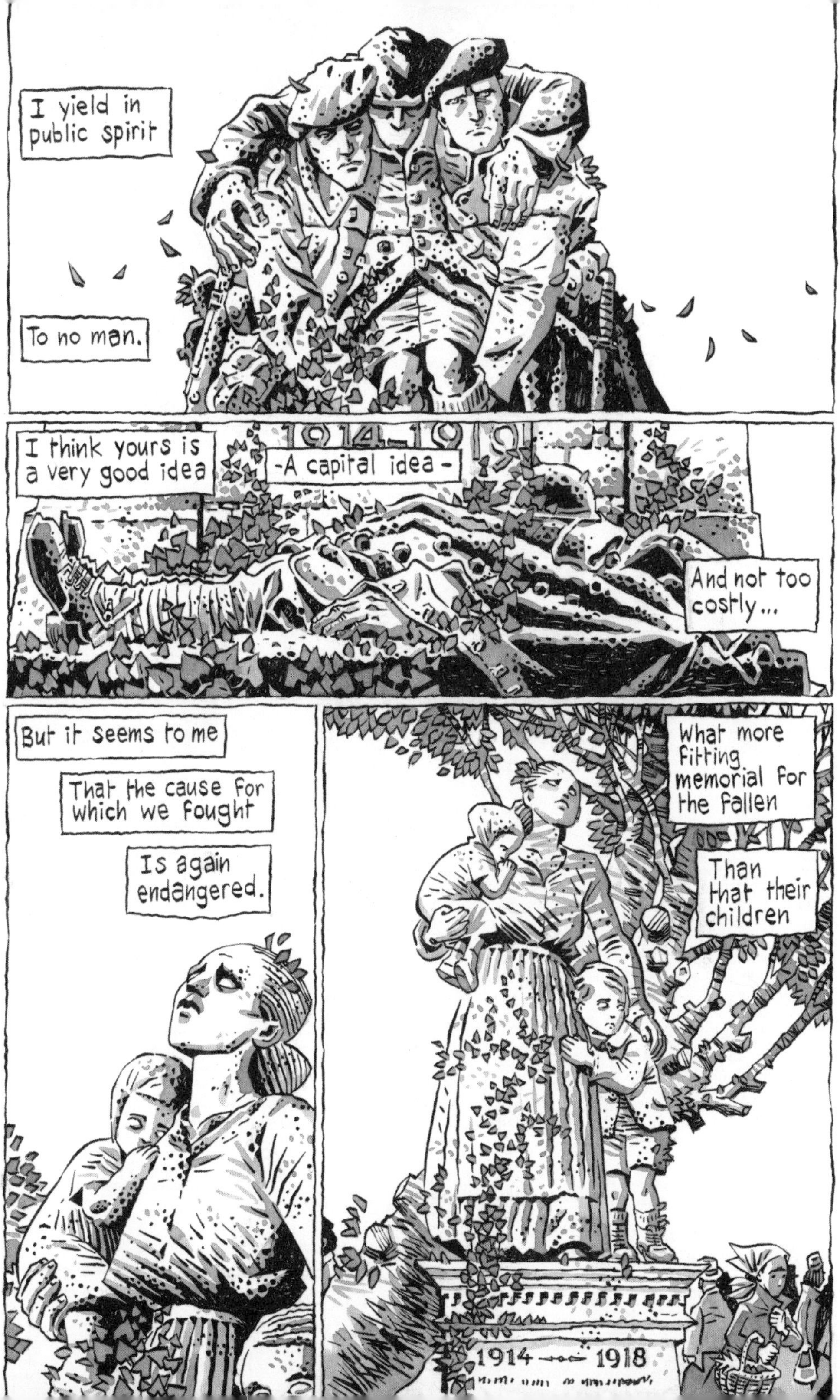
I yield in public spirit
To no man.
I think yours is a very good idea
-A capital idea-
And not too costly...
But it seems to me
That the cause for which we fought
Is again endangered.
What more fitting memorial for the fallen
Than that their children
1914 — 1918

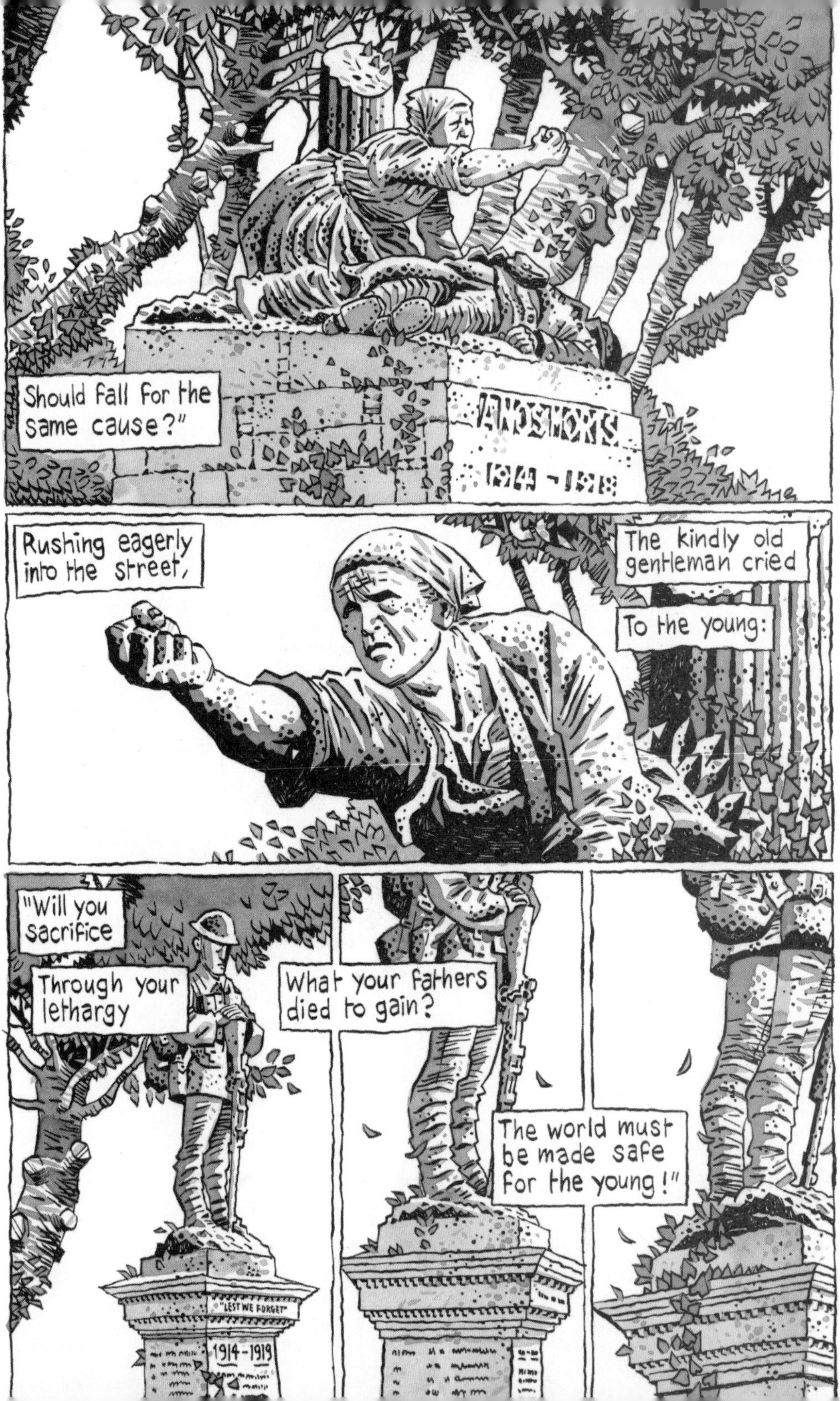
Should fall for the same cause?"
1914 - 1918
Rushing eagerly into the street,
The kindly old gentleman cried
To the young:
"Will you sacrifice
Through your lethargy
What your fathers died to gain?
"LEST WE FORGET"
1914-1919
The world must be made safe for the young!"

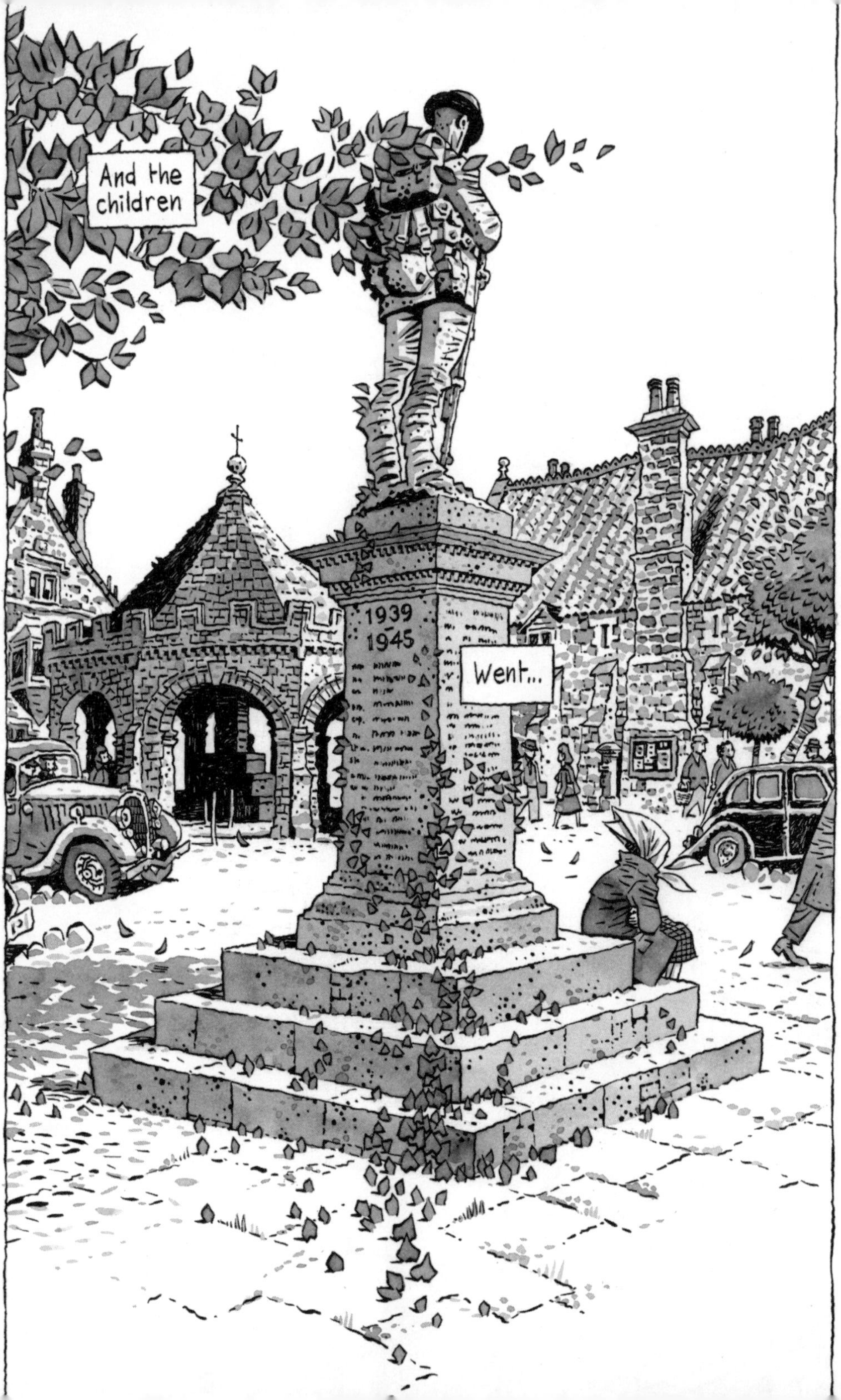
And the children
Went...
1939
1945

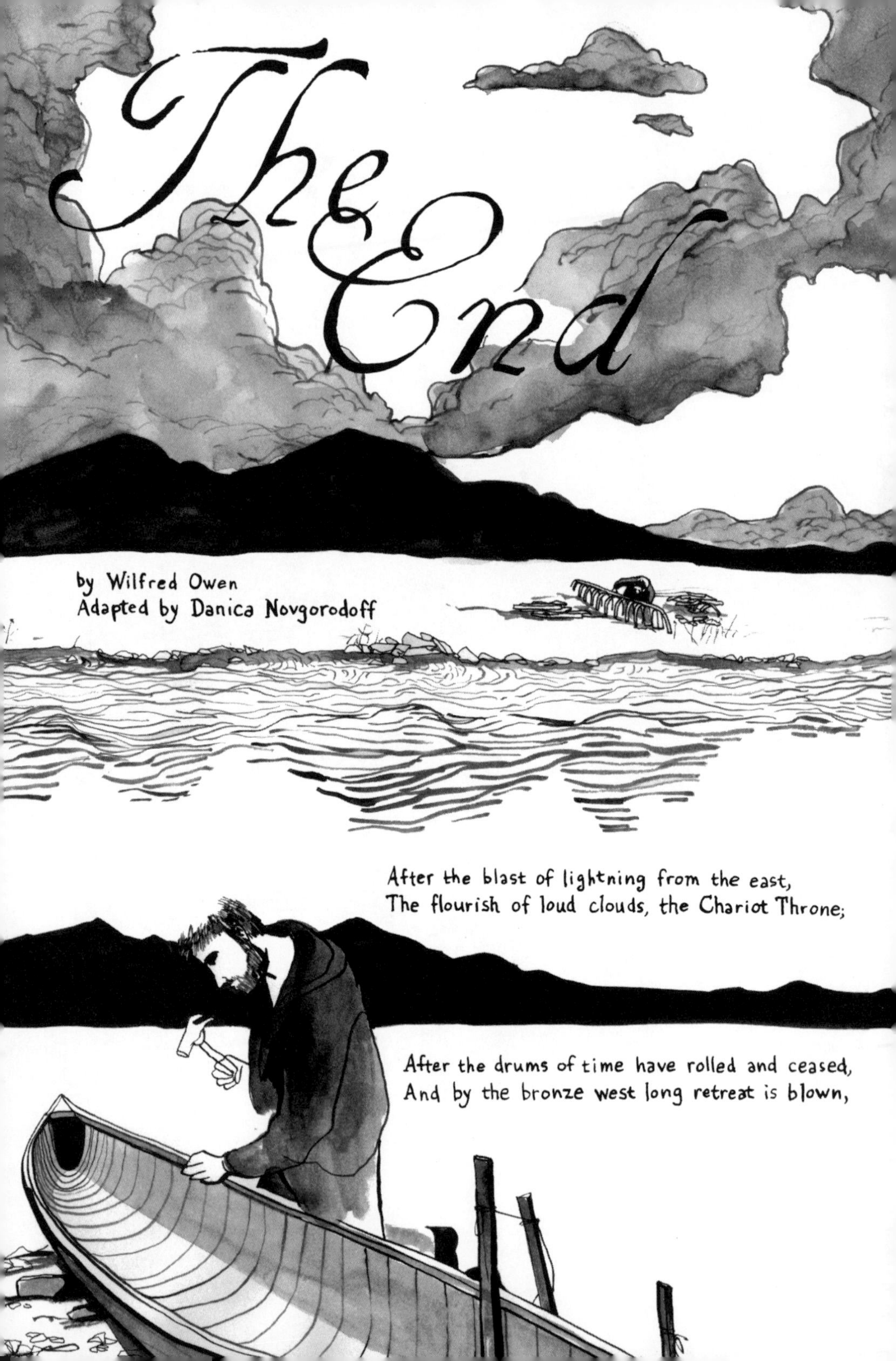
The End
by Wilfred Owen
Adapted by Danica Novgorodoff
After the blast of lightning from the east,
The flourish of loud clouds, the Chariot Throne;
After the drums of time have rolled and ceased,
And by the bronze west long retreat is blown,

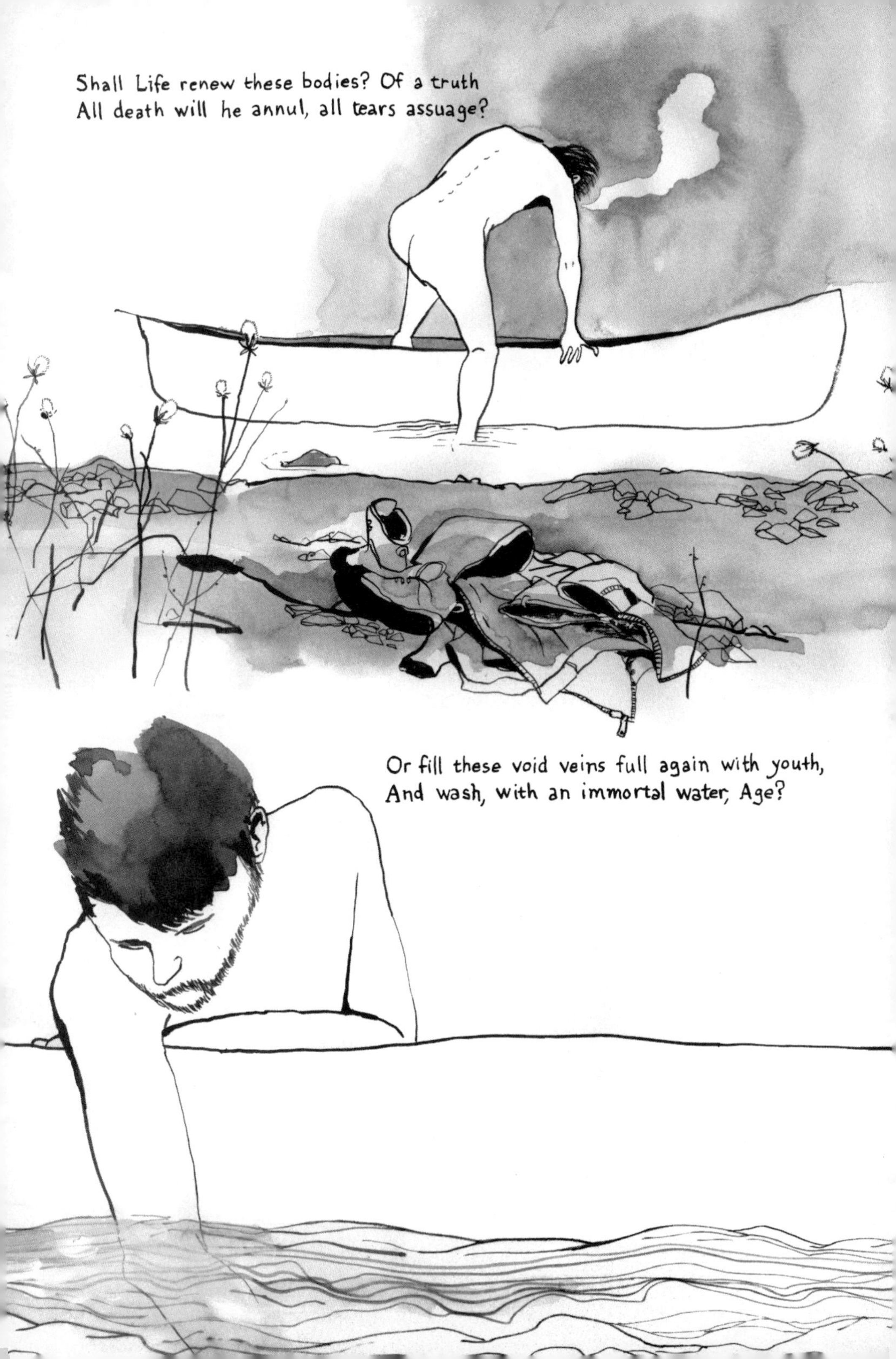
Shall Life renew these bodies? Of a truth
All death will he annul, all tears assuage?
Or fill these void veins full again with youth,
And wash, with an immortal water, Age?

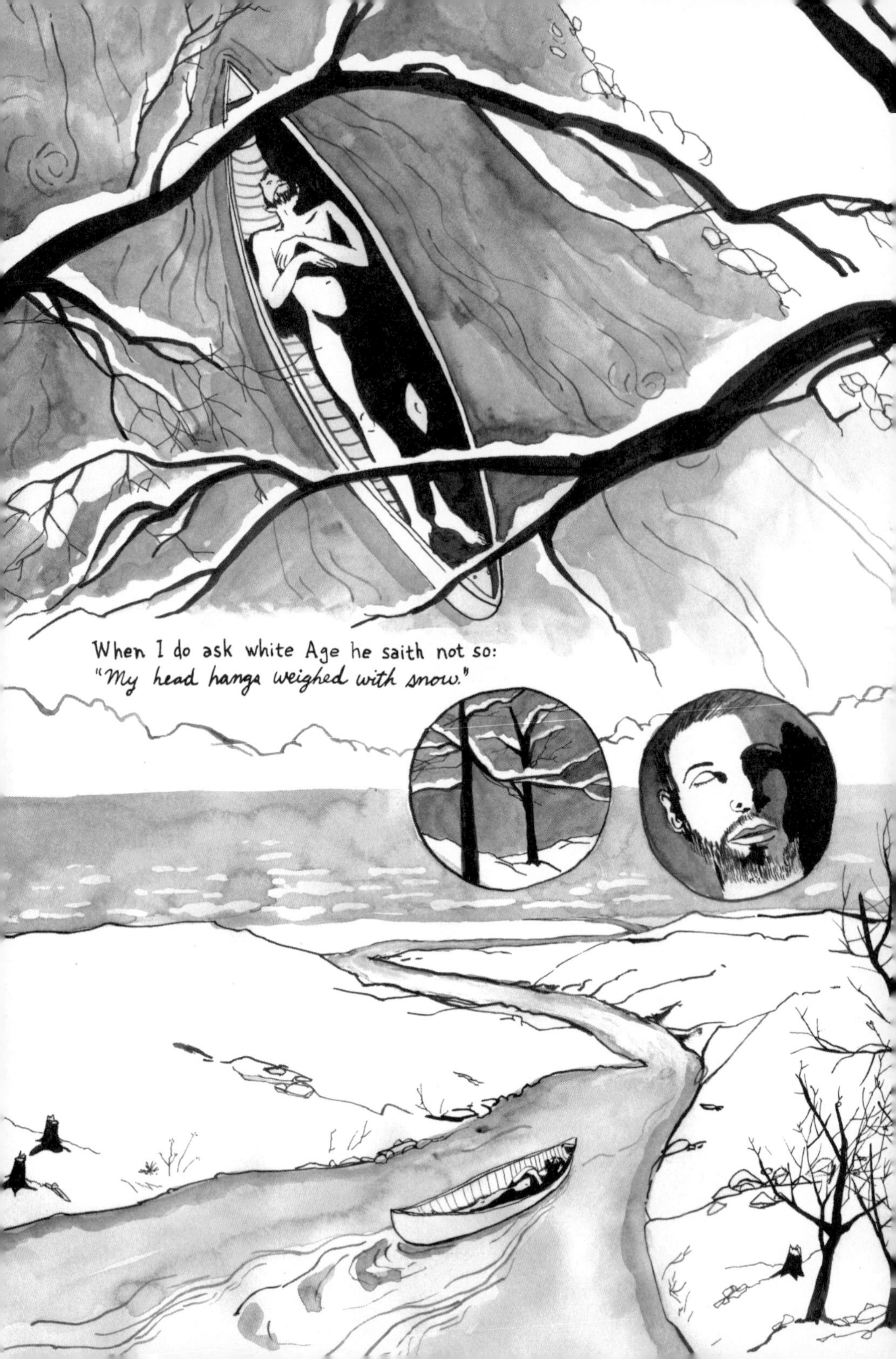
When I do ask white Age he saith not so:
"My head hangs weighed with snow."

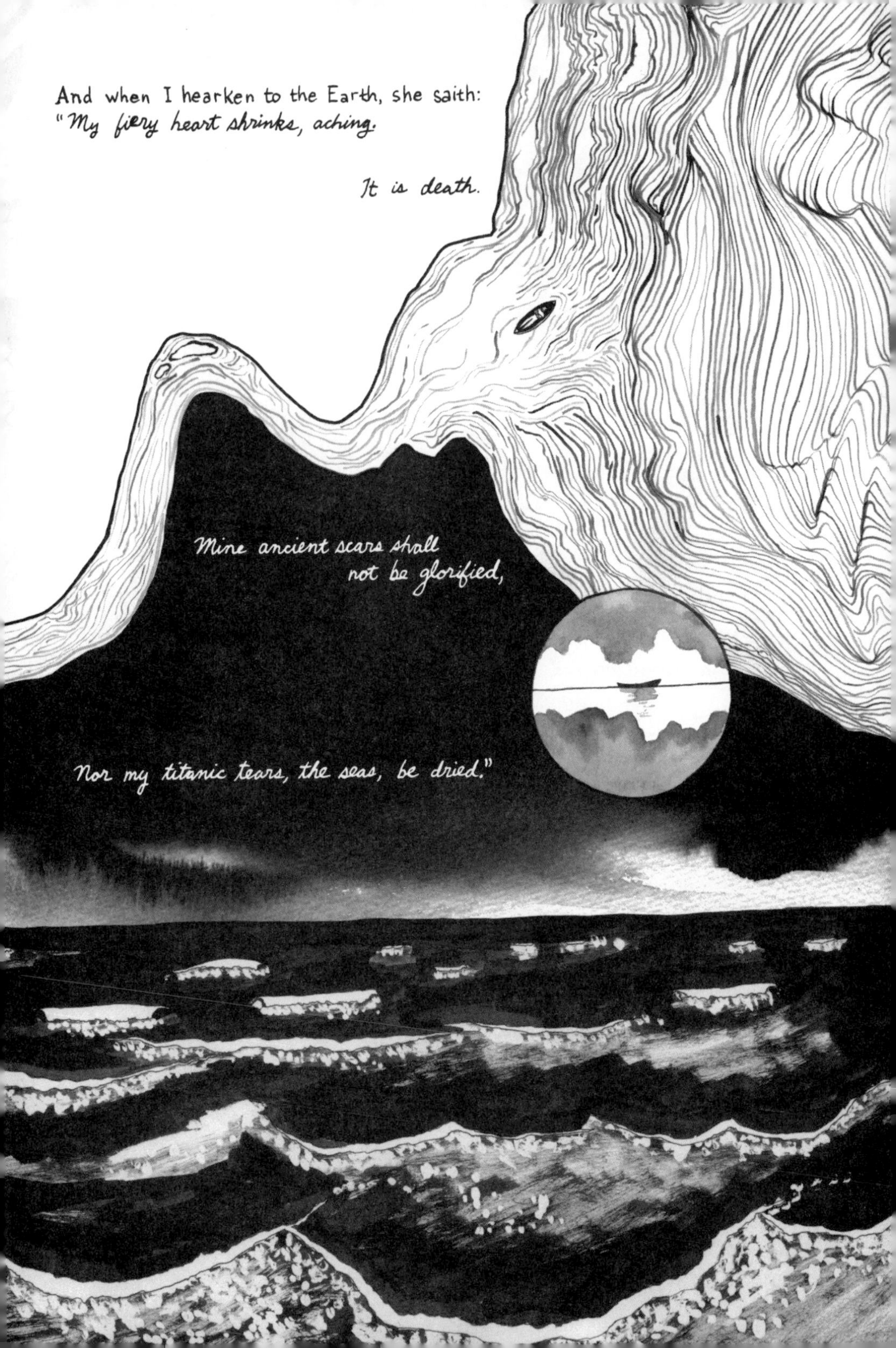
And when I hearken to the Earth, she saith:
"My fiery heart shrinks, aching.
It is death.
Mine ancient scars shall not be glorified,
Nor my titanic tears, the seas, be dried."

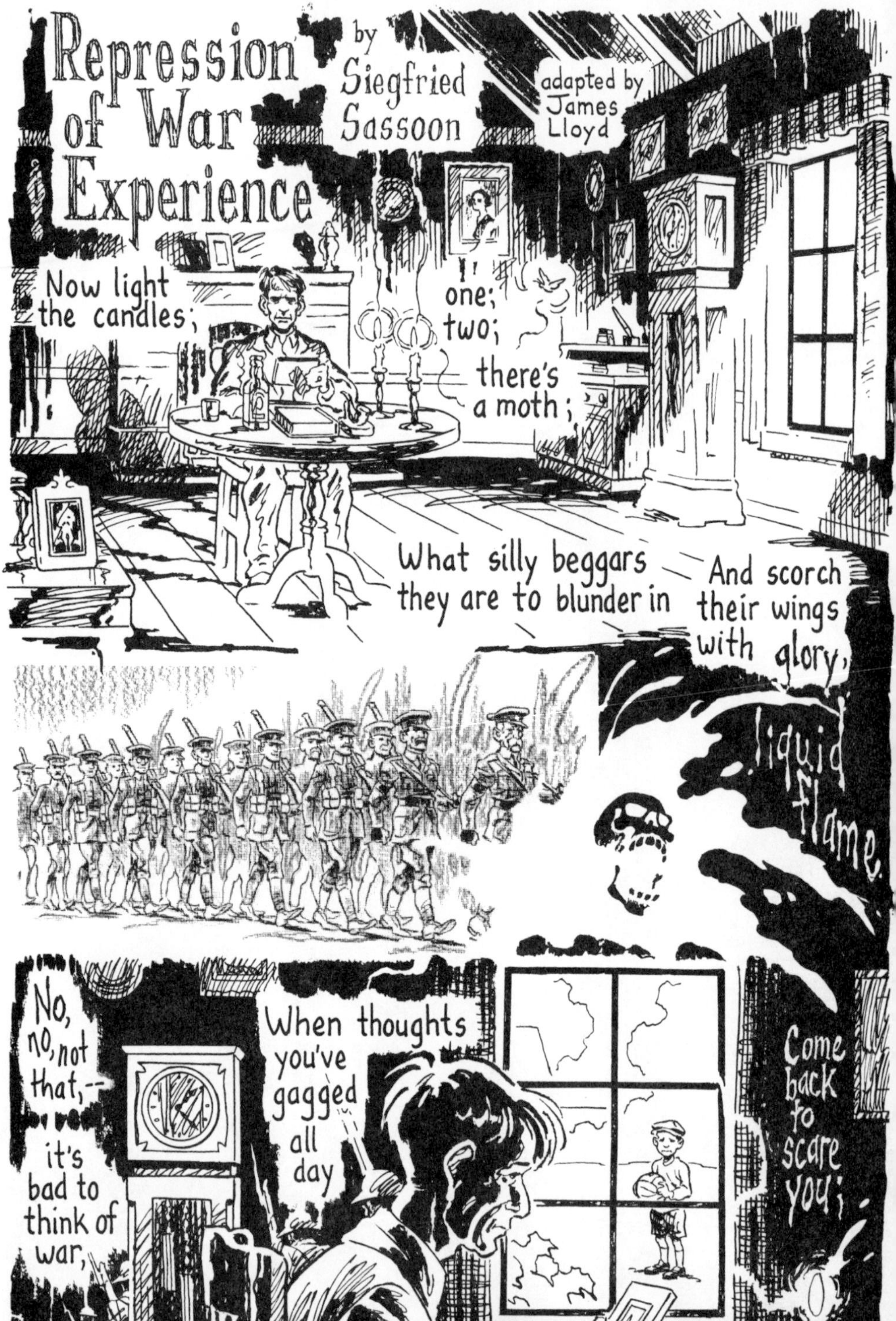
Repression of War Experience
by Siegfried Sassoon
adapted by James Lloyd
Now light the candles;
one; two;
there's a moth;
What silly beggars they are to blunder in
And scorch their wings with glory,
liquid flame.
No, no, not that,--
it's bad to think of war,
When thoughts you've gagged all day
Come back to scare you;

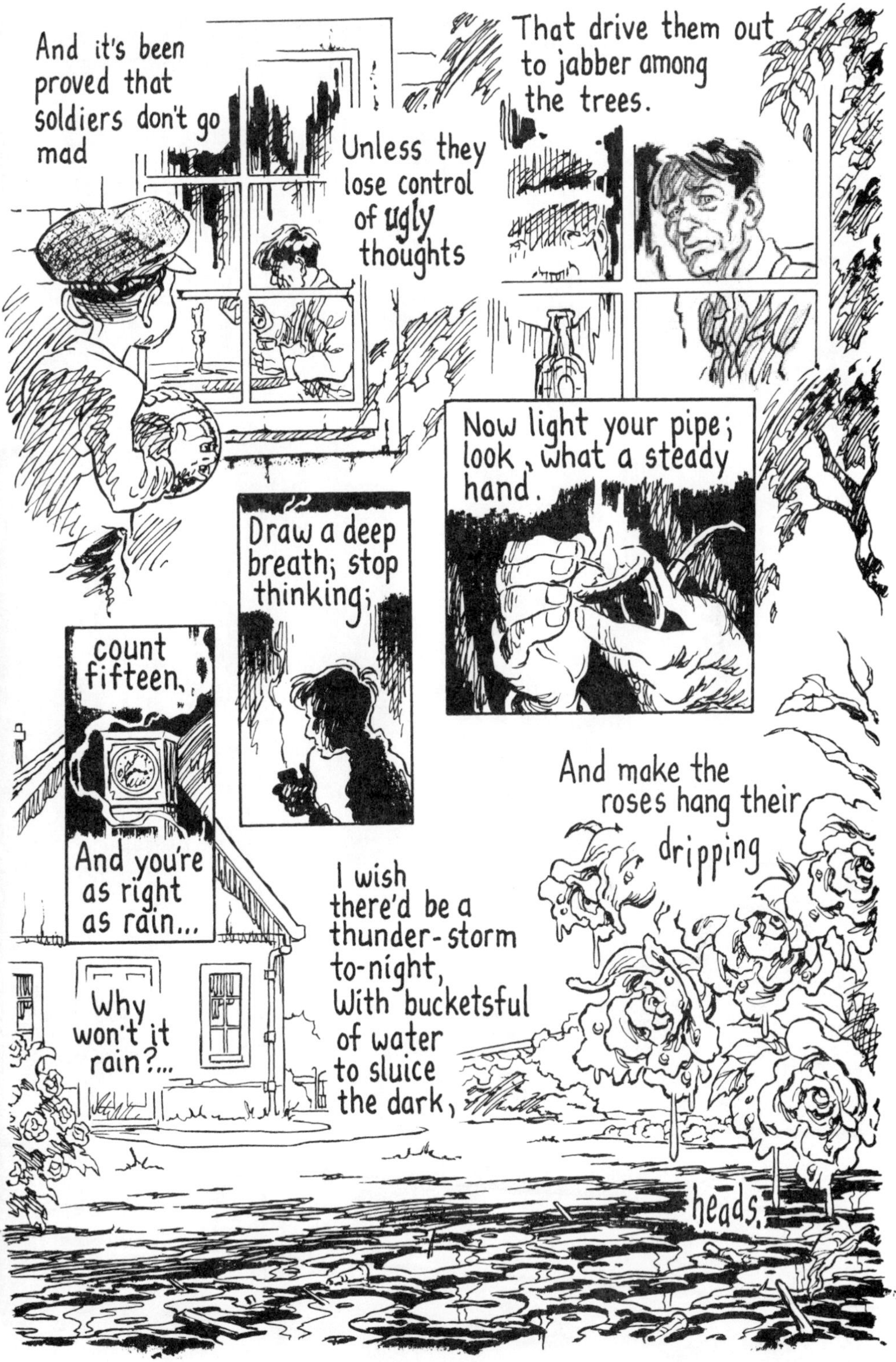
And it's been proved that soldiers don't go mad
Unless they lose control of ugly thoughts
That drive them out to jabber among the trees.
Now light your pipe; look, what a steady hand.
Draw a deep breath; stop thinking;
count fifteen,
And you're as right as rain...
Why won't it rain?...
I wish there'd be a thunder-storm to-night,
With bucketsful of water to sluice the dark,
And make the roses hang their dripping
heads.

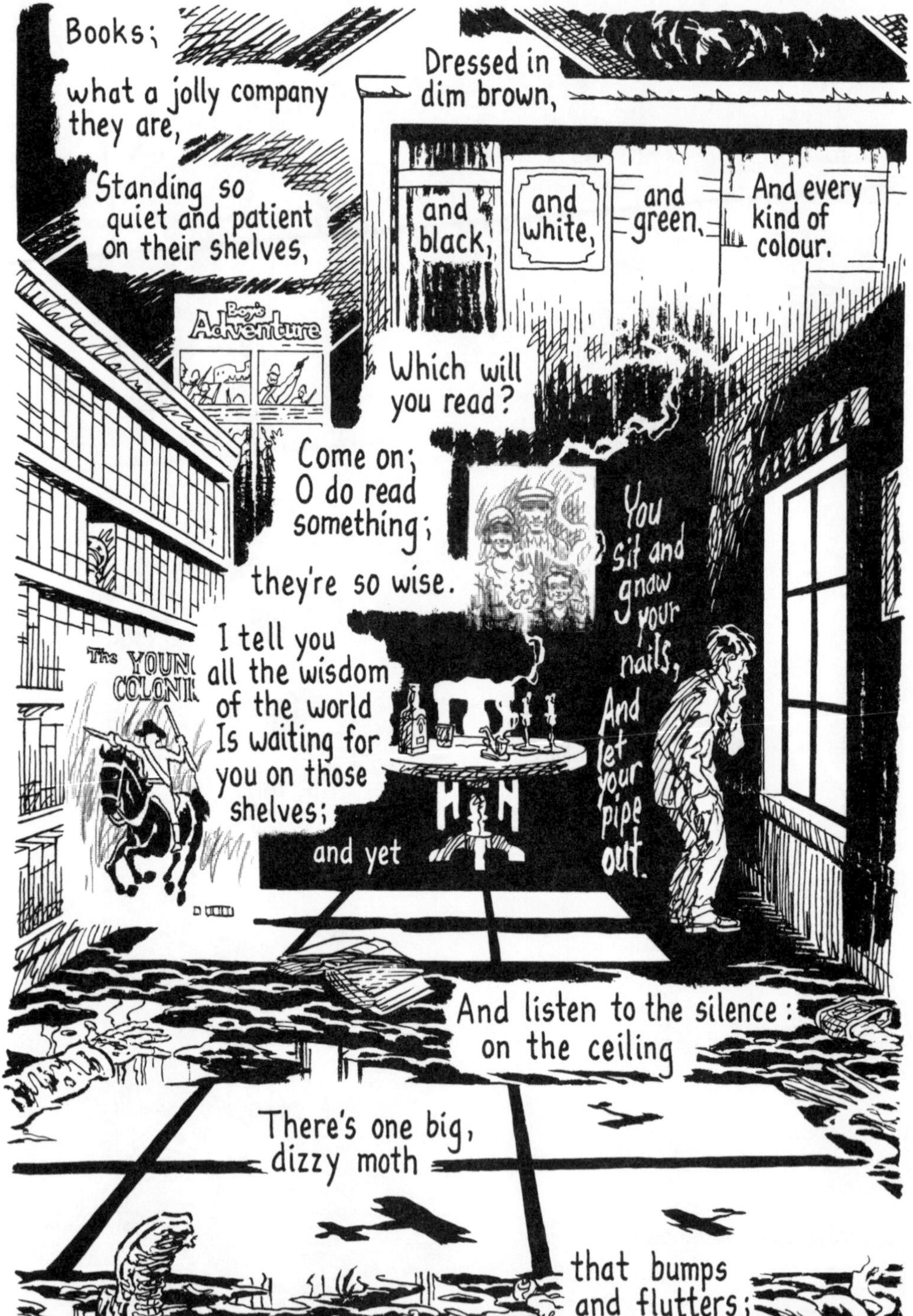
Books;
what a jolly company they are,
Standing so quiet and patient on their shelves,
Dressed in dim brown,
and black,
and white,
and green,
And every kind of colour.
Boy's Adventure
Which will you read?
Come on; O do read something;
they're so wise.
The YOUNG COLONI
I tell you all the wisdom of the world Is waiting for you on those shelves;
and yet
You sit and gnaw your nails,
And let your pipe out.
And listen to the silence: on the ceiling
There's one big, dizzy moth
that bumps and flutters;

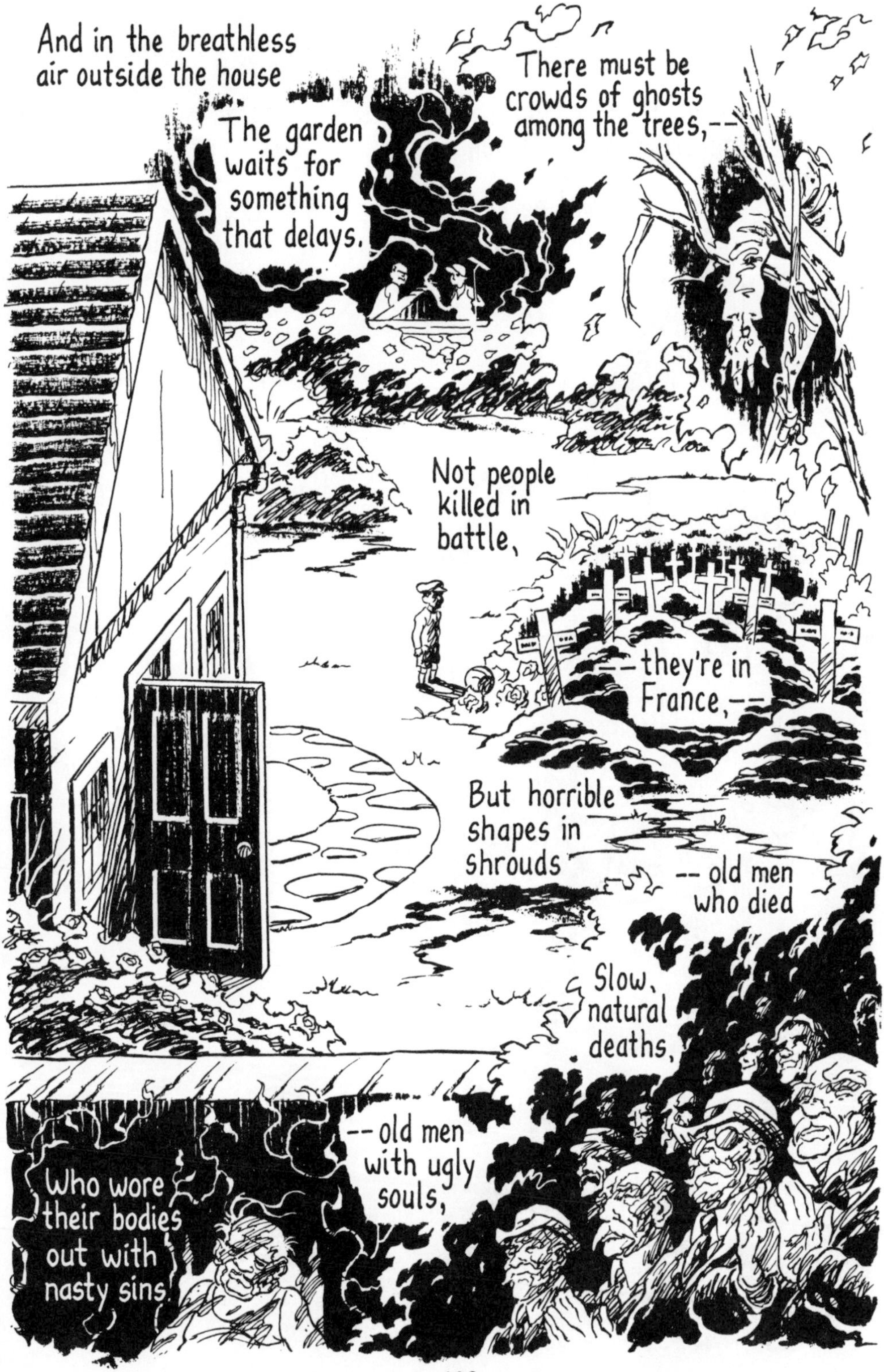
And in the breathless air outside the house
The garden waits for something that delays.
There must be crowds of ghosts among the trees,--
Not people killed in battle,
--they're in France,--
But horrible shapes in shrouds
-- old men who died
Slow, natural deaths,
--old men with ugly souls,
Who wore their bodies out with nasty sins.

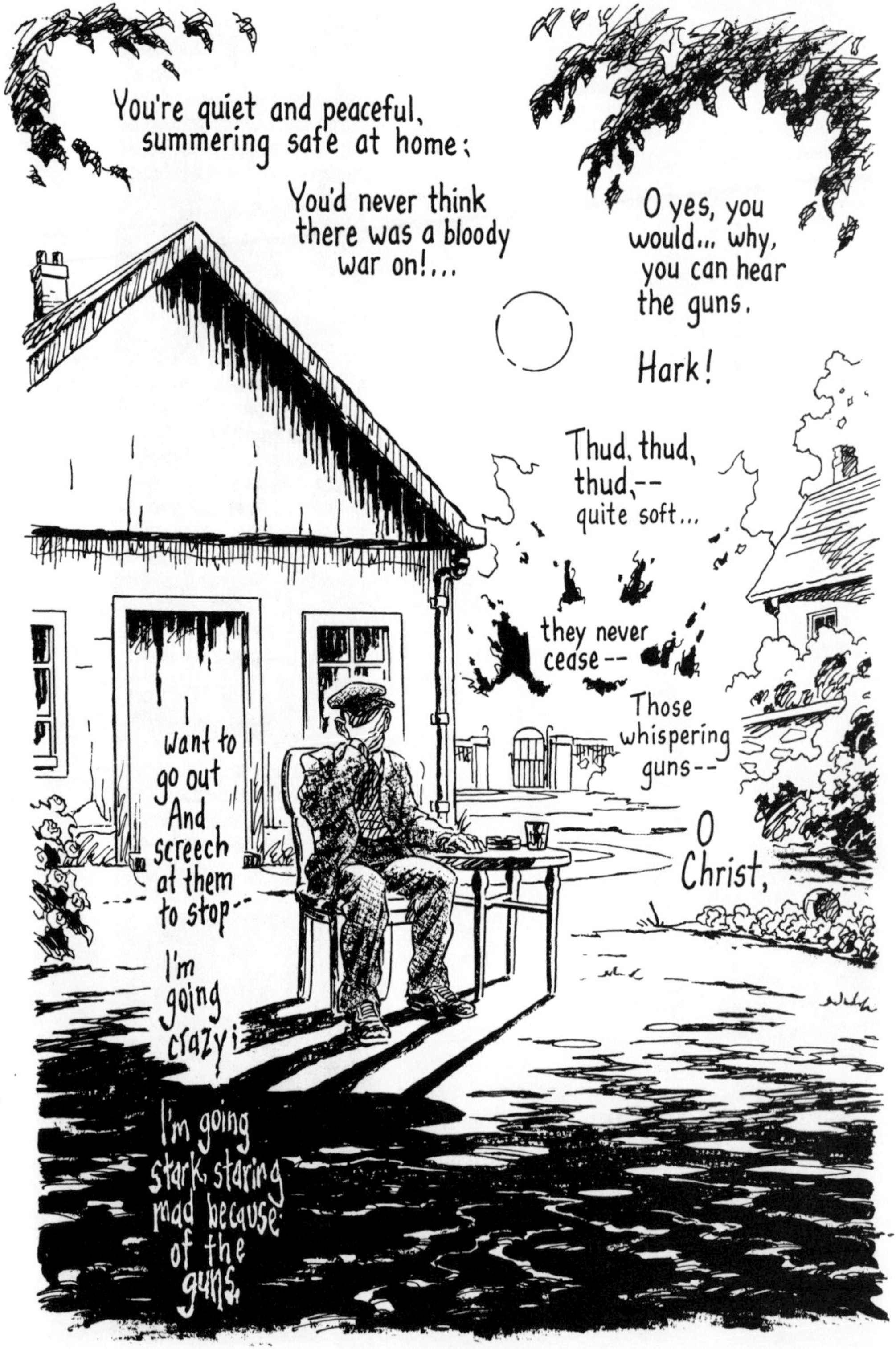
You're quiet and peaceful, summering safe at home;
You'd never think there was a bloody war on!...
O yes, you would... why, you can hear the guns.
Hark!
Thud, thud, thud,-- quite soft...
they never cease --
Those whispering guns --
O Christ,
I want to go out And screech at them to stop--
I'm going crazy;
I'm going stark, staring mad because of the guns.

In 1917 Siegfried Sassoon was diagnosed as a "neurasthenic" case, a civil term afforded the British officer class suffering the psychological effects of war. The poor working class private was simply deemed "hysterical" and left to cope, without portfolio and often employment. Ultimately, "shell shock" arose as the catch-all term applied to the lot, levelling the playing field somewhat by acknowledging a universal experience, but still not serving to widen the public's understanding. Why did these men continue to hear the guns long after they had ceased?

Shell shock, gross stress disorder, combat fatigue, Vietnam syndrome, and finally, the one that stuck, post traumatic stress disorder... name it what you will...

In the century that has passed since Sassoon penned this poem, we show no greater understanding of the psychological scars borne by the fresh wave of veterans returning to our shores post-Iraq and Afghanistan conflicts. Like their predecessors, a cultural stigma still haunts those suffering the seared elements of combat defined by the "invisible wound." Purple Hearts are awarded only to those soldiers with verifiable injuries. Multiple deployments find military psychologists pressured to give false, and even reverse, diagnoses to stave off a landslide of claims. The "old men" who still gamble with their countrymen's lives have yet to factor the cost of unending rehabilitation into their war budgets. Though suicides among veterans have become an epidemic, more U.S. soldiers dying by their own hands in 2012 than were listed Killed In Action, the deaths are not officially acknowledged as combat casualties.

And at the bottom of it all remains the resounding emptiness and profound alienation suffered by Sassoon and his mates. They are alone in the rain, and the bombs still fall.

Here's to your centennial, Siegfried.

WITH RESPECT FOR THE WORDS OF THE IRAQ AND AFGHANISTAN WINTER SOLDIERS AND ALL VETERANS WHO HAVE FOUND THE COURAGE TO BEAR WITNESS.

B.LLOYD.13

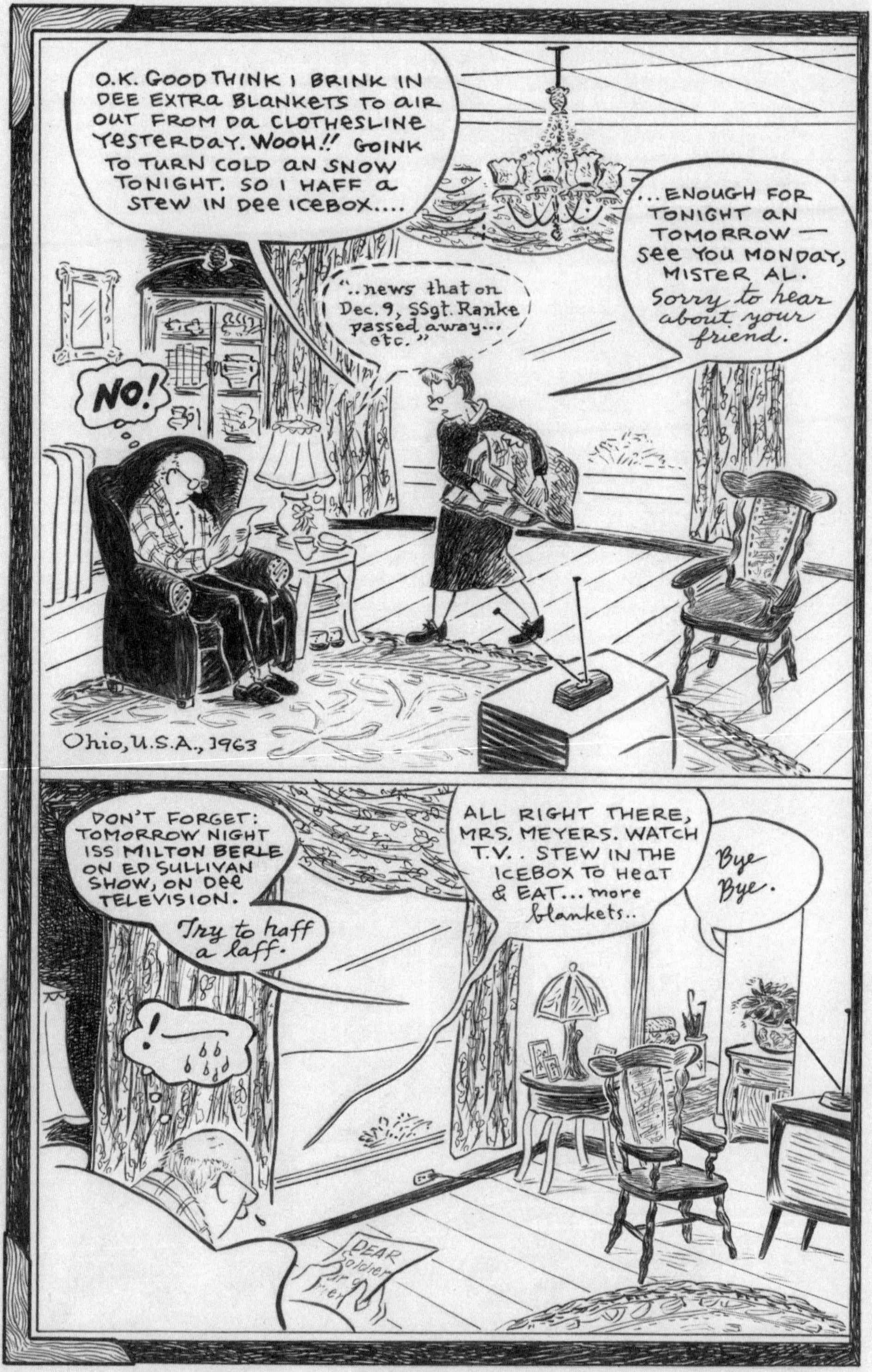
O.K. GOOD THINK I BRINK IN DEE EXTRA BLANKETS TO AIR OUT FROM DA CLOTHESLINE YESTERDAY. WOOH!! GOINK TO TURN COLD AN SNOW TONIGHT. SO I HAFF A STEW IN DEE ICEBOX....
"..news that on Dec. 9, SSgt. Ranke passed away... etc."
NO!
...ENOUGH FOR TONIGHT AN TOMORROW— SEE YOU MONDAY, MISTER AL. Sorry to hear about your friend.
Ohio, U.S.A., 1963
DON'T FORGET: TOMORROW NIGHT ISS MILTON BERLE ON ED SULLIVAN SHOW, ON DEE TELEVISION.
Try to haff a laff.
ALL RIGHT THERE, MRS. MEYERS. WATCH T.V.. STEW IN THE ICEBOX TO HEAT & EAT... more blankets..
Bye Bye.
!
DEAR Soldier

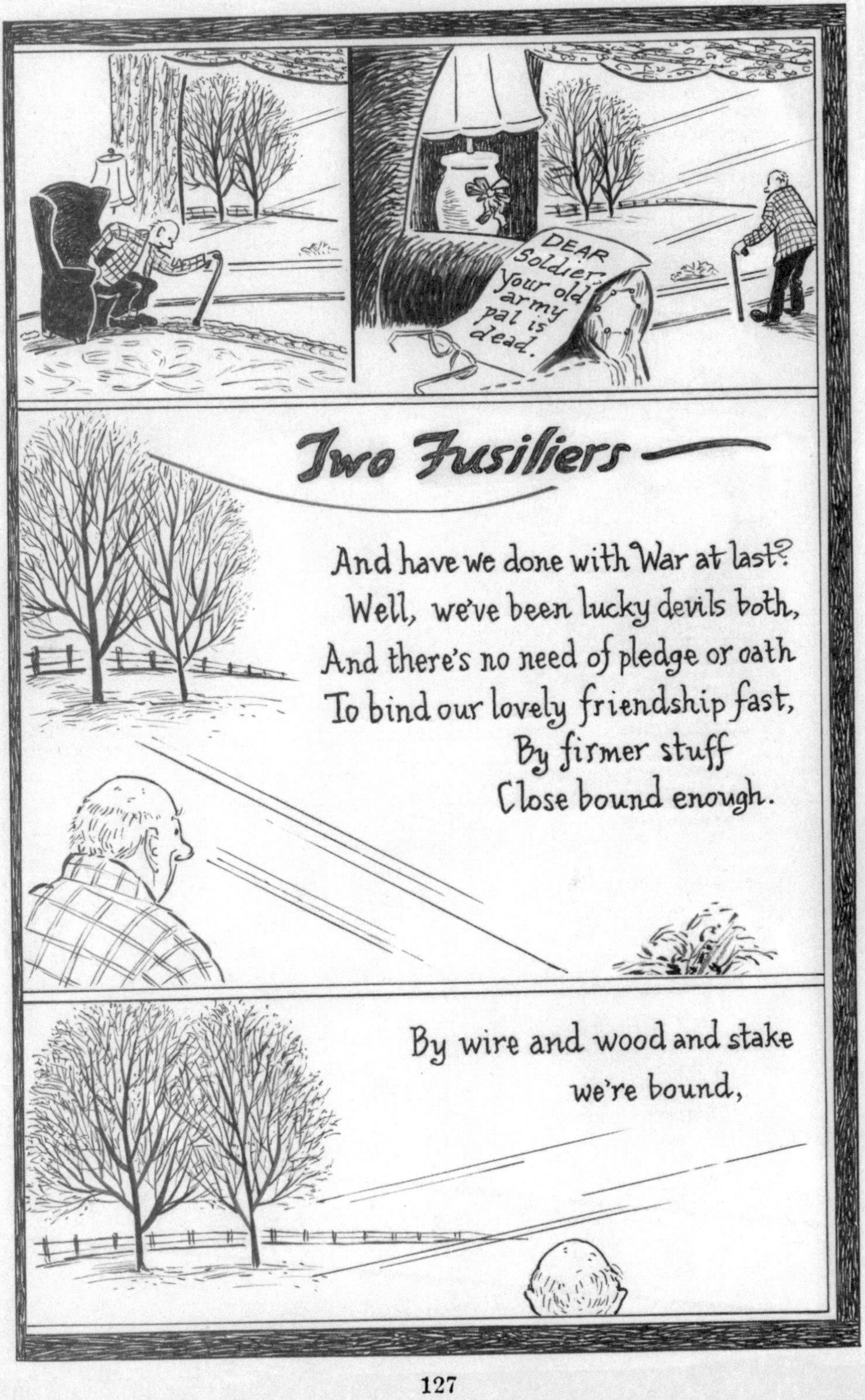
DEAR
Soldier,
your old
army
pal is
dead.
Two Fusiliers
And have we done with War at last?
Well, we've been lucky devils both,
And there's no need of pledge or oath
To bind our lovely friendship fast,
By firmer stuff
Close bound enough.
By wire and wood and stake
we're bound,

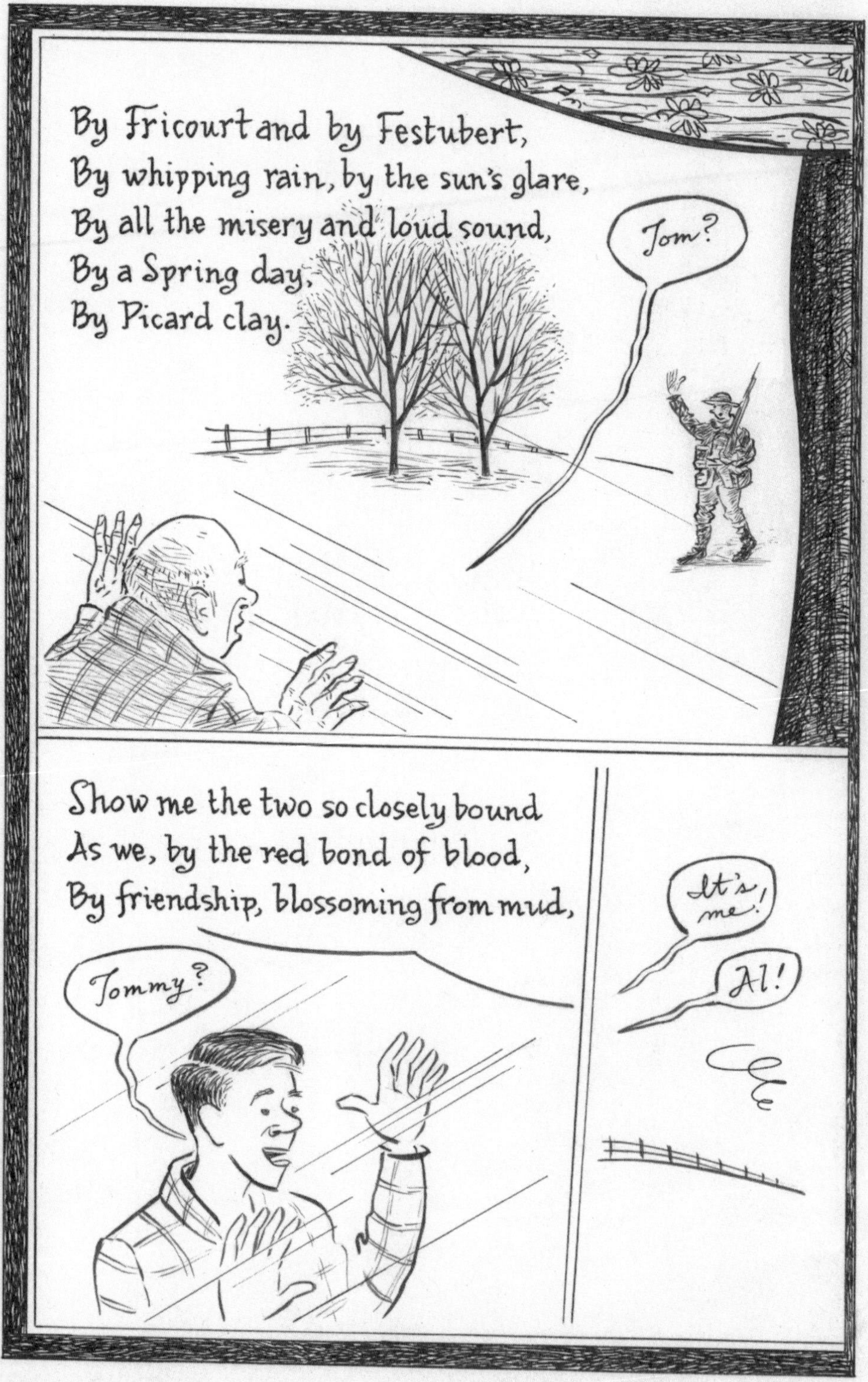

By Fricourt and by Festubert,
By whipping rain, by the sun's glare,
By all the misery and loud sound,
By a Spring day,
By Picard clay.
Tom?
Show me the two so closely bound
As we, by the red bond of blood,
By friendship, blossoming from mud,
Tommy?
It's me!
Al!

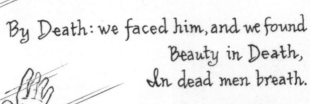

By Death: we faced him, and we found
Beauty in Death,
In dead men breath.
Robert Graves 1918
CT 14

adapted by Carol Tyler

IN TIME OF 'THE BREAKING OF NATIONS'

BY THOMAS HARDY
ADAPTED BY ANDERS NILSEN

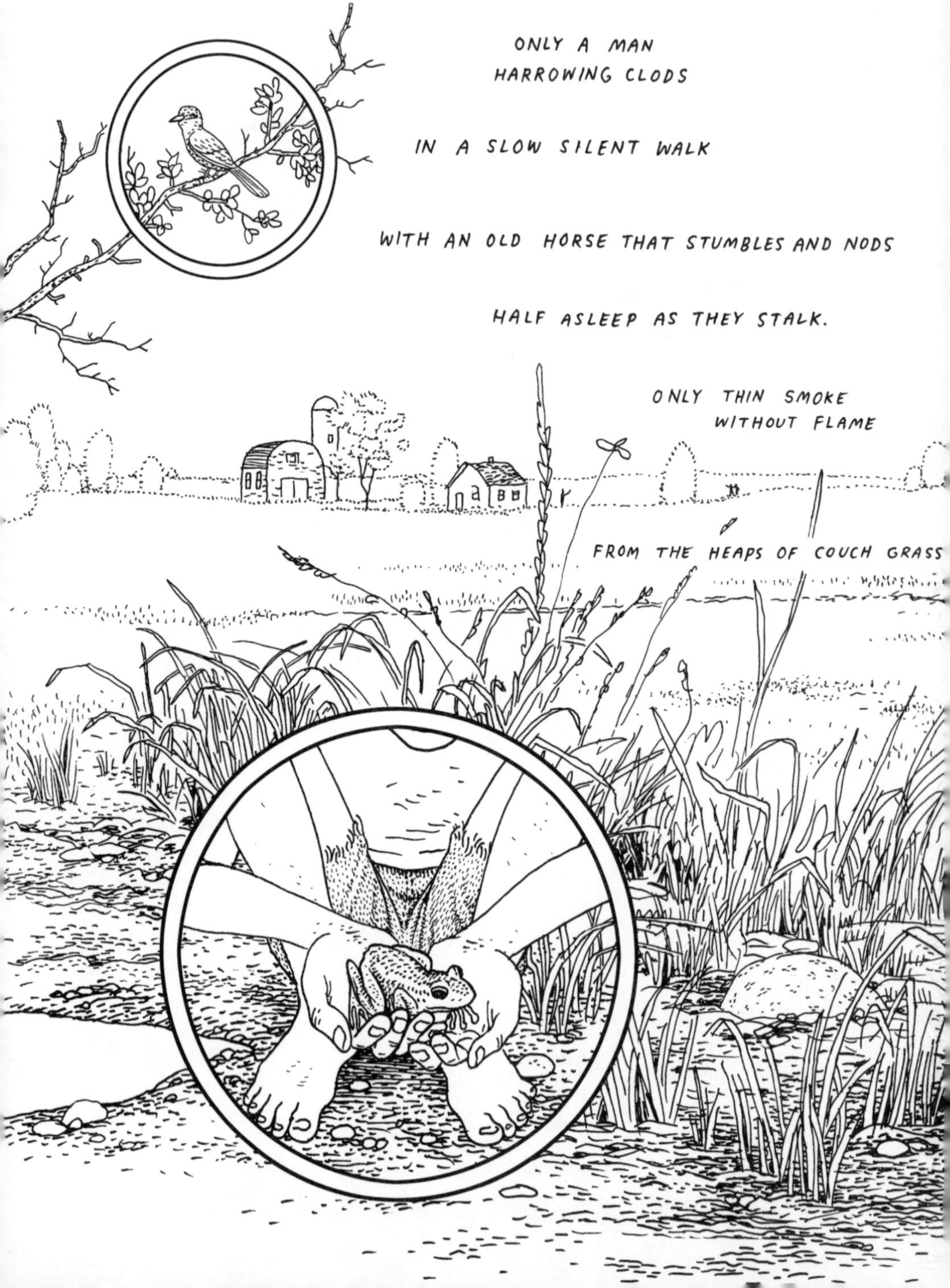
ONLY A MAN
HARROWING CLODS
IN A SLOW SILENT WALK
WITH AN OLD HORSE THAT STUMBLES AND NODS
HALF ASLEEP AS THEY STALK.
ONLY THIN SMOKE
WITHOUT FLAME
FROM THE HEAPS OF COUCH GRASS

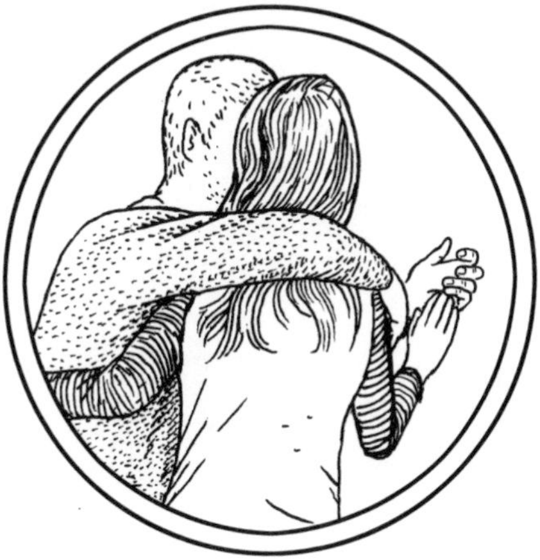

YET THIS WILL GO
ONWARD THE SAME

THOUGH DYNASTIES PASS.

YONDER A MAID AND HER WIGHT

COME WHISPERING BY:

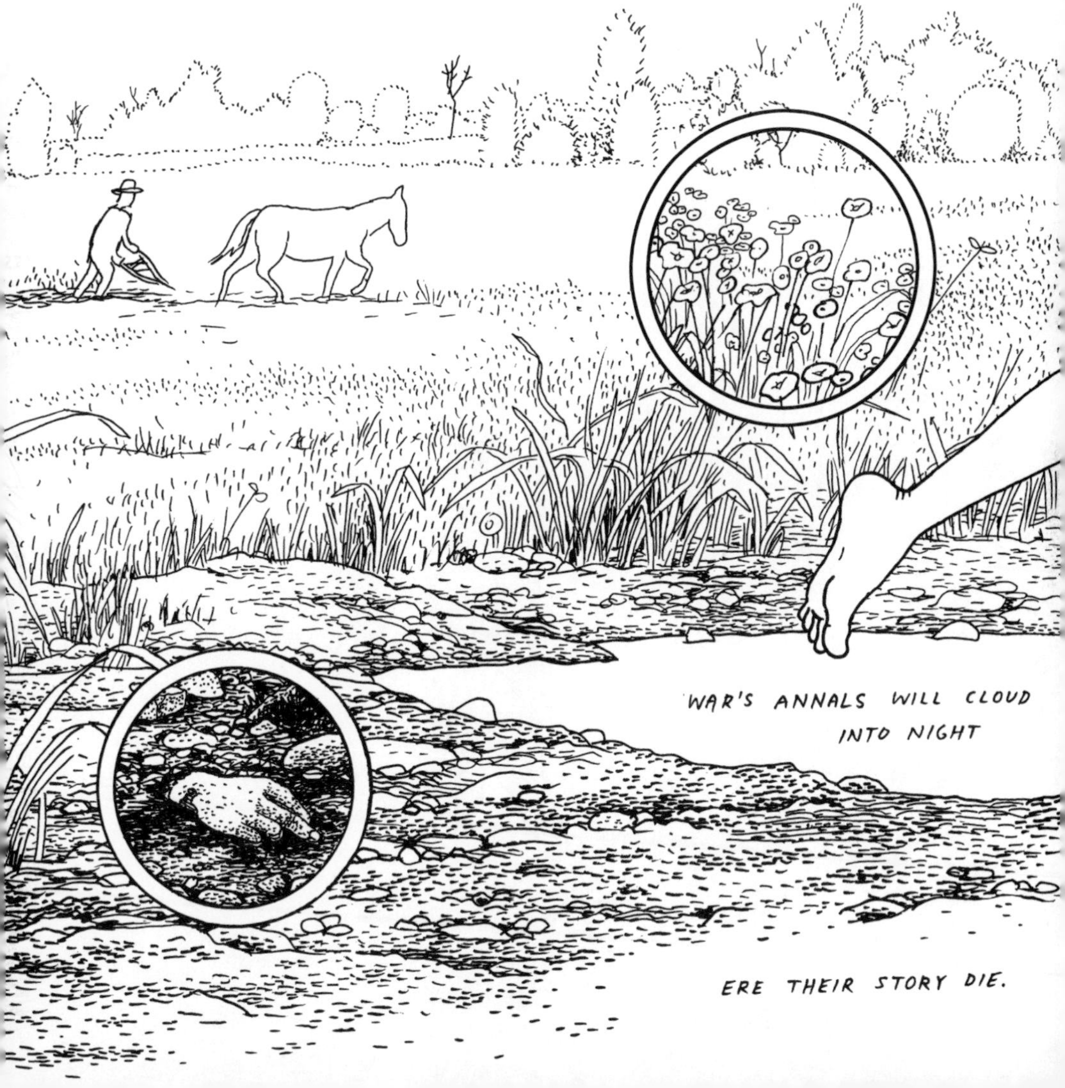
WAR'S ANNALS WILL CLOUD
INTO NIGHT
ERE THEIR STORY DIE.

NOTES

"Channel Firing" by Thomas Hardy

Stourton Tower: Also known as King Alfred's Tower. Completed in 1772 in Somerset county to commemorate the end of the Seven Years' War, it is also believed to be built on the site where Alfred the Great, King of Wessex, rallied troops before defeating the Danish army in 878.

Luke Pearson: On my first reading I was drawn to the banal humour of the skeletons, tutting and shaking their heads at man's inability to learn from past mistakes (and the nerve of him for waking them up). I decided to lean away from this in the visuals, however, as I wanted to avoid overtly literal depictions of the living dead. Written four months prior to the outbreak of war, the poem is prophetic. I wanted to focus on the way it looks back and forwards in time simultaneously to create a feeling of dread and of impending, senseless tragedy.

"I Don't Want to Be a Soldier" (soldiers' song)

Piccadilly underground: One of the busiest subway stations in London, under Piccadilly Circus. It opened in 1906.

"Peace" by Rupert Brooke

Simon Gane: The first panel depicts Lord Cardigan leading the charge of the Light Brigade. Panel four includes a bust believed to represent Spartan leader Leonidas. I felt they would hint at the history and heroic lineage Brooke believed he was joining and provide a suitable, if ironic, introduction to just how different this war would be.

The painting on page 17 is Ford Maddox Brown's *The Last of England* (1855). Brooke also sailed from England never to return.

"War" by Francis Edward Ledwidge

Sammy Harkham: Initially it was to be a man or woman on a walk, but either figure in the woods placed along with Ledwidge's verse seemed to make some obvious point about Man and Violence. The cartoon dog seemed to deflate that somewhat and throw things nicely off balance, giving the strip some tension. When I started the comic I hated drawing dogs and didn't know how to do it. By the last panel, I felt like I could draw dogs forever.

"All the Hills and Vales Along" by Charles Sorley

Kevin Huizenga: The poem has four stanzas. Each stanza adds two more lines—so the first stanza has eight lines, the next has ten, the next has twelve, and the last has fourteen. This gives the poem a feeling of increasing intensity until you arrive at the last lines of the poem, which sublimate the accumulated weight of the formal rhythm as well as the thematic ironies of life, death, happiness, war, etc.

When I divided up the lines into comics panels, I tried to follow this formal logic of building intensity in comics form. Because of how comics work, I felt like it made more sense to go the opposite way and decrease the amount of words per page, which would increase the speed at which you read the pages, but to also increase the size of the panels near the end, which is one way to add a feeling of weight and intensity in comics. Lastly I tried to rhyme the drawings whenever I could—for instance, the curve of the valley rhymes with the curve of the earth, or the musical notes rhyme with the legs of the marching soldiers, and so on.

From *The Great Push* by Patrick MacGill

Parapet: The side of a trench facing the enemy line, usually lined with a foot or more height of sandbags.

Dressing station: A first-aid station near a combat area.

Loos: Location of a major failed Allied offensive in 1915 (the subject of *The Great Push*).

Star shell: Artillery used to light up the battlefield at night.

RAMC: Royal Army Medical Corps; corps of the British army that provided medical services to soldiers.

Blighty: Britain; a "Blighty one" was a minor wound that would send one out of combat and possibly back to Britain.

Knobkerry: Club with a large knob on one end.

Eddie Campbell: It's a bit preposterous us thinking we can illustrate this stuff that we know nothing of—sitting here in our air-conditioned rooms trying to imagine the horror of being knee deep in mud with your feet rotting off.

"The Immortals" by Isaac Rosenberg

Peter Kuper: Working with this poem had the same transformative effect as adapting Franz Kafka short stories. It's as if the writer were whispering through the ages directing my pen and suggesting page design.

"Greater Love" by Wilfred Owen

George Pratt: I've been a fan of Wilfred Owen's poetry ever since I wrote and illustrated my first graphic novel, *Enemy Ace: War Idyll*. I love the poems so much, and find the words so powerful, that for this project I did not want to do straight sequential narrative; that felt a little redundant to me. I wanted the words to be the most important aspect of the adaptation. So I basically just put together images that I hope evoke the overall mood and power of the poems without taking away from Owen's words. Instead of pen and ink I chose to do the pieces in black and white acrylic, using paint rollers and putty knives as they would not allow me to noodle or get too detailed, again in the hopes of letting readers fill in the gaps with their own imaginations.

"The Question" by Wilfrid Wilson Gibson

Gey: very

Hannah Berry: I'll admit it, the idea of a war poem about a soldier worrying about his cow back home amused me. I thought it'd be a nice irony if the soldier in question was with the Royal Engineers Signal Service, charged with delivering carrier pigeons to the front in order to fly vital messages back to HQ (one of the most reliable methods of communication at the time—some 100,000 pigeons were used throughout the war): helping relay urgent correspondence but never receiving the news he was so keen to hear.

"Sing Me to Sleep" (soldiers' song)

Bully and biscuit: Typical British soldier's rations; bully is short for bully beef (corned beef).

Wipers: English soldiers' nickname for the western Belgian municipality of Ypres, the location of continuous fighting and five major battles between Allied and German forces from 1914 to 1918.

"Therefore Is the Name of It Called Babel" by Osbert Sitwell

Isabel Greenberg: This was my first adaptation of a poem into a comic, and it was a lot harder than I thought it would be; making a narrative without distracting from the words of the poem was a challenge. I also really enjoyed drawing guns and explosions, which was astonishing, as I hadn't expected to!

"The General" by Siegfried Sassoon

Arras: Site of a major British offensive in Spring of 1917, where 158,000 British troops were killed, and possibly as many German.

Garth Ennis: The trouble with writing a comic strip about World War I is that you almost immediately hit a large and obvious obstacle called *Charley's War*: grim, heartbreaking, brilliant, and to my mind the finest story ever to be told in the medium. I hope I've managed to come up with a reasonably fresh angle on the subject with my adaptation of *The General*, but—regardless—all ten volumes of *Charley's War*, by Pat Mills and Joe Colquhoun, are currently available from Titan Books. Quite simply the best there is.

Phil Winslade: The reference I found most useful and enlightening when producing this strip was *The Faces of World War I: The Great War in Words & Pictures* by Max Arthur.

"Dulce et Decorum Est" by Wilfred Owen

Five-nines: German artillary shells.

George Pratt: Books that I consistently find myself going back to for inspiration when illustrating the First World War are the *New York Times* Weekly Pictorial volumes. These were printed at the time and are chock-full of photographs from the war. I bought these volumes years ago from illustrator George Woodbridge, and they are the crown of my World War I collection. *Make the Kaiser Dance* is a wonderful book by Henry Berry that is full of firsthand accounts of the war. And any book by Lyn Macdonald is also recommended reading.

"A Private" by Edward Thomas

Bedmen: Variant of bedesman or beadsman; one who prays, often for a benefactor.

Hannah Berry: There was something about this poem, which compares a man sleeping off the drink in one field with him lying in his final resting place in another, that reminded me of the famous final episode of *Blackadder Goes Forth*. That transition from familiar, light-hearted territory to abrupt tragedy through to somber reflection sharply brings home the sobering reality.

"When This Bloody War Is Over" (soldiers' song)

Hunt Emerson: My Uncle George was a soldier in the First World War. I knew him when I was a little lad and he was an old man. (He was probably about sixty—old for the 1950s and the northeast of England.) He had a greenhouse that smelled wonderfully of tomatoes and a big shed full of interesting junk—old harness and tack, strange tools, and a steel helmet. It was a Civil Defense helmet from the Second World War, but it thrilled a war-story-obsessed little boy (me). And when I pestered Uncle George to tell me what he did in the war—did he shoot Germans?—he would say, "Oh, aye, aa killt lots o' Jarmans, bonny lad." I was too young to realize that he was saying nothing, of course, as did so many of those haunted men. They kept it to themselves.

He would stand beside me in the methodist chapel of a Sunday and sing the rich improvised harmonies of methodist hymns. When we sat to pray, I would bow my head and close my eyes, but Uncle George would sit with his hands planted on his knees, his back straight, and stare God in the eye. He was not a man to suffer fools. I can't really imagine Uncle George singing the Trench Songs—but then, he would have been just a lad himself in the trenches, keeping cheerful.

"The Coward" by Rudyard Kipling

Stephen R. Bissette: The Great War, alas, wasn't the "war to end all wars." I'll go to my grave holding in my heart and head the rage and imagery from Abel Gance's two (futile) anti-war masterworks, *J'Accuse* (1919 and 1937). Those didn't end all wars, either, but hey—Abel tried, as should we all.

"Soldier's Dream" by Wilfred Owen

Pikel: pitchfork

"Break of Day in the Trenches" by Isaac Rosenberg

Poppy: Poppy flowers were common in the fields of Belgium and France. In the 1920s, the poppy became the symbol of remembrance for soldiers killed in World War I. In many countries poppies are now worn to commemorate all war dead.

Sarah Glidden: Maybe it's because 1914 was a long time ago, or maybe it's just a way of coping with the horror of war in general, but imagining the inner lives of the men from both sides of that conflict was not something I spent much time doing until I sat down with Isaac Rosenberg's poem. In reading it over and over again for this comic, it of course became impossible for me to think of him as just another man in uniform. It was some time before I went beyond the poem to look up some biographical information on Rosenberg himself, and although it was obvious that he would be dead by now, I had just assumed (hoped) for some reason that he had made it out of the war alive. Finding out that he was shot in a battle a few years after writing "Break of Day in the Trenches" felt like a punch to the gut.

Of course many of these men wrote poetry; they were human beings. And those of them who weren't writers still looked out from their posts and thought about their lives and what tied them to those of their so-called enemies who mirrored them.

"I Looked Up From My Writing" by Thomas Hardy

Kathryn Immonen and Stuart Immonen: We both found this Open Yale course lecture helpful and enjoyable: oyc.yale.edu/english/engl-310/lecture-7

"The Dancers" by Wilfrid Wilson Gibson

Lilli Carré: I liked the eerie beauty and contrast within "The Dancers"—the protagonist is able to get lost in his own head while in the middle of a battlefield. I drew him in the pleasure of the moment, distracted and taking in the surreality of the situation of death mixed with dragonflies.

"Dead Man's Dump" by Isaac Rosenberg

Limbers: A wagon used to haul artillery or supplies.

Rusty stakes: Rosenberg is describing a limber carrying stakes and barbed wired to the front.

Pat Mills: The inspiration for my adaption was *Oh, What A Lovely War!*, a film and play I watched many times, which criticizes the generals of World War I. It's particularly loathed by current "revisionist" historians who seek to reinstate Haig as a great general and who, they claim, won the war.

David Hitchcock: It was a great honor to be working with Pat Mills on this powerful World War I poem. It was so moving I almost felt I was there on the battlefield, knee deep in the Dead Man's Dump.

"Everyone Sang" by Siegfried Sassoon

Editor's note: Robert Graves and others have interpreted this as an Armistice poem; but Sassoon himself, in his 1960s memoir *Siegfried's Journey*, said its origins are rooted in his expectations of a socialist revolution after the war.

"Ancient History" by Siegfried Sassoon

Liesbeth De Stercke: I wanted to draw Adam crawling past the olive trees bending in the rain, creating a rhythm.

"The Next War" by Osbert Sitwell

Simon Gane: The war memorials depicted can be found in the following towns and villages. *Page 110*, panel 1 and others: Somerton, England; panel 4: Château-Thierry, France. *Page 111*, panel 1 and others: Lodève, France. *Page 112*, panel 1: Alfreton, England; panel 3: Rochechouart, France; panel 4: Botz-en-Mauges, France. *Page 113*, panel 1: Oban, Scotland; panel 2: Hyde Park Corner, London.; panels 3-4: Equeurdreville-Haineville, France. *Page 114*, panel 1-2: Péronne, France.

"The End" by Wilfred Owen

Danica Novgorodoff: The poem begins after the thunderous and devastating noise of war and takes us to the long silence of death. I wanted my images to reflect that final quietness.

After the line, "My head hangs weighed with snow," the two beats of silence that break the sonnet form are visually represented in the inset panels. I was moved by the water imagery in Owen's writing—the immortal water, the heavy snow, the sea of titanic tears—and so a voyage out to the infinite ocean seemed right for this poem.

"Repression of War Experience" by Siegfried Sassoon

James Lloyd: Several key works inspired my desire to adapt Siegfried Sassoon's poem. Ron Kovic's memoir *Born on the Fourth of July* is still to me the most searing and personal account of a veteran living with the physical and invisible wounds of battle. Dylan Thomas's prose piece on Wilfred Owen and Welsh poets lost to action was fundamental to understanding the role of the war poet. "He is the common touch," wrote Thomas. "He is the bell of the church of the broken body. He writes love letters home for the illiterate dead." Many authors charged with this duty have similarly moved me, including Dalton Trumbo and Anthony Swofford.

I have also been lucky enough to attend presentations by both the War Resisters and Peace Forum Organizations here in Vancouver, in which veterans of Iraq and Vietnam provided galvanizing accounts of their time serving. One such veteran, Rodney Watson Jr., chose to share his experiences with me over the last three years. An American war resister now living in sanctuary, he strives daily for compassion and to be heard. It is to him and countless other scorned veterans that I dedicate my small contribution in this book.

"Two Fusiliers" by Robert Graves

Fusiliers: Originally a term for English regiments that guarded shipments of artillery; by the Great War, the word was used in the names of several infantry regiments.

Fricourt: A French town near the Western Front that saw fierce fighting during the Battle of the Somme in 1916.

Festubert: A French village destroyed in 1915 in the Battle of Festubert.

Picard: Region in northern France, the site of four major battles of the Great War, including the Battle of the Somme and the German Spring Offensive in 1918.

Carol Tyler: The poem honors a deep friendship forged in battle between two soldiers and is written by one of them. In my presentation, I depict that writer/soldier in old age, blanched by the news of the passing of his battlefield friend. We are never so acutely aware of the close bonds of friendship until we lose a dear someone, and so I tried to focus in on the painful convergence of connection and loss. For inspiration, I looked to the soldier I know best, my ninety-five-year-old dad, who has outlived every army buddy he ever knew.

"In Time of 'The Breaking of Nations'" by Thomas Hardy

Couch grass: A rapidly spreading grass that is treated as a weed and is often burned away.

Wight: Archaic English word meaning "human" or "creature."

Anders Nilsen: My first reading of Hardy's poem was pretty dark. The smoking grass and the "wight"—which I thought of as a ghost—seemed to point to a deeply pessimistic sentiment. The vignettes I first imposed on the farm scene were in that vein. I went back a few times, though, being a little uncomfortable with such a dark take as the book's conclusion, and I did some reading about the poem and its language. It can be easy as an artist and storyteller to default to a pessimistic, ironic view. An eloquent, open-eyed optimism like Hardy's feels, to me, important.

THE POETS

RUPERT BROOKE, 1887–1915 ("Peace"), was educated at Rugby School and King's College, Cambridge. As a young man, he associated with the Bloomsbury group, campaigned for socialist causes, helped found the Georgian Movement in poetry, and traveled in the South Seas. When the Great War began, he was already known for his book *Poems, 1911*. After enlisting, he saw action in Antwerp in 1914. Brooke died from sepsis in April 1915 while on a boat to Gallipoli. *1914 and Other Poems* (in which "Peace" and other war poems appeared) was very popular when Brooke was still living, and it was a bestseller for the duration of the war.

WILFRID WILSON GIBSON, 1878–1962 ("The Question," "The Dancers"), was born and educated in Hexham, Northumberland. An early member of the Georgian Movement, he became a close friend of Rupert Brooke and was one of Brooke's literary executors. Gibson was rejected for military service four times due to bad eyesight, but finally enlisted as a private. His war poems are notable for depicting the point of view of ordinary soldiers. After the war, he had a long career writing poems and plays about working-class men and women.

ROBERT GRAVES, 1895–1985 ("Two Fusiliers"), was born to middle class Irish and Dutch-German parents in south London. He was educated in preparatory schools and commissioned as a captain into the Welsh Fusiliers in 1914. Graves's books *Over the Brazier* (1915) and

Fairies and Fusiliers (1917) got him noticed as a war poet. He was close friends with Siegfried Sassoon; and with Sassoon and several others, signed a declaration stating that the war was being drawn out by corrupt leaders. In 1917 he was wounded and spent the rest of the war posted in England and Ireland. He had a varied writing career, with works including novels, poetry, collections of myths, and two war memoirs: *Goodbye to All That* and *But It Still Goes On.*

THOMAS HARDY, 1840-1928 ("Channel Firing," "I Looked Up from My Writing," "In Time of 'The Breaking of Nations'") was over seventy years old when the war began. Although he was by that time a famous English novelist (having written *Far from the Madding Crowd*, *Tess of the D'urbervilles*, and *Jude the Obscure*, among others), he had turned away from novels to poetry by the turn of the century. He did not write many poems about the Great War, but the few he wrote are much admired. Hardy spent nearly his whole life in Dorset.

RUDYARD KIPLING, 1865-1936 ("The Coward"), was born in India and educated at United Services College in Westward Ho!, Devon. He was a world-famous writer when war broke out—for novels, short stories, and poems, often of an unabashed imperialist bent—and had even won the Nobel Prize in 1907. His son, Jack, died in combat in 1915. Kipling was an active participant in the Imperial War Graves Commission, the group behind the creation of cemeteries for British war dead around the world.

FRANCIS EDWARD LEDWIDGE, 1891-1917 ("War"), was born into a poor family in County Meath, Ireland. He left school at age thirteen to work, but an interest in writing led to publication of his poems in local newspapers and the eventual patronage of noted writer Lord Dunsany. Ledwidge was an active Irish nationalist and at first sided with those who refused to join British forces in the war in Europe. Eventually, Ledwidge changed his mind and fought in the Dardanelles, Serbia, and on the Western Front with an Irish regiment. While doing construction work near Ypres, he was killed by shelling in 1917. His first book of poetry, *Songs of the Field*, was published in 1915. Two more volumes were published after his death.

PATRICK MACGILL, 1889-1963 (*The Great Push*), was born in County Donegal, Ireland, where he attended school until age eleven. At age twenty-one, while working on the Scottish railways, he self-published a book of poetry, *Gleanings from a Navvy's Scrapbook*. The book's success propelled him into a long career as a poet, novelist, and journalist of the poor and oppressed. In 1914, he volunteered and joined the London Irish Rifles, serving on the Western Front, where he was wounded at the Battle of Loos. MacGill wrote five books (novels and poetry) about the Great War during the war and two after. His family moved to the Unites States in the 1930s, where he continued to write novels until prolonged illness ended his career late in that decade.

WILFRED OWEN, 1893-1918 ("Greater Love," "Dulce et Decorum Est," "Soldier's Dream," "The End"), is probably the most well known of the Trench Poets today. The son of a railway official in Ostwestry, Shropshire, he attended Shrewsbury Technical School. He did not, however, score high enough in university entrance exams to gain a needed scholarship. After working in France as an English teacher from 1912 to 1915, he enlisted as an officer in the Manchester Regiment. He had written poems since a young age, but he found his greatest inspiration when he met poet Siegfried Sassoon while on sick leave in 1917. The two became great friends, and, encouraged by Sassoon, Owen published several poems during the war. Owen was killed in action on the Sambre-Oise canal one week before the Armistice in 1918. Most of his poems were published after his death, the result of support from Sassoon and poets Edith Sitwell and Edmund Blunden.

ISAAC ROSENBERG, 1890-1918 ("The Immortals," "Break of Day in the Trenches," "Dead Man's Dump"), was the oldest son of working-class Lithuanian Jewish immigrants. He grew up in London and became an apprentice engraver at age fourteen. He studied painting at age twenty-one and soon began writing poetry as well, gaining the attention and support of poets Laurence Binyon and Gordon Bottomly. Despite chronic bronchitis and personal opposition to the war, Rosenberg enlisted in 1915 to support his mother; he had no other prospects at the time. He served as a private on the Western Front and was killed in April of 1918 near Arras. Rosenberg's war poems were seen by hardly anyone until their publication in 1922 by Binyon and Bottomly in *Poems by Isaac Rosenberg*.

SIEGFRIED SASSOON, 1886-1967 ("The General," "Everyone Sang," "Ancient History," "Repression of War Experience"), was born in Kent and attended, but did not matriculate from, Clare College, Cambridge. He enlisted in 1914 and was soon commissioned a second lieutenant in the Royal Welsh Fusiliers. He served in France, Ireland, and Palestine, gaining the rank of captain by end of the war. Although known for heroic exploits, in 1917 he publically expressed his belief that the war was being unnecessarily drawn out. For this he was sent for psychiatric treatment in Scotland. Two books of his poetry were published during the war, *The Old Huntsman and Other Poems* (1917) and *Counter-Attack and Other Poems* (1918). He had a long literary career after the war, including three fictionalized war autobiographies: *Memoirs of a Fox-Hunting Man*, *Memoirs of an Infantry Officer*, and *Sherston's Progress*.

OSBERT SITWELL, 1892-1969 ("Therefore Is the Name of It Called Babel," "The Next War"), the son of a baronet, was born in London and educated at Eton. He enlisted in the Grenadier Guards in 1912 and after war began saw active duty in France, where he wrote poetry in earnest for the first time. In 1916, his military career ended after he contracted blood poisoning from an injured foot. He would go on to become an important English writer, devoting his life to poems, novels, art criticism, travel-writing, and a four-volume autobiography. With his sister, Edith, he edited the influential journal *Wheels*.

CHARLES SORLEY, 1895-1915 ("All the Hills and Vales Along"), was born in Aberdeen and educated at Marlborough College. When war broke out in 1914, Sorley had been studying in Germany. He returned to England and enlisted in the Suffolk Regiment, despite a newly won scholarship to Oxford. In May 1915, he shipped to France as a lieutenant. By August he was a captain, and in October he was killed in action at Loos. Sorley's war poems were found after his death and published in 1916 in *Marlborough and Other Poems*.

EDWARD THOMAS, 1878-1917 ("A Private"), attended Oxford and married as an undergraduate. He was a prolific critic, biographer, and novelist before trying his hand at poetry at the start of the war—encouraged by friend and neighbor Robert Frost. Thomas enlisted in 1915 as a private in the Artists' Rifles and was commissioned as a lieutenant in 1916, but he did not go on active service until 1917. He was killed only a few months after arriving in France, at the first battle of Arras. Most of his war poetry was not directly about war experiences, but a mix of military and pastoral themes.

COMICS CONTRIBUTORS

HANNAH BERRY ("The Question," "A Private") is a British graphic novelist, writer, illustrator, teacher, and proselytizer of comics. Her first graphic novel, *Britten and Brülightly*, was released to much critical acclaim and published in several countries, with the French edition chosen as part of the official selection at the Angoulême International Comics Festival in 2010. Her latest, *Adamtine*, has been steadily giving people the willies since its publication, and a third, *Livestock*, is currently in progress.

STEPHEN R. BISSETTE ("The Coward"), a pioneer graduate of the Joe Kubert School, currently teaches at the Center for Cartoon Studies and is renowned for *Swamp Thing*, *Taboo* (launching *From Hell* and *Lost Girls*), "1963," *Tyrant®*, co-creating John Constantine, and creating the world's second "24-Hour Comic" (invented by Scott McCloud for Bissette). He writes, illustrates, and has co-authored many books; his latest include *Teen Angels & New Mutants* (2011), the short story "Copper" in *The New Dead* (2010), and *The Vermont Monster Guide* (2009). Forthcoming: *S.R. Bissette's How to Make a Monster, Tales of the Uncanny*.

EDDIE CAMPBELL (excerpt from *The Great Push*) is the artist of *From Hell* with writer Alan Moore, turned into a Hollywood film starring Johnny Depp. He recently produced *The From Hell Companion*, a linear narrative containing all the other stuff you would want to know about it, including alternative scenes and unpublished art.

LILLI CARRÉ ("The Dancers") lives and works in Chicago, where she makes comics, experimental animation, illustration, and sculpture. She has created several books of comics, most recently the short story collection *Heads or Tails*, published by Fantagraphics. lillicarre.com

LIESBETH DE STERCKE ("Ancient History") was born in Belgium in 1987. She graduated from Sint-Lucas School of Arts in Ghent. She currently has her studio in Ghent, where she spends her time filling sketchbooks, drawing comics, and printing woodcuts.

HUNT EMERSON ("I Don't Want to Be a Soldier," "Sing Me to Sleep," "When This Bloody War Is Over") has been drawing and publishing comix since the early 1970s and is now officially a Footnote in Comics History. His work appears regularly in publications as diverse as *The Beano* (U.K.'s cornerstone children's comic weekly), *Fiesta* (a magazine for men!), and *Fortean Times* (a magazine for nutters!), and he has contributed to countless other magazines and comics. Hunt has published around thirty comic books and albums, mainly with Knockabout Comics (London). The latest is his version of *Dante's Inferno*. In 2000 he was named as one of the seventy-five Masters of European Comics by the CNBDI, the noted French comics Academy. Hunt's books and comics can be accessed through his Web site and shop: largecow.com.

GARTH ENNIS ("The General" script) is a British comics writer living and working in the United States. His credits include *Preacher*, *Hitman*, *The Boys*, *Crossed*, the war comics *Battlefields* and *War Story*, and successful runs on the Marvel Comics titles *Fury* and *The Punisher*. Originally from Belfast, Northern Ireland, he now lives in New York City with his wife, Ruth.

SIMON GANE ("Peace," "The Next War") lives and works in Bristol, U.K. Other comic book projects include *Paris*, *Dark Rain: A New Orleans Story*, and *Godzilla*. You can see more of his work at simongane.blogspot.com.

SARAH GLIDDEN's ("Break of Day in the Trenches") first book, a graphic memoir called *How to Understand Israel in 60 Days or Less*, was published by Vertigo in 2010 and was later translated into five languages. She has had work published in *Ha'aretz*, *Symbolia Magazine*, *Medium*, *Cartoon Movement*, and the *Jewish Quarterly*. In 2012, she was an artist in residence at the Maison des Auteurs in Angoulême, France. Her second book, *Rolling Blackouts*, will be published by Drawn and Quarterly in 2015.

ISABEL GREENBERG ("Therefore Is the Name of It Called Babel," "Everyone Sang") is a London-based illustrator and comics artist. Her first graphic novel, *The Encyclopedia of Early Earth*, is published by Jonathan Cape in the U.K. and Little, Brown in the U.S. She also self-publishes minicomics and zines.

SAMMY HARKHAM ("War") was born in 1980. He writes and draws the comic book *Crickets* and edits the acclaimed comics and art anthology *Kramer's Ergot*. A collection of his short strips, *Everything Together*, was published by PictureBox and awarded a *Los Angeles Times* Book Prize for Graphic Novel of the Year. He currently lives in Australia.

DAVID HITCHCOCK ("Dead Man's Dump" art) is an Eagle Award-winning artist/creator, self-publishing since the mid-80s. His work is set mainly in the Victorian era as he finds it visually interesting. He is mostly known for his take on the penny dreadful mainstay Springheeled Jack and other gothic tales.

KEVIN HUIZENGA ("All the Hills and Vales Along") is the author of the ongoing comic book series *Ganges*, as well as several other books. He lives in Saint Louis with his wife, Katie, and several animals.

KATHRYN IMMONEN AND STUART IMMONEN ("I Looked Up from My Writing") have been making comics together for more than twenty-five years. Perhaps best known for their work on Marvel Comics flagship characters, they have been equally recognized for their independent work, such as *Moving Pictures* for Top Shelf and *Never as Bad as You Think* for Boom! Studios. They live in the woods of northern Ontario with amazing wildlife, including their very bad dog.

PETER KUPER's ("The Immortals") illustrations and comics have appeared in magazines around the world including *MAD*, where he has written and illustrated *SPY vs. SPY* for every issue since 1997. His latest books include *Drawn to New York*, *The System*, and an anthology collection of *World War 3 Illustrated*, a political comics magazine he has co-published since 1979. He has taught courses in comics and illustration at Parsons, School of Visual Arts, and is a visiting professor at Harvard University.

JAMES LLOYD ("Repression of War Experience") is a Vancouver-based cartoonist who got his start in the 1990s in the independent comics scene and in the animation industry. He has been the regular artist on the *Futurama* comics series (published by Matt Groening's Bongo Comics) since its launch in 2000 and has contributed to *Simpsons Comics* and Boom!'s *Adventure Time* title as well. He keeps his hand in gallery shows and illustration, and in recent years Lloyd has been helping to illustrate the story of an Iraq verteran.

PAT MILLS ("Dead Man's Dump" script) is the creator and first editor of *2000AD*. He developed *Judge Dredd* and is the writer-creator of many of *2000AD*'s most popular stories. He created *Charley's War* with artist Joe Colquhoun, and this ten-volume, acclaimed anti-war story is now the subject of international interest from museums and schools. His current projects include the lead story for *NW1*, a graphic novel commissioned by the Edinburgh Book Festival, illustrated by Hannah Berry, and *Brothers in Arms*, a World War I saga with artist David Hitchcock.

ANDERS NILSEN ("In Time of 'The Breaking of Nations'") is the author and artist of *Big Questions*, *Rage of Poseidon*, *The End*, and *Dogs and Water*, among other works. He has received three Ignatz awards as well as the 2012 Lynd Ward Graphic Novel prize. His work has appeared in the *Yale Anthology of Graphic Fiction*, *Kramer's Ergot*, and *Best American Comics* and has been translated into numerous languages. His drawing and painting has been shown internationally. He lives in Minneapolis.

DANICA NOVGORODOFF ("The End") is an artist, writer, graphic novelist, graphic designer, and horse wrangler from Kentucky who currently lives in Brooklyn, New York. Her graphic novels include *A Late Freeze* (2006), *Slow Storm* (2008), *Refresh, Refresh* (2009), and *The Undertaking of Lily Chen* (2014).

LUKE PEARSON ("Channel Firing") is a cartoonist and illustrator from the U.K.. His comics include the Hilda series (*Hilda and the Midnight Giant*, *Hilda and the Black Hound*) and *Everything We Miss*.

GEORGE PRATT ("Dulce et Decorum Est," "Greater Love," "Soldier's Dream") is an award-winning painter, writer, and photographer. His work is in numerous private collections worldwide. Among other honors, he is a recipient of the Eisner Award, a Spectrum Gold Medal, and Best Feature Documentary Award at the New York International Independent Film Festival for the film *See You in Hell, Blind Boy*. In addition to his gallery work, he is currently working on the International Black Light Project on the genocide in West Africa and on his blues novel, *See You in Hell, Blind Boy*. He teaches full-time at the Ringling College of Art and Design and summers with the Illustration Academy in Kansas City.

CAROL TYLER ("Two Fusiliers") is no stranger to the military theme. Her graphic novel trilogy, *You'll Never Know*, details the damage World War II did to her father and how his

PTSD affected her life. *You'll Never Know* has received eight Eisner nominations, four Ignatz nominations, and was a finalist for the *Los Angeles Times* Book Prize. It has received numerous other awards and accolades, including an Award of Excellence from the Ohio Arts Council. Carol has been doing comics since the R. Crumb *Weirdo* days and is a Professor of Comics, Graphic Novels & Sequential Art at the University of Cincinnati DAAP School of Art.

PHIL WINSLADE ("The General" art) has been employed as an artist for nearly a quarter of a century. He has worked with such writers as Garth Ennis (*Goddess*), Steve Gerber (*Nevada, Howard the Duck*), and Keith Giffen (*Threshold*) for various publishers, including Marvel and DC.

FURTHER READING

WORLD WAR I POETRY
Lost Voices of World War I, edited by Tim Cross, Bloomsbury, 1998.
Men Who March Away, edited by I.M. Parsons, Chatto & Windus, 1965.
The Penguin Book of First World War Poetry, edited by George Walter, Penguin, 2006.

SOLDIERS' SONGS
When This Bloody War Is Over, Max Arthur, Piatkus Books, 2001.

MEMOIRS OF THE TRENCH POETS
Good-Bye to All That, Robert Graves, Anchor Books, 1998.
The Great Push, Patrick MacGill, Birlinn Limited, 2000.
Memoirs of a Fox-Hunting Man, Siegfried Sassoon, Penguin Classics, 2013.

BIOGRAPHIES OF THE TRENCH POETS
Wilfred Owen: A New Biography, Dominic Hibberd, Ivan R. Dee, 2002.
Isaac Rosenberg: The Making of a Great War Poet: A New Life, Jean Moorcroft Wilson, Northwestern University Press, 2009.
Siegfried Sassoon: A Life, Max Egremont, Farrar, Straus and Giroux, 2005.

WORLD WAR I
The Experience of World War I, J. M. Winter, Oxford University Press, 1989.
The First World War, John Keegan, Vintage, 2000.
The Great War and Modern Memory, Paul Fussell, Oxford University Press, 2013.

ONLINE RESOURCES
BBC online: *bbc.co.uk/ww1*
The First World War Poetry Digital Archive: *oucs.ox.ac.uk/ww1lit*
Move Him Into the Sun (analysis of WWI poetry): *movehimintothesun.wordpress.com*
A Multimedia History of World War One: *firstworldwar.com*